wer and Resistance in the New World Order

Also by Stephen Gill

THE GLOBAL POLITICAL ECONOMY: PERSPECTIVES, PROBLEMS AND POLICIES (*with David Law*)

ATLANTIC RELATIONS: BEYOND THE REAGAN ERA

AMERICAN HEGEMONY AND THE TRILATERAL COMMISSION

GRAMSCI, HISTORICAL MATERIALISM AND INTERNATIONAL RELATIONS

INTERNATIONAL POLITICAL ECONOMY: UNDERSTANDING GLOBAL DISORDER (*with Robert Cox, Björn Hettne, James Rosenau, Yoshikazu Sakamoto and Kees van der Pijl*)

CHIKU SEJI NO SAIKOCHIKU: REISENGO NO NICHIBEIOU KANKEI TO SEKAI CHITSUJO (RESTRUCTURING GLOBAL POLITICS *in Japanese translated and edited by Seiji Endo*)

GLOBALIZATION, DEMOCRATIZATION AND MULTILATERALISM

INNOVATION AND TRANSFORMATION IN INTERNATIONAL STUDIES (*with James Mittelman*)

Power and Resistance in the New World Order

Stephen Gill

Professor of Political Science
York University, Toronto, Canada

First published 2003 by
PALGRAVE MACMILLAN
Houndmills, Basingstoke, Hampshire RG21 6XS and
175 Fifth Avenue, New York, N.Y. 10010
Companies and representatives throughout the world

PALGRAVE MACMILLAN is the global academic imprint of the
Palgrave Macmillan division of St Martin's Press LLC and of
Palgrave Macmillan Ltd.
Macmillan® is a registered trademark in the United States,
United Kingdom and other countries. Palgrave is a registered
trademark in the European Union and other countries.

ISBN 1 4039 0389 1 hardback
ISBN 1 4039 0390 5 paperback

This book is printed on paper suitable for recycling and
made from fully managed and sustained forest sources.

A catalogue record for this book is available
from the British Library.

Library of Congress Cataloging-in-Publication Data
Gill, Stephen, 1950–
    Power and resistance in the new world order / Stephen Gill.
        p. cm.
    Includes bibliographical references and index.
    ISBN 1–40390–389–1 (cloth)
        1. International relations. 2. Balance of power. 3. Economics.
    I. Title.

JZ1310 .G55 2003
327.1'01—dc21
                                                          2002028751

10   9   8   7   6   5   4   3   2
12   11   10   09   08   07   06   05   04

Printed and bound in Great Britain by
Antony Rowe Ltd, Chippenham and Eastbourne

For Isabella

Contents

Preface

This volume has two basic purposes. First, it is intended to outline and explain aspects of the new world order created after 1945, for example its geopolitical and political economy elements, and to highlight the central role of American power.[1] Second, the book tries to show how power and resistance have multiple forms and moments in the making of world orders more generally. Various forms of power and resistance include hegemonic leadership, supremacy, counter-hegemonic resistance and what I call *transformative resistance*: forms of resistance that may serve to constitute historical alternatives.

The different forms of power identified in this book – whether they are direct or relational, structural or constitutive, overt or covert – are connected to different forms of knowledge and political agency. Power structures and power relations emerge from and are connected to agency and to political actors: this involves the consciousness and collective action of elites, classes, and movements. Power is also related to how social forces are imagined, motivated and organized. Power is mediated, channelled, mobilized and institutionalized through political and civil society, that is states, political associations and other organizations, in ways that serve to constitute historical structures of global politics.

At the same time, various forms of power are connected to different forms and patterns of resistance. Resistance can be active or passive, localized or global, negative or creative. Transformative resistance involves not only negation but also creation and the personal and the political. It is often connected to actions and conduct of leaders that exemplify and inspire collective action. Examples of leaders who succeeded in this regard – despite extreme conditions of oppression, poverty or incarceration – include Gandhi, Gramsci and Mandela.

So what of issues of power and resistance at the start of the new millennium? After a period when the power of capital has been ascendant,

---

1. My concept of 'new world order' should not be confused with the usage of President George H. Bush who used the term to describe the nature of international relations after the 1991 Gulf War. As will become clear, I see the post-1991 situation as a third phase in the development of a new world order that arose from the ashes of World War II.

as articulated for example in the ideology and practice of globalization, perhaps one of the most important, and in some senses optimistic developments in global politics is the emergence of globalized forms of resistance. Many of these are associated with movements geared towards securing a more just, sustainable and democratic world order. Of course, many forms of resistance are simply opposed to the dominant projects associated with the globalization of capitalism. Others, for example social democratic perspectives, tend to be concerned with creating a more humane form of capitalist globalization. However the social democratic perspective tends to underestimate the degree to which globalization of capitalism and politics (states play a central role) is a revolutionary, intensifying process that involves both the integration of the world through the creation of a world market, as well as social disintegration as the radically new supplants the old. This process seems to now be globalizing what feminists call a crisis of social reproduction, involving tremendous social dislocations.

In this sense, capitalist globalization involves a hierarchy of power and resistance linked to basic changes in the everyday lives of people. This great transformation is associated with the intensification and extension of exchange relations and the mediation of social relations by money, a process that is largely shaped by the discipline of capital. It means greater aspects of human activity and numbers of life forms are now subject to exploitation and commodification. Indeed, as obscene levels of global inequality intensify, capital seems to become increasingly akin to the alien power theorized by Marx. To reverse Schumpeter's proposition: capital is now perhaps more destructive than creative.

So, notwithstanding evidence of more sophisticated coercive capacities of states to control and to discipline resistance (see Chapter 10), there is now a pattern of resistance to neo-liberal restructuring and globalization that goes beyond capillary forms of resistance within local communities, and indeed goes beyond traditional nationalist forms of resistance to foreign power associated with the balance of power.

Of course, resistance to aspects of the new world order and the globalization of capitalism can take on a reactionary, xenophobic or fundamentalist form that is anti-modernist in its perspective on the world. Much of this resistance is in fact connected to nationalism and some versions of the ideology of 'the national interest' propagated by traditional elites. By contrast, what I call transformative, global resistance is associated with innovative forms of political agency that are global in scope and that stem from popular movements (see Chapter 11).

This form of resistance is transformative since it involves more than simply the negation, or counter-action of dominant power within the context of a power relation (or the balance of power). It involves movement rather than management and it implies therefore a transformation in the political limits of the possible. As a consequence it points towards social possibilities and intimations of new forms of social and political order.

In this book I am therefore interested in analysing and explaining a central aspect of the redefinition of the political on a world scale, and how this relates to our civilizational possibilities. This involves analysis, first, of the changing nature of dominant power, and second, sketching the contours of the historical dialectic between dominant power and forms of resistance. Third, this involves identification of those forms of transformative resistance associated with a universalism that is premised on opposing all forms of oppression and violence and affirming a diversity that is tolerant and pluralist relative to the coexistence of different civilizations and a variety of political economy forms. The issue is perhaps the most fundamental one of our times, although it is not to be confused with Samuel Huntington's post-Cold War thesis of a 'clash of civilizations', or 'the West versus the rest'. The issue is more complex since it cuts across different civilizational forms, which should be understood as cultural processes in movement, not objects that are frozen in time. It is, at one and the same time, a global and a local issue mediated by the spread and deepening of the social relations of globalizing capitalism. It involves a clash between a singular market civilization, shaped by corporate power, versus the possibility of civilizational diversity.

In this respect it is important to stress that forms of transformative resistance can come from 'the power of the powerless', particularly when apparently powerless groups interconnect and link up with other social movements and forces throughout the world. For example, the landless peasant movements in Brazil have managed to develop new concepts of power and production through collective action, seizing control not only of unused land of absentee landlords, but also of their own lives and destinies. Such movements, which include other groups in Latin America and elsewhere (e.g. the Zapatistas in Mexico or the U'Wa in Colombia) have provided inspiration for other groups in their struggle to assert their identity, dignity and rights to livelihood. They also offer an epistemo-logical alternative to dominant ways of seeing and interpreting the world. At the same time they have connected with and become significant in much wider political groupings such as those that congregate at and network through the World Social Forum in Porto Alegre (a city that is well known for its self-government by and for the people).

In a broader sense many of these groups are coming together to form a novel transnational political party that is multiple in form and is a set of forces in movement. They may be beginning to point towards alternatives to an ordinary politics that is constrained by constitutional law and other political-juridical 'new constitutional frameworks' that underpin the dominant power of the propertied and the globalizing elites discussed in Chapter 9, for example the World Economic Forum in Davos. Thus the new world order should be understood as comprising ideas, institutions and processes in movement. It involves different constituencies, moments and frameworks of power and knowledge. It is associated with the changing conditions of existence that people face in their everyday lives. In this new world order there is a clash of globalizations – as the forces represented by the World Social Forum and popular movements from below challenge the World Economic Forum of the globalizing elites and this clash concerns, along with basic issues of political economy, human security and human rights, the question of what it means to be civilized.

It may be clear by now that the term 'world order' is not used in this book to indicate a normatively desirable condition. Rather it is an analytical construct. Indeed world order refers not simply to the relations between states and the capacities and potentials for organized violence (as in traditional Realist thought). It also refers to how forms of power and resistance, and production and destruction produce patterns of world order. My work is based upon a non-atomistic *social* ontology that involves the way human beings are constituted in and through social processes and institutions. Thus social relations and social structures (including what feminist theorists call the structures of social reproduction) form the starting point for the analysis of world orders, understood as specific configurations of social forces in historical situations.

Thus the 'new world order' can be understood as a *social process* that involves dominant power, and resistance to that power under conditions of intensifying globalization. This involves not only a hierarchy of states but also new forms of power and authority linked to the globalization of capital and the globalization of resistance (both of passive resistance and direct action). It involves struggles over issues of war and peace and those related to the contradictions of political economy, culture and civilization. The point is however, that contradictions cannot simply be resolved at the level of theory: this requires the movement of social and historical forces in collective action.

A word on the structure of the book

This work was originally intended to be a representative collection of my essays published since the mid-1980s. It has become something different. In the same way that an intellectual dialectic between the old and the new in my thinking about world order has emerged in the past decade, so I began to perceive that a coherent work about the new world order would require reworking some of the earlier essays as well as the inclusion of new, previously unpublished work (the Preface, and Chapters 1, 3 and 10 are new pieces). So I have liberally edited, abridged and reworked some of the earlier essays, but have ensured that their original argument has been preserved. The original sources of these works are listed in the Acknowledgements below. I have tried to make lengthy essays shorter and where an essay has been abridged, this is indicated by means of ellipses.

With this in mind, the book is constructed in three interconnected parts: the specification of its theoretical apparatus and key concepts (Part I: 'Social and International Theory'); elements of the historical constitution of power structures of, and contradictions in, world order (Part II: 'Political Economy of World Order'); and contemporary patterns of power and resistance (including transformative resistance) connected to emergent political possibilities (Part III: 'Global Transformation and Political Agency'). Each part has an introduction to the chapters within it, written with the invaluable help of Tim DiMuzio, who was an imaginative and exemplary Research Assistant for this work. Readers who wish to get an overview of the work may want to read these introductory pieces before embarking upon specific chapters.

In this framework several concrete aspects of the new world order are identified and articulated. For example, structures of global social stratification associated with the supremacy of the globalizing elites and disciplinary neo-liberalism (e.g. Chapter 9) as well as other political forms connected to new constitutionalism, panopticism and surveillance power (Chapters 7 and 10) are outlined. They form part of the dialectic of power and resistance, dominance and subordination, hegemony and supremacy that shapes the problematic of this book.

In conclusion the task of critical social and international theory is twofold: epistemological and political. It involves the explanation of the constitution of world orders and the determination of the nature, limits and potentials for political action in any given era. Second, critical theory is part of the global movement of social and political forces. It forms a moment in the politics of a transformative resistance as it seeks to conceptualize and to identify potentials for emancipation and liberation, sustainable social and human development, and conditions for human security. Of course this includes resistance to illegitimate power. As Shakespeare once put it in *Macbeth*:

Fare you well.
Do we but find the tyrant's power to-night,
Let us be beaten, if we cannot fight.[2]

---

2. Siward, Act 5, Scene 6. <http://classics.mit.edu/Shakespeare/macbeth/macbeth.5.6.html>.

Acknowledgements

I wish to thank the following institutions for their support: Wolverhampton University; UCLA; Manchester University; the UK's ESRC; Canadian SSHRC; St Antony's College, Oxford; Faculty of Law, University of Tokyo; Japan Association for the Promotion of Science; Meiji Gakuin University, La Trobe University, Department of Political Science and Office of the Dean of Arts, York University, Toronto.

Second, I would like to thank Nicola Viinikka for commissioning this book and Amanda Watkins, Guy Edwards and Oliver Howard at Palgrave Macmillan for their fine editorial work.

Third, I most gratefully acknowledge permission to reproduce, edit, rework and update material from the following: Millennium, Monthly Review Foundation, Cambridge University Press, Palgrave Macmillan and the United Nations University.

Chapter 2 is a reworked and edited version of an essay originally published as: 'Epistemology, Ontology and the "Italian School"', in Stephen Gill (ed.) *Gramsci, Historical Materialism and International Relations* (Cambridge University Press, 1993) pp. 21–48. Chapter 4 is a longer version of a very short piece, 'Hegemony, Culture and Imperialism'. It was the foreword to Matt Davies' *International Political Economy and Mass Communications in Chile* (Basingstoke and New York: Macmillan/St Martin's Press, 1999) pp. vii–xi. Chapter 5 is a radically abridged version of 'American Hegemony: Its Limits and Prospects in the Reagan Era'. It previously appeared in *Millennium*, Vol. 15: 3 (1986) pp. 311–36. Chapter 6 is a shortened version of Stephen Gill and David Law, 'Global Hegemony and the Structural Power of Capital', in Stephen Gill (ed.) *Gramsci, Historical Materialism and International Relations* (Cambridge University Press, 1993) pp. 93–124. Except for a reduction in its extensive footnotes, Chapter 7 reprints the complete text of 'Globalisation, Market Civilisation and Disciplinary Neoliberalism', *Millennium*, Vol. 24: 3 (1995) pp. 399–423. Chapter 8 is a slightly enlarged version of a short essay originally published as 'The Geopolitics of the Asian Crisis', *Monthly Review*, Vol. 50: 10 (1999) pp. 1–10. Chapter 9 is a radically abridged and slightly reworked version of 'Political Economy and Structural Change: Globalizing Elites in the Emerging World Order', in Yoshikazu Sakamoto (ed.) *Global Transformation: Challenges to the State System* (Tokyo, United Nations

University Press, 1994) pp. 169–99. Chapter 11 was originally 'Toward a Postmodern Prince? The Battle in Seattle as a Moment in the New Politics of Globalisation' *Millennium*, Vol. 29: 1 (2000) pp. 131–41. It is reprinted as in the original, with a small but important footnote added at the end of the piece.

Fourth, this book is indebted to many other scholars. Most of this book was written whilst I have been at York University, Toronto. So I would like, initially, to thank the following colleagues and students who helped form the intellectual community that has supported my work in Canada: Cemal Acikgoz, Rob Albritton, Nicole Anastasopoulos, Tyler Attwood, Mitchell Bernard, Elaine Brown, Greg Chin, Melodie Cilio, Robert Cox, Jessie Cox, George Comninel, André Drainville, Bob Drummond, Grace-Edward Galabuzi, Randy Germain, Andrea Harrington, Eric Helleiner, Ahmed Hashi, Derek Hall, Seiko Hanochi, Gigi Herbert, Martin Hewson, Gibin Hong, Greg Jacobs, Matina Karvellas, Samuel Knafo, David Leyton Brown, Marie Josée Massicote, David McNally, David Moore, Hepzibah Munoz Martinez, Rob O'Brien, Leo Panitch, Marlene Quesenberry, Nigmendra Narain, Jonathan Nitzan, Hélène Pellerin, Scott Redding, Magnus Ryner, John Saul, Tim Sinclair, Noli Swatman, Angie Swartz, Jacqueline True, Douglas Verney, Silvia Waterman-Anderson and Ellen Wood.

I also extend my sincere thanks to other (non-York) colleagues helpful to my work: Georges Abi-Saab, John Agnew, Esref Aksu, Giovanni Arrighi, Dennis Altman, Richard Ashley, Elmar Altvater, Donatella di Benedetto, Lourdes Beneria, Leo Bieling, Janine Brodie, Steve Burman, Joseph Buttigieg, Alan Cafruny, Joseph Camilleri, James Caporaso, Phil Cerny, Fantu Cheru, David Coates, Bruce Cumings, Matt Davies, Georgi Derlugian, Bob Denemark, Martin Durham, Seiji Endo, Diane Elson, Richard Falk, Jeff Frieden, Harriet Friedman, John Haslam, Jeff Harrod, Richard Higgott, Michael Holdsworth, Glenn Hook, Otto Holman, Makato Itoh, Tony Jarvis, the late Takehiko Kamo, Shigeru Kido, Bradley Klein, Makato Kobayashi, Robert Kudrle, Robert Latham, Jong won Lee, David Law, Michael Loriaux, Neil Malcolm, Adam Morton, Henk Overbeek, Ronen Palan, Mustapha Kamal Pasha, Harry Magdoff, Rianne Mahon, Phillip McMichael, Craig Murphy, Kinhide Mushakoji, Michael Loriaux, Hidetoshi Nakamura, Chris Reus-Smit, Adam Roberts, Carlos Parodi, Frank Pearce, Spike Peterson, Kees van der Pijl, Heather Rae, David Rapkin, James Rosenau, Bill Robinson, Steve Rosow, Mark Rupert, Yoshikazu Sakamoto, Mike Schechter, the late Hiroharu Seki, Tim Shaw, Steve Smith, Tetsuya Tanami, Ann Tickner, Roger Tooze, the late Susan Strange, John Vogler, Takeo Uchida, Brigitte Young, John Vogler and R.B.J. (Rob) Walker.

The final stages in the production of a book involve the talents of many people, and this one is no exception. The team that worked with me to finish this book included Tyler Attwood and Tim DiMuzio who did the bulk of the painstaking work preparing the index. Tyler assisted in proofreading with Tracey Day. Ray Addicott supervised the proofs and the printing of the text in a timely, efficient and thoroughly professional manner. Isabella Bakker took the author photograph, and an artist friend, Peter Scarth, produced the striking image on the livery of the book based on his painting 'Hard Rain' (1994). Gregory Scarth transformed the original painting into an electronic version for the jacket, which was designed by Tony Hooper. My sincere thanks go to all of them.

Finally, very special thanks are due to Isabella Bakker, Adam Harmes and Randolph Persaud for suggesting that I produce this book, and to Randy for so graciously insisting on the title. I also especially thank David Sarai, Lori-Ann Campbell and particularly Tim DiMuzio for their research assistance in the production of this book. I am grateful to Isabella and Tim for very carefully reading and commenting on the final manuscript. Of course I remain responsible for errors and omissions and hope that anyone whose help I have forgotten will forgive me.

Toronto, 16 July 2002

1
Personal, Political and Intellectual Influences

This introductory chapter is written partly at the request of the several colleagues and students who prompted me to produce this book. They felt it would be useful if I were to sketch out, as a background to this selection of my work, some of the personal, intellectual and political influences that have motivated me, and that have shaped my thinking.

I was born on the last day of 1950. Thus my political perspective on the world was a product of the new world order that followed the most lethal war in history, World War II. A then reformed capitalism confronted a communist alternative, in an era of decolonization and creation of many new states that comprised what came to be known as the Third World. Since then, the world order has gone through a number of phases or mutations and it has become progressively more capitalist: (1) the period between the late 1940s and the early 1970s that corresponds to its creation; (2) the period between the early 1970s and the late 1980s involving its transformation; and (3) the period since the early 1990s associated with its extension on a global basis: a world order with a single 'hyper-power' and a potentially universal form of capitalism. However, at the start of the twenty-first century there is also a new moment in the making of global politics. I call this moment the 'clash of globalizations' and it involves global resistance – to both the power of the USA and the power of capital.

So in what follows I will narrate those parts of my intellectual journey that correspond most directly to my interpretations of the phases of the new world order, and I will also indicate some of the lineages of the theoretical principles in my work. I conclude with a brief sketch of a central theme of the book.

Politics in the classroom and the politics of class

My political inclinations can be traced back to the effects of, and resistance to some of the pernicious effects of the British class system. My

1

understanding of the class system emerged during my education and upbringing in the north of England, in the city of Leeds in Yorkshire, during the 1950s and 1960s. This system helped forge a sense of injustice and resistance to illegitimate power that have been driving forces in much of my intellectual and political work. The British class system is a form of social power that is cruelly designed to create subservience to the rulers and to prepare working-class children for subordinate, largely menial wage-labour. It is also a tactile, almost material force that systematically configures life-chances. Indeed I vividly remember, as I grew up during the era of the welfare state system, I could not help noticing how young, working-class women seemed to grow old, long before their time. I also recall how the class system in its manifold manifestations served to lower the expectations of the majority of the population. Indeed I also remember the old truism of one law for the rich and another for the poor in British society, and how the drama of daily events furnished evidence of its verisimilitude.

My parents – Rowland and Millicent Gill – grew up in this world, having met and married following World War II. They produced two children and David, now a businessman, is by 14 months the younger of the two brothers. My father had spent two years in a military hospital during World War II recovering from severe injuries received in the service of his country. Prior to enlistment, my father had been a very successful young footballer. The war resulted in a permanent disability and he limped for the rest of his life (although he never once complained about what had happened). Thus a promising career was foreclosed to him, although in those pre-televisual days, soccer was played for the glory and not for wealth. Players were employed under a regime of low (maximum) wages and had few opportunities for sponsorships and other cash spin-offs associated with the inflated celebrity culture of our times. My father and mother left school at the then normal age of 14 and both worked in various manual and semiskilled jobs. My father was a popular and generous man, and my mother a loving person. Indeed, although our family was relatively poor, I have little recollection of feeling deprived as a child, although I remember growing up in the centre of a large industrial city, where often the playgrounds were the streets and the roofs of factories.

In my primary school (ages 5 to 11) most of the other children had the expectations that had been prescribed to them – that the right and proper thing to do was to go to the 'secondary modern', that is schools for working-class children designed, in accord with the intentions governing the class system, to provide them with the minimal literacy required for manual jobs. By contrast, I wanted to further my education and I received a lot of encouragement to do so from my teachers, as well as from my parents and relatives.

I became the first child at the school for many years to pass the infamous '11 plus' exam and so I qualified to go to grammar school.[1] The grammar school was a place where one could gain higher qualifications, and if one was lucky, perhaps go on to university. However at this stage the idea of a university seemed like a fictional idea: like the gleaming city on the hill in Thomas Hardy's novel *Jude the Obscure*. I remember at the time choosing to go to City of Leeds School because it allowed me to play soccer, rather than rugby (my ambition was to become a professional soccer player). There, I became Captain of Newton House (named after the great scientist) and Captain of the Football XI. However despite some academic and sporting success, my Headmaster considered me (with some justification) to be an irredeemable rebel. Since he believed I could not be tamed by the system, he frequently threatened to expel me. My parents, however, failed to see things the same way as he did. The threatened expulsion was never carried out.

So despite such local difficulties I subsequently became the only member of my extended family who went to university (my father had ten siblings and my mother four sisters – I have numerous cousins). Perhaps it was my love of soccer and arts, including music that largely kept me out of other political trouble at the time. On the other hand, some of my musical influences came from blues music and protest songs. Indeed my later years in school coincided with the peak of the worldwide student movement. My final year of school was in 1968. So it is hardly surprising that I played a minor part in this moment when the old order was shaken to its foundations.

At a series of universities I took several degrees in different subjects including English, French, Economics, Industrial Administration, Government and Politics and Education. Of importance for my subsequent thinking was the class on liberalism that I took at Essex University with John Gray, later to become a professor at Oxford and the London School of Economics, and, for a period, a supporter of Thatcherism. Gray was an

---

1. The 11 plus exam was sat by all 11-year-olds and the exam decided one's educational future. In the mid-1960s, this exam was abolished. Secondary modern schools and grammar schools were replaced in the state system by comprehensive schools. However, some grammar schools were allowed to opt out of the state system, and effectively became 'public' (i.e. private) schools. The public school is a peculiarly British oxymoron. Public schools are in fact expensive private schools, designed for offspring of the ruling and owning classes. The vast majority of Oxbridge graduates have come from public schools.

excellent teacher who really understood the liberal mind and was particularly expert on Hayek and Popper, two of the most influential thinkers of the twentieth century. This training helped me subsequently to understand the intellectual basis of liberalism. The other main influence in my university education of direct significance in terms of later work was my reading for the doctoral degree in Sociology that I took as a part-time student at Birmingham University under the thoughtful and generous supervision of Dr Stephen Burman (now at Sussex). This degree allowed me to study transnational class formations and to begin to think about world order in a more complex way than orthodox theorizations of International Relations seemed to allow. Nevertheless it was a long, hard task to complete the thesis, which I eventually defended before the formidable presence of the late Susan Strange, my external examiner. I studied for the degree part-time since at the age of 25 I had obtained a full-time position at Wolverhampton Polytechnic (now University). Sadly, my father passed away after a long struggle with cancer just before the PhD degree was conferred, something that he had looked forward to witnessing.

In retrospect, I was one of a small minority who managed to break free of some of the intellectual and political shackles of the British class system, and the fact that this happened was because collective action had created the social reforms that followed the Great Depression and World War II. The war brought broad pressure from working-class forces to create a new form of state in Britain – one that would be more democratic and inclusive of the various interests of society. The sacrifices made during World War II in the Herculean struggle against the Axis powers meant that the ruling class had to agree to changes in the framework of politics – partly in order to preserve British capitalism. This meant post-war reconstruction and the creation of the welfare state was shared by both major parties (Conservatives and Labour) in a political consensus that lasted until the early 1970s. Real gains were made for working people in healthcare and in the socialization of risk through pensions and unemployment benefits. In this sense it seems absolutely right to re-state the central theme of E.P. Thompson's magisterial work: the English working classes are indeed always present at their own creation (Thompson 1980). However it must be stated that my appreciation for and support of working-class culture is and has always been tempered with a healthy combination of 'pessimism of the intelligence and optimism of the will'.[2] Coming from a working-class background, and having had many factory

---

2. This was Gramsci's favourite maxim, and motto of the revolutionary newspaper *L'Ordine Nuovo*. Romain Rolland originally coined the phrase.

and other manual jobs, I held few illusions about the English working classes that some of my middle-class contemporaries at university sometimes indulged in.[3]

A sociological perspective on world order

It was in Wolverhampton that the next and most important stage in my intellectual formation took place. It was there that I developed what C. Wright Mills would have called a 'sociological perspective' on world order. It was where I became an international theorist, although one who had never taken any courses in International Relations. It was also where I learned to discipline my time and learn more systematically. Up to that point, my studies had allowed me to understand some themes and topics well, but often I was left with a knowledge structure that resembled a patchwork quilt with many holes. Teaching full-time at university level, often on topics that I had little or no knowledge of, forced me to learn quickly, systematically and comprehensively. Moreover, since Wolverhampton was a new institution, and just beginning to provide degree programmes, it meant that the recently hired, younger faculty members were thrown in at the deep end. We were required to work in teams to write entire degree programmes, and not just specific courses, and then to justify our proposals before an external review body, the Council of National Academic Awards, which we called, with due deference to Monty Python, 'The Spanish Inquisition'.

During this period I had a number of fine colleagues. Of these the most influential were Frank Pearce and David Law. Together they and our young group of faculty endlessly debated social and political theory, political economy and philosophy. We discussed the works of great modern thinkers such as Althusser, Gramsci and Foucault; Smith, Ricardo and Keynes; Marx, Durkheim and Weber; Popper, Kuhn and Feyerabend; as well as many others. Indeed, our young faculty not only survived The Inquisition, with no one burned at the stake, but several also began to publish their work and enjoy what was for them the magical status of print. Indeed in the mid-1980s members of the Politics Group were

---

3. E.P. Thompson sought to rescue the English working classes from the intellectual savagery of the elites, or, as he put it from 'the enormous condescension of posterity'. I share Thompson's aversion for the elitism that characterized some of the British left as it filled the university expansion of the 1960s and 1970s. To this extent, I considered myself to be an outsider relative to much of left-wing intellectual culture in Britain.

astonished to learn they had been ranked highly for teaching of politics in the venerable *Times Higher Education Supplement*. In an act of apparent heresy, the editors of the *THES* ranked Wolverhampton in front of several universities normally associated with the ethos of 'effortless superiority'. This period made me appreciate that creativity is often a collective practice. It also allowed me to develop a global political economy and world order viewpoint grounded in a sociological perspective (what a reviewer of my work in *THES* called 'the big picture'). Also at Wolverhampton I developed courses on American politics and society, allowing me to extend my lifelong interest in the relationship between the USA as a society and the modern world – a necessary part of the 'big picture' if you like.

Although many intellectual relationships were significant in this period, the most important was with David Law. David and I worked together consistently for about ten years. David is an extraordinarily widely read person whose insights go well beyond the nuances of economics and political economy. He is a person of great integrity, patience and loyalty, with little of the ego that often accompanies great minds. We had little trouble in agreeing that the most persuasive form of politics and pedagogy was based on an open debate that allows the reader to make an informed decision about problems and policies with an awareness of different explanations and perspectives. So we wrote our (very long) book *The Global Political Economy* partly to outline and partly to engender as a debate between the major perspectives in International Political Economy. We made a point of trying to highlight our own argument and if possible to contribute to the most innovative approaches, as well as seeking to shape agendas for further study and research. This commitment to innovation and emancipatory forms of knowledge has been a foundation of my subsequent work, which I consider to be a combination of the philosophical, political and pedagogical.

During the time I was at Wolverhampton, British society was transformed by reforms introduced by the Conservatives under Margaret Thatcher. The post-war consensus referred to earlier, broke down in the early 1970s, and the shift to neo-liberalism in Britain was consummated in 1976. At that time, the Labour government went to the IMF and the Bank for International Settlements for loans to deal with a balance of payments crisis. The change in policy split the Cabinet, and although only a small minority favoured the 'narrow path to growth', Labour shifted towards the rudiments of what today would be referred to as the 'Washington consensus'. Thatcher came to power in 1979 following the so-called 'winter of discontent', involving widespread public sector strikes and general dislocation. The Conservatives intensified the application of neo-liberalism, and in the early 1980s there was a very deep, indeed planned, recession designed to restructure the political economy, that led, as a side effect, to rioting in over 40 towns and cities throughout Great Britain.

In education, Thatcherism produced a productivity miracle, as student numbers rose and as faculty complements fell in the polytechnics (where the experiments were initiated), and thereafter in other universities, although, as usual, the elite universities were largely insulated from the cuts. During the 1980s Wolverhampton was transformed from a relatively collegial, small-scale university into a large 'provider' of degrees and other, increasingly vocational courses. It was now run by a centralized 'management' that sought to increase the productivity of its faculty through the application of Taylorist, factory principles of scientific management, through promotion of Thatcherite fellow-travellers and, if possible, elimination of slackers or dissidents. Hierarchical management, 'quality control measures' and new businesslike incentives were the order of the day. The university was dedicated to producing varied menus in the new cafeteria system to service its 'educational consumers'. With the effort at abolition of the traditional language of teacher and student and its replacement with the newspeak of provider and client, came widespread panopticism in the workplace. Shortly after I had left England for Canada, it transpired that senior members of faculty were required to wear beepers and report directly to their 'line managers', that is their deans, on a 24-hour basis. With varied degrees of success the management sought to overcome traditional forms of resistance and produce a normalized, conformist and business-oriented consciousness amongst faculty members (see Chapter 10 on other aspects of panopticism). These educational 'reforms' were a prototype for subsequent efforts to restructure state institutions along more marketized, commodified lines and to shift British society towards what I have called a market civilization (see Chapter 7).

In sum, there was collapse of the post-war consensus in Britain and the beginnings of a conservative counter-revolution intended to rollback working-class gains of the post-war period, and also to prevent the challenges of the 1960s and 1970s from making any further progress. In many respects, Thatcherism was inspired by the political thought of Friedrich von Hayek and the economics of Milton Friedman and it became the emblem of global neo-liberal reform, its trademarks including privatization, monetarism and deregulation. However, the crucial forces in the shift towards disciplinary neo-liberalism came from the USA. This was when American macroeconomic policy featured a combination of very tight monetary policies, and tax cutting and military Keynesianism of the Reagan Administration. Reaganomics allied to the second Cold War drove the global shift towards neo-liberal globalization under American dominance (see Chapter 5).

Disciplinary neo-liberalism and the end of history

The third stage of my intellectual formation coincided with my life living outside of the UK after 1990 when I immigrated to Canada, as an intellectual refugee from Thatcherism. In 1990, I took up a position in Political Science at York University in Toronto following a brief appointment at Manchester University. My change of country coincided with the onset of a major shift in the structures of world order. The period 1968–79 was one of economic and political crises in many of the OECD countries, with the old order being challenged from below, as well as at the inter-state level. Increasing militancy in the Third World and the rise to superpower parity by the Soviet Union were features of these changes. However, as we have noted, and as the *coup d'état* in Chile in 1973 underlined (see Chapter 4), in the 1970s there was a powerful conservative and neo-liberal counter-offensive. During the 1980s, following the world's deepest recession since the 1930s (1979–82), the neo-liberal right largely succeeded in rolling back the challenge of the socialist left, Third World militancy and Soviet-led communism.

Indeed 1989 saw the beginnings of the collapse of communist rule in Eastern Europe. The 'transition' to capitalism involved increasing use of what I call new constitutional measures in the former East Bloc, as well as in the OECD and the Third World (see Chapters 7–9 on the sequencing of this process and the use of legal and institutional measures to lock in the property rights and power gains of capital). My new home country, Canada, of course was not immune to these changes. After I took up my appointment in Political Science at York University, Canada had entered into a neo-liberal phase in its policies at both federal and provincial levels, both of which are significant in Canadian politics. Moreover, Canada entered into free trade agreements with the USA in ways that many felt would create constitutional subordination of Canada to the USA, as well as constrain progressive forms of public policy. On the other hand, as in many other countries, domestic forces were at work pressing for neo-liberalism. For example in Ontario, under the banner of the balanced budget, the Conservative government pursued harsh neo-liberal policies after its election in 1995. One of the results of Federal and Provincial cutbacks in education, health and social spending was an enormous increase in deprivation, child poverty and homelessness whilst the numbers of Canadian millionaires rose rapidly.

In this context, the social settlements and forms of state created after World War II have been transformed and in some respects destroyed. They have been transformed in the context of much more marketized and commodified world order under the dominance of a single superpower, the USA. The USA presides, in an imperialist manner, over global governance in concert with other powerful capitalist states in the G7.

More broadly, the period 1989–97 was one of American triumphalism as well as intensification of disciplinary neo-liberalism under the political slogan 'the end of history', the neo-Hegelian proposition that all meaningful political alternatives to the absolute idea of liberty had been exhausted or were buried under the rubble of communism. Since 1979 there has been an acceleration of historical time connected to the emergence of intensified globalization (see Chapters 2 and 3 for a discussion of the structure of political necessity in connection with rhythms and tempos of historical time).

It is now very well documented that the neo-liberal period of restructuring in the new world order has been a process of 'creative destruction'. However, by the late 1990s many people throughout the world were wondering whether the new world order had become more destructive then creative. Indeed despite successful efforts to incorporate some forms of opposition into the neo-liberal globalization project (e.g. social democracy), other forms of global politics began to challenge the 'end of history' hypothesis and its political constraints. Partly because of increasingly obscene levels of global inequality and massive social dislocations connected to crises and restructuring, challenges from the left and the right to the supremacist political project of globalization have become increasingly manifest. I have called this 'the clash of globalizations' (Gill 2002). The clash is linked to the emergence of a 'Post-modern Prince', that is an innovative form of global collective political agency that goes beyond localized resistance to disciplinary neo-liberalism to create real alternatives (see Chapter 11). In a word, the clash involves the old and the new, the right and the left, including what I have called transformative resistance.

Part I

Social and International Theory

Part I is concerned with outlining (1) the need to unite both social and international theory, and (2) to do so by providing an epistemological, ontological and methodological framework adequate to understanding and explaining world orders. Of course there is no single way to approach these issues. What follows are three chapters that, in the context of other work, form preliminary theoretical sketches for a critical, historical materialist perspective on political economy and international relations – one that seeks to critique and to go beyond the conventional wisdom and the theoretical and practical restrictions imposed by prevailing orthodoxies, whether of Realists, Liberals, or the adherents of orthodox Marxism.

Chapter 2 sketches four arguments that serve as a critique of political economy in order to go beyond ahistorical, determinist and orthodox theorizations to explain complex social transformations in world order. In this regard three major differences are highlighted that distinguish between a Gramscian approach to the study of International Relations and Political Economy and other, more positivist theorizations: (1) its non-structuralist historicism and critique of positivism; (2) its critique of all forms of methodological individualism and methodological reductionism; and (3) its insistence upon an ethical dimension to the study of social relations.

The chapter then distinguishes between historical materialism and historical economism. It argues that a historical materialist framework is much more reflexive and dynamic in so far as its theoretical development is premised upon the study of social structures that change through and over time. Indeed, in the current conjuncture of crisis, social relations and structures (constituted by collective action) are undergoing a great transformation as the power and logic of capital becomes more and more entrenched in everyday life in global society. How social formations will evolve under the new conditions of transnational production, circulation and exchange, is therefore also a question to be decided by the collective action of humankind. This is another way of emphasizing that the theoretical and practical analysis of world order should be from 'the bottom upwards, as well as the top downwards' in an approach

11

concerned with *'movement, rather than management'*. By contrast, the managerial approach reflects the needs of dominant power and its intellectual orthodoxy.

Chapter 2 concludes with a critique of vulgar Marxism and other orthodox discourses, paying particular attention to how much US scholarship seeks to insulate itself from critical attack. Dominant discourses seek to discipline theoretical alternatives that might challenge their power by creating and sustaining their identity as orthodoxy, with its high priests, acolytes and deviants clearly demarcated. This not only inhibits theoretical innovation, but it also serves to consolidate and reinforce a particular way of conceiving the world that assumes the status of universal 'truth'.

Chapter 3, 'Transnational Historical Materialism and World Order' is also animated by the goal outlined in Chapter 2: the search for a more comprehensive framework for analysing world order. It demonstrates an attempt to develop a new historical materialist method of analysis that goes beyond traditional forms of Social and International Relations theory. Building on some of the ideas of Fernand Braudel, Karl Marx and Antonio Gramsci, it seeks to provide both a conceptual map and a methodology that can serve to highlight the historical dialectic of the 'old' and 'new' in the constitution and transformation of world orders. Thus the chapter begins with an explication of rhythms and tempos of social or historical time (event, conjuncture and the *longue durée*). It links these to issues of power, production, and the broader reproduction of social relations in historical time.

Chapter 3 shows how the object of analysis of Political Science (and Political Economy) is a concrete historical situation. This idea is explored in a novel way through articulating the concepts of hegemony and the relations of force (structural, political and strategic). Of interest here is that despite conjunctural changes in the constitution of capital, its *longue durée* is characterized by a remarkable structural continuity and extension of its basic social form associated with exchange value and the 'monetization and commodification' of social relations. Some of the lineage of these developments is illustrated by the example of an original revolution that served to constitute the onset of modern (bourgeois) state formation in Britain. The English case is exemplary, not only because it illustrates how the expansion of capitalist social relations coincides with the early modern capitalist state formation with a particular legal apparatus that privileges the rights of private property owners. This case also shows how the rise of capital is linked to earlier patterns of globalization associated with incipient British imperialism. All of this helps to prepare the ground for analysis of the twentieth century with specific emphasis on restructuring in the former communist-ruled states in Eastern Europe as a form of 'passive revolution'. The chapter concludes with a discussion of the formation of historic blocs in the context of world order and the argument that the new world order of the 1990s can be characterized by a politics of supremacy (rather than hegemony) dominated by an American-led 'transnational historic bloc'.

'Hegemony, Culture and Imperialism' is a brief chapter that stresses links between culture and hegemony in the context of American imperialism in Latin America. Central to the maintenance of hegemony is a system of rule premised more upon consensual aspects of power rather than direct coercion. In the modern world, the production of consent involves the creation and distribution of cultural products (not only by the state but also by private media and entertainment firms). Understood instrumentally, a cultural apparatus serves to consolidate and create (directly and indirectly) the cultural 'limits of the possible' for social thought and political action. The establishment of hegemony involves more than simply propagation of the dominant ideas of a ruling class in a particular epoch. Hegemony involves persuasion and relatively legitimate forms of rule. Moreover, it must encompass not only ideas but also institutions and material potentials but also a whole way of life. Thus cultural hegemony is difficult to achieve, particularly in a society subjected to external dominance and subordination, and it involves intense struggle and resistance. In this sense, cultural dominance can never be totalizing, since humankind will always create alternative modes and channels of communication that will seek to redefine the language of cultural reality. This creative, human process is an aspect of radical collective action and the ongoing production of alternative cultural and communicative forms that emerge partly through transformative resistance.

2
Epistemology, Ontology and the Critique of Political Economy

This chapter discusses literature in International Political Economy (IPE) and International Relations (IR) in order to compare and contrast orthodox and critical perspectives on knowledge, power and world order. Using Gramsci's distinction between historical materialism and historical economism it attempts to highlight and critique a widespread tendency to use transhistorical theorizations based upon sets of *a priori* categories that appear to take on an ontological autonomy: a characteristic associated with American neo-realism and mechanical, economistic forms of Marxism.

Epistemology and politics

My approach assumes that 'there is no symmetry between the social and natural sciences with regard to concept formation and the logic of inquiry and explanation' (Gunnell 1968: 168). The key contrast between social and natural science is that the structure of social relationships and the meaning of social events are not principally functions of the scientist's theory, since what social scientists confront is 'not a first but a second order reality'. The 'world' of the social scientist is a second order one because it has been logically pre-ordered by its participants, 'in whose terms action is conducted and justified'. This implies that social scientific explanation entails limited generalizations and a conditional vocabulary. In order to avoid conceptual reification, this entails continual interaction between social scientific constructs and 'social reality'. 'Such a requirement will be viewed as a limitation only if it is assumed that the science of physical mechanics must somehow serve as a standard for all explanation' (Gunnell 1968: 186). Underlying this contention is the argument that social science explanation cannot develop if it rests either upon a Cartesian dualism concerning subject and object or theorizes in terms of cause and effect. In this context, I understand social structure as a conceptual abstraction that corresponds to how the collective agency of human beings produces regularities that are more or less institutionalized over time and space – as people struggle to objectify and transform their relations with each other and with nature.

So how can we understand this process, in particular its social and political aspects? To return to epistemological argument, rather than following Cartesian dualism, and a positivist search for invariant transhistorical relationships that are supposed to reveal some *a priori* transhistorical 'human nature', I follow Vico and especially Gramsci. As Vico observed, in the *New Science* of 1725, human beings make society and thus the social world is a human creation. Thus its explanation is to be found within changes in thought that configure action. It was Vico, therefore, who first propounded the essential aspects of Marx's maxim that human beings make their own history but not necessarily under conditions of their own choosing.

Gramsci took this further in what he called the philosophy of *praxis*. He rejected the positivist separation of the subjective and objective aspects of social life. The two needed to be united in concept and practice so that alienated thought and action might be epistemologically and politically transcended. For example, in asking the question what does the term objective really mean, Gramsci noted that this implied something universal and, as such, independent of any sectional, group or class interest or particular point of view. Thus in real, historically constituted human relations:

> Objective always means 'humanly objective' which can be held to correspond exactly to 'historically subjective': in other words, objective would mean 'universal subjective'. Man knows objectivity insofar as knowledge is real for the whole human race *historically* unified in a single unitary cultural system. But this process of historical unification takes place through the disappearance of the internal contradictions which tear apart human society, while these contradictions themselves are the condition for the formation of groups and for the birth of ideologies which are not concretely universal but are immediately rendered transient by the practical origin of their substance. (Gramsci 1971: 455)

In other words a process of resolution of historical contradictions involves an ongoing struggle amongst competing ideological hypotheses and theoretical and political projects. In this sense collective action is the means and the form through which historical structures are created and are transformed.

Differences between Gramscian and positivist IR and IPE

In this context we ask: how does a critical Gramscian approach to International Political Economy differ from prevailing orthodoxy? There are three main differences that can be outlined initially.

First, in international studies the Gramscian approach is an epistemological and ontological critique of the empiricism and positivism that underpin the prevailing theorizations in the field, as well as the cruder forms of 'mechanical Marxism'. This is because the Gramscian approach is a specific form of non-structuralist historicism and it stands in contrast to abstract 'structuralisms' in so far as it has a human(ist) aspect. Historical change is understood as, to a substantial degree, the consequence of collective human activity.

More specifically, Gramsci's historicism might be said to have at least three main components: (a) transience, (b) historical necessity, and (c) a dialectical variant of (philosophical) realism (Morera 1990). Point (a) implies that history and social change is a cumulative, endless, yet non-repetitive process, with different rhythms and tempos, applying respectively to structural developments and to patterns of apparently discrete events. Thus the critique of political economy for Marx and Gramsci begins with the concept of the historicity, or historical specificity of the capitalist market system, rather than seeing it as natural or eternal.

The idea of historical necessity, point (b), implies that social interaction and political change takes place within what can be called the 'limits of the possible', limits which however, are not fixed and immutable, but exist within the dialectics of a given social structure (comprising the inter-subjective aspect of ideas, ideologies and theories, social institutions, and a prevailing socio-economic system and set of power relations). The dialectical aspect of this is historical: although social action is constrained by, and constituted within, prevailing social structures, those structures are transformed by agency (for example through collective action in what Gramsci called 'the war of position'). Thus the problem of historical necessity is understood in dialectical terms in ways that challenge the subject/object dichotomy of positivist epistemology. In this sense, Gramscian historical materialism builds upon and extends aspects of the Marxian critique of classical political economy.

Marx, in the *Grundrisse*, showed how, by abstracting from the social relations of production, Ricardo developed an ahistorical and therefore misleading conception of the freedom of the individual:

In money relationships in the developed exchange system ... individuals appear to be ... independent, to collide with one another freely and to barter within the limits of this freedom. They appear to do so, however, only to someone who abstracts from the conditions of existence in which these individuals come into contact ... close investigation to these external circumstances or conditions shows, however, how impossible it is for individuals forming part of a class, etc., to surmount them *en masse* without abolishing them. (Marx 1973: 83–4)

Gramsci's variant of philosophical realism, point (c), identifies the intellectual process as a creative, practical yet open-ended and continuous engagement to explain an apparently intractable social reality. This process is, like the processes of change within a given necessity, a dialectical one, and is thus a *part of* the historical process; it does not stand outside it. Indeed, Gramsci developed the unique concept of the 'organic intellectual' to show how the processes of intellectual production were themselves in dialectical relation to the processes of historical change. Intellectual work directed towards social explanation was often directly or indirectly linked to political strategies, themselves developed from different perspectives. Such perspectives exist in political time and space. Thus by linking the theory of knowledge production to a theory of identity and interests, Gramsci was able to show how, at least in this sense, theory is always for someone and for some purpose.

This Gramscian viewpoint can be contrasted with the technocratic assumptions that inform the outlook of most professional economists in the West and Japan, and those working in major international economic organizations like the IMF and the World Bank. More generally these assumptions are associated with those working within the neo-classical tradition in modern political economy, for example Keynesians, with their engineering assumption that the role of the economist is to build a behaviourist apparatus enabling the fine-tuning of the economy. Again, this assumption is founded upon the positivist separation of subject and object.

Second, the Gramscian approach provides a general critique of methodological individualism, and methodological reductionism. The latter, of course, is frequently found in some variants of Marxism, as well as in other traditions. Indeed, analytical Marxism seeks to synthesize methodological individualism and methodological holism, for example in developing a theory of exploitation. In the Gramscian approach history and political economy are not understood as a sequence or series of discrete events or moments which when aggregated equal a process of change with certain governing regularities: for Gramsci it is the *ensemble* of social relations configured by social structures ('the situation') which is the basic unit of analysis, rather than individual agents, be they consumers, firms, states or interest groups, interacting in a (potentially) rule-governed way in the 'political market-place' at a given moment or conjuncture, as in modern public choice theory.

Third, the approach insists upon an ethical dimension to analysis, so that the questions of justice, legitimacy and moral credibility are integrated sociologically into the whole and into many of its key concepts. This is reflected in Gramsci's dual conception of politics and the state: on the one hand there is a classical Marxist concern to analyse the state as a class-based apparatus of rule; on the other is something akin to the Aristotelian view of politics as the search to establish the conditions for the good society, where the state is seen as at least potentially able to be transformed from an apparatus based upon social inequality into an ethical public sphere.

In consequence, unlike the prevailing orthodoxy with its priority given to political order and the pragmatic need for systems management, the normative goal of the Gramscian approach is to move towards the solution of the fundamental problem of political philosophy: the nature of the good society and thus, politically, the construction of an 'ethical' state and a society in which personal development, rational reflection, open debate, democratic empowerment and economic and social liberation can become more widely attainable. It is important to emphasize here that this is a rather negative definition, concerning minimum conditions, of the 'good society', and it offers no promises nor prescriptions for the form that such a society might take: historical structures can be changed by collective action in a 'war of position', but there is no historical inevitability. The key contrast here would be with teleological Marxism, with its promise of possible utopia(s), or Francis Fukuyama's much-publicized dystopia of the 'end of history': the eventual unfolding of the logic and spirit of liberal democratic capitalism. In Gramscian terms, *telos* is 'myth':

> From Sorel, (Gramsci) took the notion of social myth (e.g. the modern prince as a myth). Myth presupposes a psychic force, a compelling movement combined with a rejection of the prevailing norms (e.g. as hypocritical, demystified). It is a normative force but not a normative plan or set of normative criteria. It can generate movement but not predict outcome. Thus the normative element is crucial but not as teleology.[1]

---

1. Note from Robert Cox to the author, 29 September 1990.

To summarize, then, in contrast to the tendency in much of the (American) literature to prioritize systemic order and management, from a vantage point associated with the ruling elements in the wealthy core of the global political economy, the historical materialist perspective looks at the system from the bottom upwards, as well as the top downwards, in a dialectical appraisal of a given historical situation: *a concern with movement, rather than management.* This highlights the limits of a narrow political economy approach to the analysis of International Relations. For Gramsci, a broad-based and more integrated perspective is achieved by the elaboration of a historicist version of the dialectical method developed from Hegel and Marx, also influenced by Machiavelli. In the *Prison Notebooks*, this took the form of a critique of and polemic against the German historicists and more specifically, the Italian idealist, Benedetto Croce.

The critique of political economy: four arguments

Here I attempt initially to identify and develop some of the key theoretical and applied features of a *historical materialist* approach to social and historical explanation, and to contrast them with narrower *materialist* theories, which can be associated with Gramsci's notion of *historical economism.* To indicate initially how Gramscian historical materialism develops concepts to help explain aspects of the normative structure of society we can bear in mind Gramsci's concept of myth (e.g. *telos* as myth), which suggests how apparently normative forces may have the social power normally associated with 'material forces' (such as technology, the forces of production).

A *materialist* theory of knowledge assumes that nothing exists (e.g. God, the idea of liberty, providence) outside and apart from nature and society. In my view, this also implies that no *telos* or spirit exists as a guide to or purpose for that process. Nevertheless, for materialists, metaphysics and idealist thinking are a part of the social reality to be explained, since they help to constitute the social outlook and predispositions of individuals and more broadly, groups and movements within social formations. In a recent book on Gramsci's historicism, Morera argues that to be a *materialist* theory, at least four conditions need to be met (Morera 1990: 122):

1. Materialism acknowledges the existence of an object of knowledge, independent of a knowing subject, the process of knowledge production and the system of knowledge itself.

2. The adequacy of the object of knowledge provides the ultimate standard by which the cognitive status of thought is to be assessed.
3. Thought and ideas are recognized as realities in their own right and thus an object of knowledge.
4. Those realities are theorized as not *sui generis* but as the result of causal mechanisms.

I will now attempt to show how conventional materialist epistemology has severe limitations, particularly in its more positivist representation. Here I will attempt to indicate that a creative historical materialist approach transcends rigid theories of causality and moves towards a reflexive and dynamic form of political economy *explanation*. As will be argued below, for example, the concept of mechanical causality is inconsistent with historicism, since historicism is concerned with explanation, rather than causality. This entails the rejection of technological, economic or indeed any form of reductionism. This line of argument relates to the difference between what Gramsci called 'historical economism' and 'historical materialism'.

Beyond the intransigence of 'social reality'

Of course, we can accept that there is a certain intransigent 'reality' to society and nature (which we can never fully know or explain because of its scale and complexity). Therefore, this reality is to a certain extent independent of, but nonetheless interdependent with the processes of knowledge production. Further, the 'truth' of social reality is made more intractable because it involves the thought and inter-subjective meanings of individuals who have different forms of self-consciousness and awareness as to the social nature of their action/inactions. The social organization of production, as an aspect of the social world, is thus necessarily constituted partly by inter-subjective meanings, which can be identified and understood, however imperfectly. Thus our second-order, social 'reality' has different dimensions that cannot be understood fully or completely recorded, although abstractions concerning the structural components of such social reality can and must be intellectually produced for explanation to be possible.

With regard to the interdependence of theory and reality, following Hegel, we can argue that there can be no immediate knowledge, since this would imply that we have no consciousness, which mediates with such a reality. Consciousness, then, implies an explicit or implicit conceptual apparatus and language. As outlined in the *Grundrisse*, Marx's adaptation (or inversion) of the Hegelian dialectical method (further extended and elaborated by Gramsci) applies a particular materialist approach to society and continually extends, refines and elaborates its conceptual apparatus generating new concepts and discarding others. This occurs in the context of historical explanation that is seen to entail a dialectical process. With regard to concept formation our senses are partly theoreticians; our ideas of what is or can be are produced conceptually and our conceptual frameworks are partly produced by the environment or society.

With regard to the process of knowledge, one version of how the historical dialectic, as I have defined it here, might be approached is though Marx's ideas concerning the 'concrete-real' (which determines theory) and the 'thought-concrete' (which is an understanding of the concrete, or the significance of social action and structure generated by the process of reflection and thought). Implied here is that each conceptual framework produces its own version of 'concrete-real' and 'thought-concrete'. For Marx, then, knowledge was the process of change in which the two 'concretes' are interconnected and are mutually transformed to provide a new synthesis.[2]

At this point we can emphasize a key issue which differentiates historical materialism from empiricism and positivism: a change in thinking is a change in the social totality and thus has an impact on other social processes; a change in the social totality will provoke change in the process of thought. Hence the process of thinking is part of a ceaseless dialectic of social being.

The limits of ontological objectivity

How are thought-concretes developed and elaborated? A way to move towards the answer to this question is by making an initial distinction between the appearance and essence or inner and outer manifestation of social reality. This process of abstraction-concretization allows us to move theoretically to a better correspondence with such a reality, a position which presupposes the possibility of a never complete, but a closer approximation of, ontological objectivity. Following Marx's *Grundrisse*, this is attempted through an ongoing and endless process of the generation of abstractions and concepts, which are reconstructed and refined as they

---

2. Here we might distinguish between logical contradictions, and historical contradictions. The former characterize formal logic and mathematics (e.g. as discussed in Hegel's *Science of Logic*). The latter result from human beings acquiring self-consciousness and capacity to understand and act in historical situations.

encounter a mass of data. This method, to use the metaphor of Engels, enables the theorist to approach a more comprehensive and consistent explanation of social reality, rather like the way an asymptote approximates a straight line (an asymptote is a curve which increasingly approximates, but never touches, a straight line stretching to infinity). This position seems to be superficially similar to that of John Stuart Mill and the sceptical empiricists, who argue that the senses or their surrogates can never yield social knowledge which can truthfully approximate social reality. However, historical materialists take this argument one step further, by arguing that society is a totality or system which is regulated or conditioned by structural relations and can thus never be understood through the method of empiricist atomism. Further, the process of development of thought-concretes is ongoing and thus is simply arrested and incomplete if it rests with or is explained through transhistorical abstractions or theories, like those associated with the Cassandras of the rise and (inevitable) fall of (Roman, Dutch, British and) American hegemony. Marx when developing his critique of political economy, for example his criticisms of Ricardo and Malthus, of course originally made this type of argument. This point is further developed below with regard to structuralism and Gramsci's critique of Bukharin.

Thus whereas much modern International Relations theory takes the rise and decline of hegemonies and balances of power in the inter-state system as largely given, with its primordial anarchic form constitutive of the development possibilities in international relations since at least the time of Thucydides, historical materialists argue that this structure, in so far as its existence can be substantiated, is a particular configuration of states and social forces, corresponding to a particular epoch and having certain conditions of existence which are corporeal and transitory. In other words, Marxists stress the conditional and historical application of what for Robert Gilpin seems to operate as a something akin to a sociological abstraction.[3]

By contrast, there are different forms of state and world orders, whose conditions of existence, constitutive principles and norms vary over time. These conditions include different social modes of production and social structures of accumulation, with their own characteristic ethics and politics, and which vary in political time and space. Thus no transhistorical essentialism or homeostasis is imputed to any given social system or world order. Moreover, the state itself, and the forms of state action

---

3. For the archetypical Realist statement see Gilpin (1981).

are themselves differentially constituted in complex ways by blocs of socio-economic and political forces, which operate within the limits of a given historical necessity.

Indeed, whereas empiricists move towards the understanding of social reality from the perspective of methodological individualism, historical materialists develop a theory based upon social structures as the fundamental unit of analysis. In this sense although all 'social realities' are theorized, though some are more theorized than others. Thus the inter-state system is viewed in individualistic terms, with states as atomized actors interacting within the structure of anarchy. Indeed much of American International Relations and to a lesser extent International Political Economy operates within what has been called the anarchy *problématique* (Ashley 1988).

To make some applications of this point clearer, and in a more substantive way, let us sketch some aspects of the post-war system from this perspective.

First, and most fundamental, is that it is assumed that any historical materialist approach to understanding and explaining a given world order system must analyse it as a whole. The particular ontology used is by no means self-evident and must, on one level, be a theorized one. Synthesizing insights of different writers from within this perspective influenced by Gramsci, then, our ontology must be founded upon the idea of a global social formation constituted in part by the degree of integration/disintegration of basic social structures, social forces and forms of state. This is the fundamental basis for understanding the 'international': that is what is usually seen as a relatively autonomous inter-state system articulated with related forces, mechanisms and institutions of production and exchange at separate 'domestic' and 'international' levels.

In other words, our understanding of the dynamics of the political economy is founded upon certain sociological ideas concerning, for example, the degree of 'embeddedness' of world orders in socio-political structures at the national or transnational levels (Polanyi 1975). Thus, in the contemporary era (i.e. since 1945), we can call such a historically specific yet changing ensemble of social structures and social forces the global political economy (Gill and Law 1988).

Thus since 1945, in the era of the *pax americana*, a new world order structure emerged which was in some ways qualitatively different to its predecessors. However, this new system cannot simply be explained with regard solely to apparently unique features, for example the existence of weapons of mass destruction or the long-term threats to the survival of the species through ecological catastrophe (previous weapons systems caused mass destruction and former civilizations were either displaced or eliminated partly because of adverse environmental and ecological changes). Hence the conventional focus of much International Relations theorizing, the inter-state system, and the transition from a balance of power/hegemony (Westphalian) international political system towards a 'post-Westphalian' system needs to be explained through the examination of the ways in which social forces and social structures are entering a period of transition so that, in classical Marxist terms, there is both a growing socialization (universalization) of aspects of social life, and a disintegration of previous forms of identity and interest: crudely speaking between, for example, 'internationalist' and 'nationalist' groups of interest. This transformation and struggle, amongst other things then, involves a dialectical interplay between forces, some of which are relatively cosmopolitan, and others that are more territorially bounded, such as nationalist movements and ideologies, military-security structures, particular linguistic forms and patterns of identity.

In a more specific sense, the formal system of state sovereignty, which was in some ways reinforced and constituted by earlier forms of international economic activity (hence the term the 'international' political economy), appears now to have been cumulatively undermined by more pervasive and deep-rooted economic integration and competition (including inter-state competition to attract supplies of capital and investment from overseas, and to promote the competitiveness of 'home' industries). This has created a new force-field of constraints, opportunities and dangers, that is new conditions of existence for all states, groups and classes in the system, as well as extending, albeit in still limited and contradictory ways, a growing structural power for internationally mobile transnational capital (see Chapter 6).

Some are more constrained than others in this world order system. Not only does this new order coincide with a decisive change in the productive powers and balance of social forces within and between the major states, but also state structures in the major capitalist countries have been transformed into different variants of a neo-liberal form, that is more oriented to the integration of their economies into the emerging global system of production and exchange, in which knowledge, finance and information play a more decisive role, when contrasted with the inter-war period. This largely is what Cox means by the process of the internationalizing of the state, involving coalitions, class alliances and historic blocs of social forces across as well as within countries (Cox 1987).

At the same time, peripheral economies have become more tightly geared to the economic activity of the core, and their developmental rhythms partly subjected to the imperatives of Cold War politics and liberal neo-classical economic doctrines and associated institutions and social forces. They have entered a period of widespread social restructuring as their domestic arrangements have both begun to disintegrate and become ever-more attuned to the growing integration of trade, investment, production and finance. The story of the 1980s attests to some of the social costs of this transformation: a period of arrested development potential, with the Third World debt crisis involving huge transfers of resources from the poorer countries to the richest.

In the emerging post-Westphalian system, then, the cosmopolitanism of international economic forces was accompanied by a disciplining of social groups in the Third World, in order to deepen the structural power of internationally mobile capital and undermine prevailing mercantilist arrangements. This has occurred, with varying degrees of effectiveness, through a combination of market power and the surveillance of the Bretton Woods international organizations under US leadership (Augelli and Murphy 1988).

This capitalist cosmopolitanism is also important in any explanation of the breakdown of the Cold War bloc structure between the USA, USSR and in Europe. Here changes occurred in large part because of the intensification of technological innovation and military rivalry, especially between the USA and USSR. In the context of a deep crisis in the social structure of accumulation and thus of the productive power of the various nations of the Soviet-led bloc, the social myth of the communist utopia, which had reached its *apogée* in an earlier period of history, was vaporized almost completely. This hegemonic, organic crisis of 'actually existing communism' proved to be especially severe in Poland, Romania, East Germany and most important, the USSR. In the context of the brittle (and economistic) legitimacy of the communist states, with the relations between state and civil society co-ordinated by an authoritarian and paternalist structure of political power, the inability of the USSR to respond to the long-term challenges posed within the context of existing forms of post-Stalinist political economy led to its collapse as an alternative social myth (to capitalism).

In the world capitalist order, then, power appeared to be re-concentrated in the metropolitan countries, which were, however, also undergoing substantial transformation in what is, clearly, a global process of restructuring. The social forces and political arrangements associated with 'embedded liberalism' (Ruggie 1982) were progressively undermined by the growing extension, resources and power of internationally mobile forces, undermining the historic blocs of social forces which constituted, at the national level, the structural underpinnings of the post-war international political economy. In Gramscian terms, the ensemble of these blocs and welfare-nationalist forms of state was politically synthesized within the context of the twin pillars of American hegemony (the Cold War structures and the liberalizing international economic order) into an *international historic bloc* initially in a transatlantic, then later Trilateral (i.e. including Japan) format. However, the recessions and restructuring of the 1970s and 1980s, allied to the cumulative internationalization of production, consumption and exchange, and the integration of global economic forces, meant that the integral nature of these historic blocs was undermined, and an underdeveloped, yet clearly emergent *transnational historic bloc of forces* (associated with dominant interests in the metropolitan countries and elsewhere) began to emerge, particularly during the 1970s and 1980s. The contradictions of this development, which involves a crisis of the old hegemonic structures and forms of political consent, negotiated internationally, are now unravelling the former international historic bloc and are bound up with the new and emergent transnational bloc (see Chapters 3, 5 and 6).

Even here, however, the contradictions of the system may be intensifying. Developments in the metropolitan heartland of the system, with ripple effects in the Third World, have been linked to a situation in which production and exchange structures are becoming disarticulated in an era of shortening time-horizons and speculative capitalism (e.g. growing disparities between productive investment, international trade and capital and exchange markets). This suggests that, on one level, the ethical appeals of the social contracts of the era of embedded liberalism are rapidly being laid to waste. As Susan Strange points out, the game of economic life comes to resemble a combination of snakes and ladders and (Russian) roulette (Strange 1986).

How are we to begin to explain the nature of these changes? In the conventional literature in International Political Economy what has just been discussed is usually understood as the disjuncture between 'domestic' and 'international' forces in the international exchange system, along with an international diffusion of inter-state power leading to a move away from the stability of the superpower duopoly towards a more complex plural system. The question then is how is order possible 'after hegemony'? (Keohane 1984). Theories have been developed to ascertain how the metropolitan capitalist nations at the centre of the system can co-operate fruitfully in a post-hegemonic world characterized by slower growth and economic instability. Much debate centres on the problem of the highly imperfect co-ordination at the summit of the system, that is how to cope with the complexities of 'two-level' or 'multi-level' or mixed 'games between larger numbers of national actors', that is governments (Axelrod and Dawkins 1990). Thus, the question, which continues to constitute, and has constituted the research agenda for orthodox IPE theory during the last decade is: 'how can co-operation be achieved under anarchy?'

Another way of looking at this question, however, is to situate a discussion of inter-state forums, international organizations and informal councils like the Trilateral Commission, in the context of the development and application of hegemonic strategies on an increasingly transnational basis. Yet this level of analysis is still insufficient to explain adequately the emergence and salience of these strategies, and the political struggles that are entailed by them. The political gods at the summit of the system, and the various forums in which they interact, such as the Group of Seven (G7) summits, operate within the limits of the possible, limits situated within the context of the historical transformations discussed above, as well as the blocs of social forces with which they are associated at the domestic level in their own countries and elsewhere (Gill 1990).

Given the historical complexity of these forces, the importance of, and interaction within, these elite forums cannot simply be explained with abstract formulations such as the Prisoner's Dilemma (that Axelrod claims can explain biological evolution and trench warfare in World War I equally well). Since such inter-governmental and transnational forums have existed for some time, their growing importance can only be explained historically. Apart from being concrete institutional responses to the crisis or transformation in the post-war world order system, corresponding to an uneven globalization of the political economy, they are also initiatives which are bound up with the birth and early development of an international political and civil society which is in some respects new and suggestive of a reconfiguration of the world order in the late twentieth century.

From a World-Systems viewpoint the above developments would appear to correspond to a situation where power appears to have been re-concentrated in the 'core' states, whilst Realists, agreeing to a point, would lament the dissolving of the glue of bloc structures associated with the balance of terror and the decline of American power and leadership. However, what may be the most important aspect of the current epoch is the fact that social relations and social structures are in a period of extended and deep-seated transformation or crisis, on a global scale: a crisis which is in fact, a crisis of both the existing Cold War and inter- and intra-capitalist order.

In so far as there are leading elements in this process, the principles of organization of this restructured world order system are increasingly those associated with liberal economic ideas and interests (e.g. transnational capital and the Bretton Woods institutions), which are engaged in a dialectical struggle *vis-à-vis* embedded mercantilist and statist perspectives (often associated with the public sector, the security complex, and protected industries which are non-competitive inter- nationally). This struggle and transformation involves not only the states in the capitalist core, but also configures the agenda of social transformation in Latin America, in Central and Eastern Europe, and in the successors to the Soviet Union.

A good recent example of the globalizing thrust of capitalism, and of the internationalization of political and civil society and, to an extent, of the internationalization of authority under these new conditions was the way in which the Bretton Woods institutions, the OECD, and metropolitan capitalist governments and a range of private interests (e.g. leading figures from banking and transnational companies, as well as think tanks and private universities) rapidly came together to produce a radical and draconian package of reforms, to swiftly transform the Polish economy, in January 1990 (in 1991–92 this approach was also applied in Russia, after the collapse of the USSR). The Polish experiment was, as the OECD put it at the time, the launching of an unprecedented strategy of social transformation from a communist, protected and mercantilist society, into a market-based, capitalist society, a 'great transformation' which took at least 70 years to accomplish in nineteenth century England (Polanyi 1975). The plan for Poland was itself based upon a learning process amongst capitalist elites in light of the experiences of the 1970s and 1980s, and the experiments with the use of IMF/World Bank conditionality. The new strategy applies macro/micro restructuring and the idea of hard budget constraints (on state expenditures and also on individual enterprises) in ways which will extend and deepen the structural power of capital (Kornai 1980). This strategy, which, to say the least, is by no means certain of success, is nonetheless not a pure market strategy: there is some political direction and internationalization of authority in order to prevent the mistakes of the 1970s (over debt recycling) and the 1980s (over the debt crisis) from being repeated. This strategy then, in so far as it has an internal logic, represents the use of direct political power in order to develop the structural power of capital.

In this context the ultimate form of 'conditionality' was reflected in the economic, monetary and social unification of East Germany with the Federal Republic started on 1 July 1990. This was, of course, soon followed by full political unification on 2 October 1990, when the Volkskammer dissolved itself and a crowd estimated to be over a million people gathered in front of the Reichstag in the old Prussian (now all-German) capital of Berlin. Observers reported that the mood of the vast, emotional crowd was:

A mixture of joy, bewilderment, anxiety and catharsis. The West German political establishment gathered in the Schauspielhaus and its cocktails were made headier by the echoing song of the 'Ode to Joy' from the Ninth Symphony. Not wishing to dampen their euphoria, the normally sober Bundesbank was denying the prospect of economic hopelessness in East Germany. As the Germans celebrated to the strains of Schiller and Beethoven, Mrs. Thatcher offered her congratulations after earlier ominous warnings about German dominance in Europe. The Soviet Union announced that unification was caused by the logic of the enlightened policy of *perestroika*, and the European Commission said that it meant that the process of economic and political unification in Europe would be accelerated.[4]

The structure of necessity and political consciousness

In the above examples, then, the structure of necessity varied partly according to the viewpoint of different agents, be they individuals, unions, firms, government bureaucracies, or international organizations. Further, the nature of this structure changes over time. The post-war changes just described are not simply the result of impersonal cumulative structural transformations, although, following Fernand Braudel, those changes relating to the *longue durée*, that is the *gestes répétées* of history, have created the structure of necessity in which the *évènements* or events of history occur in particular conjunctures (Braudel 1980). Of course, this twofold chronological rhythm is itself an over-simplification, although changes of long-standing structural importance in this context are the spread and deepening of commodification and monetization of social relations.

Yet social reality involves not only the structural constraints that are often taken as the limits of the possible: it also involves consciousness and thus encompasses philosophical, theoretical, ethical, and common

4. Editorial. *Financial Times*, 3 October 1990.

sense ideas. Beethoven, rather than Wagner was chosen to symbolize the cathartic emotion of the united Germany for its present generation of political leaders. In the case of Gramsci this aspect of society is reflected in his interest in the questions of consciousness and political culture, the role of the intellectuals and philosophy, and the substantive attention given to the superstructures, notably civil society, in his conceptions of hegemony and of the constitution of society:

> Critical understanding of self takes place therefore through a struggle of political 'hegemonies' and of opposing directions, first in the ethical field and then in politics proper, in order to arrive at the working out at a higher level of one's conception of reality. Consciousness of being part of a particular hegemonic force (that is to say political consciousness) is the first stage towards progressive self-consciousness in which theory and practice will finally be one. Thus the unity of theory and practice is not just a matter of mechanical fact, but part of a historical process, whose elementary and primitive phase is to be found in the sense of being 'different' and 'apart', in an instinctive feeling of independence, and which progresses to the level of real possession of a single and coherent conception of the world. This is why it must be stressed that the political development of the concept of hegemony represents a great philosophical advance as well as a politico-practical one. (Gramsci 1971: 333)

Here then, Gramsci is arguing that critical understanding is not an automatic process: it involves reflection and effort within oneself, as well as within the context of the wider struggle of ideas and political programmes. 'Progressive self-consciousness' is thus defined developmentally and politically: the awareness of self is re-constituted through an appreciation of prevailing thought-patterns and the nature and distribution of life-chances. Hence the moment of self-awareness leads to a more complex and coherent understanding of the social world and is a form of historical change (and thus in the balance of social and political forces). Thus the achievement of self-consciousness is understood dialectically. Politics and the individual are central to the definition of structures and of change, and are not abstracted 'falsely' out of a theory of history.

This argument does not imply that Gramsci was an idealist or that he subordinated 'economics' to 'politics'. In his social theory society is conceived, as in classical Marxism, as a totality primarily constituted by a mode of production. This can be separated analytically into ideas, institutions and material forces but remains a general, integrated if contradictory entity. Certain systems of thought such as religion or common sense (or philosophies as Gramsci would have it) or social institutions (like the family) can outlive any given mode of production, or social structure of accumulation, and thus there is no necessary congruence between 'base' and 'superstructure'. The same would apply to systems of government and politics more generally: a capitalist mode of production can go with authoritarianism, dictatorship or parliamentary democracy. What is crucial is to place each of these sets of ideas and social institutions in its proper socio-historical context, since their importance and meaning can change over time.

Likewise if we take the case of the revolutions of 1989 in East and Central Europe, a key structural aspect of the explanation of this type of change was an implosion of economic performance and a deep-rooted and long-term crisis in the irrational social structure of accumulation of 'actually existing socialism' – which lost momentum since its leaders could not reconcile its contradictions. For example, Kornai shows how, at least in the Hungarian case, the practice of politically allocated but largely open-ended subsidies allied to the system's overall centralization and the setting of abstract and unrealistic plan targets resulted in an inefficient system of allocation and incentives: there were no real market signals as exist in capitalism, and no financial or market constraints to punish the inefficient (Kornai 1990). The allocation of labour was distorted (massive underemployment, hoarding of labour and factors of production). The system simply did not provide the goods and services that people either wanted or needed. In Habermasian terms, this represented a deep rationality crisis of a social system premised upon, as it were, the perfect computation of social needs and economic activity (Habermas 1976).

This organic crisis was intensified; on the one hand, by the long-term economic challenges being posed by the advanced capitalist countries, and on the other, by the military and economic implications of the strategic challenge of Reaganism to the USSR. The lack of any substantive legitimacy under conditions of declining economic performance merely underlined the increasingly brittle legitimacy of the Stalinist anti-democratic system. This crudely materialist and anti-democratic form of legitimacy was of course made more fragile by the virtual elimination of any autonomous political activity and thus arrested the creation or rebirth of a civil society. Thus like a snowball gathering size as it rolls down a hill, when it reached its point of destination, the contradictions of the system had reached the scale of an avalanche.

Kees van der Pijl places these developments in the context of what he calls an organic crisis of the Hobbesian, repressive state form (Pijl 1993). At its worst in Romania, this process (which was condoned if not welcomed during the 1970s and 1980s by Western leaders because of Ceaucescu's opposition to Moscow and his ability to pay his bills to foreign bankers) involved the abuse of the political and human rights of the population and its virtual starvation to pay for, amongst other things, a grotesque marble palace for the 'butcher of Bucharest'. Here the key point is that a Gramscian analysis might have suggested that a Hobbesian state structure is inherently unstable for two reasons; it lacks ethical credibility and, since its political system is not embedded in the 'fortresses and earthworks' of a strong civil society, like Ceaucescu's palace, it can be toppled by an insurrectionary form of revolutionary spontaneity.

In van der Pijl's theorization, then, hegemonic state–civil society complexes in the West have been historically associated with the idea of the 'Lockeian state', that is one in which there is a vigorous and largely self-regulating civil society. This type of state–civil society complex is exemplified by the Anglo-Saxon countries, and to a certain extent, by many of the member states of the European Community. The international counterpart to this type of hegemonic formation is the British Commonwealth, which is rooted in the history of British imperialism and colonialism but represents, at the international level, the transformation of coercion into consent and informal regulation of inter-state relations. Here the contrast can be made with the usual idea of a strong state found in the bulk of International Relations theorizing, which is often associated with what van der Pijl calls the Hobbesian state form: a strong state which dominates civil society from above, with the political capacity to centralize political power so as to develop and mobilize the national material resources. This type of state form, then, is generally non-hegemonic, since it is not socially embedded in a strong civil society, and by implication has fragile legitimacy. At least in Eastern Europe, this crisis reflects not only the feeble legitimacy of communist rule (e.g. the coming to power of Vaclav Havel as a symbol of the ethico-political rejection of the social myth and concrete form of communist order in Czechoslovakia), but also the cumulative pressure of international forces for each of these countries.

Thus instead of the tendency to reify the state and the inter-state system, the Gramscian approach explains the nature of the state in terms of the complexity of state–civil society relations, and shows how the nature of state power is related to the strength of the dynamic synthesis between the key forces in the economy and society, operating politically on an inclusive basis. The synthesis between these forces creates what

Gramsci called a historical bloc, which may at times have the potential to become hegemonic. For ethical hegemony to be possible the state must necessarily be constituted primarily by general legitimacy and active consent, which implies inclusion of the interests of the subordinate elements within the system. Precisely what the components are for any particular social formation, of course needs to be explained by historical analysis. In its most fundamental and complete sense, however, the achievement of hegemony is concerned with the transcendence of narrowly based economistic or corporate perspectives, so that a genuinely universal position, synthesizing particular with general interests could come to prevail.

We might also compare the revolutions in Eastern and Central Europe (which were largely peaceful with the exception of Romania) with the crisis of legitimacy in China, as well as with the decay of state author-itarianism and military dictatorship in Latin America. As I have mentioned, van der Pijl suggests that each of these variants of the Hobbesian state form has undergone or is undergoing a fundamental crisis during the 1970s, 1980s and 1990s. However, the case of China may turn out to be a problematic one for van der Pijl's general thesis. Another problematic case would be the development of Japan since the Meiji Restoration.

To summarize, at the international level, the movement towards a more liberal and integrated global political economy and the beginnings of social reconstruction in Eastern Europe and Latin America are two sides of the same coin of a profound restructuring of the international order. Not only the Hobbesian states, but also many others are moving in a more market-oriented direction and thus towards the internationalization of something resembling a Lockeian form of self-regulating civil society (although the German model of the social market economy is a key variant in the pan-European context). Despite the contradictions and conflicts involved in the transformation of Eastern and Central Europe, we may see this development, at the European level, sooner, rather than later: the Cold War appears to have been eclipsed. On 6 July 1990 NATO finally announced that it no longer regarded the Warsaw Pact as its enemy, and in early August 1990 Prime Minister Thatcher of Britain was advocating a seat for Mikhail Gorbachev at the next G7 summit in London in 1991. Gorbachev attended the summit, and was then forced to resign as the Soviet Union was formally dissolved. As noted above, some of the members of the CIS, notably Russia, are embarking on a Polish-type form of draconian economic restructuring, with guidance being given by the IMF and the senior financial and political ministers of the G7, albeit under rapidly deteriorating economic conditions in the CIS. The 'great transformation' of the former Soviet bloc may well occur under conditions akin to those of the Great Depression of the 1930s in the West. This can be viewed as an aspect of what Gramsci called 'passive revolution', the development of mimetic political and economic structures in subordinated parts of the world. What seems to characterize the world order of the late twentieth century, then, is a series of profound crises of identity, ethics and socio-economic restructuring at the domestic/international level encompassing all three categories of country we have discussed: in metropolitan capitalism, the communist/post-communist states, and in the Third World. These crises are linked together by the forces at work in the global political economy. From this vantage point, the outcome of these developments is likely to be determined mainly at the domestic level, that is, within each of these countries. Nevertheless, the globalization of the political economy, and the transnationalization of social and political forces, means that new conditions prevail. These changes cannot be captured simply through a theorization of historical structures which is static, non-dialectical and premised upon the separation of the 'domestic' and the 'international', the 'economic' and the 'political'.

Historical change and counter-hegemony

It is clear that the achievement of hegemony within a particular social formation is a complex and contradictory process, since counter-hegemonic forces will come to challenge the prevailing institutional and political arrangements. Hegemony is even more difficult to achieve (and therefore much rarer if not theoretically impossible) at the international level, where there is no single world state or a fully developed international civil society, although it can be argued that there is both a substantial framework of international law, international organization (and thus a set of international norms, rules and values) which is partly interwoven with an internationalized structure of production and exchange (and thus a complex web of private and informal linkages, some of which involve state agents). International hegemony, as normally defined in the literature, has been associated with the dominance and leadership of a powerful state within the system of international relations, achieving power over other states. However this is an unsatisfactory definition, since it associates social forces with a territorial entity, whereas the global system needs to be conceived as a totality, and the social forces that operate within that system are not territorially bounded or determined (see the following chapter for elaboration). ...

Discussing one of the major instances of global hegemony, Giovanni Arrighi points to some of the reasons why the term 'hegemonic' seemed to apply to the leading strata and dominant social forces emanating from Great Britain during the nineteenth century as industrial and commercial capitalism began to internationalize. Whilst keeping its domestic market relatively open, and with comparative advantage in trade, Britain had substantial control over the world market. It also had a general mastery of the global balance of power, and a 'close relationship of mutual instrumentality with *haute finance'* (and thus the ability to manage the international monetary system under the Gold Standard). This enabled Britain to govern the inter-state system 'as effectively as a world-empire', and thus helped to sustain 'the unprecedented 100 years' peace among the great powers. Material power was not a sufficient condition for this to be possible. According to Arrighi, the key to British hegemony was:

> The *capacity to claim with credibility* that the expansion of the power of the United Kingdom served not just its national interest but a 'universal interest' as well. Central to this hegemonic claim was a distinction between the power of rulers and the 'wealth of nations' subtly drawn in the liberal ideology propagated by the British intelligentsia ... presented as the motor force of the universal expansion. Free trade might undermine the sovereignty of rulers but it would at the same time expand the wealth of their subjects, or at least their propertied subjects (Arrighi 1993: 174.[5]

Thus the combination of material, coercive and hegemonic capacities created the possibility for and reality of British supremacy, particularly in the middle decades of the nineteenth century. At least for the European ruling classes this made for a more or less legitimate capacity to restructure the world to suit British national interests. However, this was not hegemony in a fundamentally Gramscian sense, although Arrighi's analysis shows how a 'situation', that is the intersection and interaction of sets of social forces which produce a synthesis of interests, explains the *credibility* of British leadership in the international economy of the nineteenth century. What would strengthen this account is reference to the fact that the Gold Standard and its operation was constituted by, and depended heavily upon the co-operation of other European states, and in this sense was a European system. The key element here is that in so

---

5. Emphasis added.

far as Britain's rulers were hegemonic in the nineteenth century, they required the consent of other leading elements within metropolitan states. Moreover, in a global sense, the costs of adjustment under the Gold Standard tended to be borne most heavily by the poorer colonies under the control of each of the imperial, metropolitan European nations, and as such were by no means globally embedded nor consensual, a fact which Arrighi notes in his remarks concerning the siphoning of 'tribute' by the British state from India.

Thus social change, and in the above case, international political stability, at any historical moment is the result of the interaction of structural, or relatively permanent aspects of social reality, and specific conjunctures of events, that is the product of synchronic and diachronic forces. Hegemony, in other words, can never be the simple product of the preponderance of a single state or grouping of states exerting power over other states. This is of course partly because human beings have consciousness and a degree of free will or agency within the limits of the possible.

Hence any attempt to construct a hegemonic system of rule will tend to generate, dialectically, a set of counter-hegemonic forces, which may or may not be progressive. The corpse of the *pax Britannica* was buried in the trenches of Ypres and the Somme. The theoretical point here is that the social world is a qualitatively different, 'second-order' reality from that explained by the natural sciences (which can be likened to elaborating systems of causal regularity). Hence mechanical theories like the neo-realist theory of hegemonic stability have limited scientific validity, as well as a lack of plausibility in explaining complex social transformations and the constituents of world orders. Social crisis, and social transformation in this sense, is in large part explicable by the disintegration of social hegemonies, and the formation of counter-hegemony in the global political economy, rather than by 'long waves' of capitalist development.

Finally, in this context, no unilinear, pseudo-chronological concept of time can be applied to understand and explain plausibly constellations of social forces and historical conjunctures. Processes that reflect different rhythms and historical tempos constitute social structures and social events: from events time to the *longue durée* (see Chapter 3).

Beyond vulgar Marxism and the orthodox discourses

I have not yet addressed in detail the problem of how to go beyond these epistemological questions and move in a more detailed way towards an ontology, social theory and analytical method which avoids the lapse into arguments concerning the determinacy of either 'politics' or 'economics', or some underlying or ultimate causality, although my position on this question is implicit in much of the above. However we develop a given social ontology, it is crucial to remember the abstract, momentary and necessarily incomplete nature of all thought-processes and knowledge systems. Thus, we should heed Marx's warning in his admonition of the classical political economists:

> The vulgar mob [i.e. the classical economists] has therefore concluded that theoretical truths are abstractions which are at variance from reality, instead of seeing, on the contrary that Ricardo does not carry true abstract thinking far enough and is therefore driven into false abstraction. (Marx, *Theories of Surplus Value*, Vol. II, cited in Resnick and Wolff 1987: 58, note 44)

Here falseness is not simply equated with the approximation of an abstraction to some independent reality, since both Marx and Ricardo conceptualize the relation of thought to the 'concrete-real' quite differently. At issue is how and why and with what consequences classical economists and Marxists arrive at different 'thought-concretes' (Resnick and Wolff 1987). Two points seem relevant here. First, there is relativity in each claim to truth. Second, social conditions interact with and influence the survival, 'scientific' status and consequences of rival social theories: knowledge is also a process of social struggle, again between hegemonic and counter-hegemonic perspectives and principles. Thus, from this point of view, the hegemonic perspectives within International Political Economy and International Relations can be criticized for not probing deeply enough into the complex role of ideas and consciousness and the interaction of knowledge systems with the rest of the historical process: an extreme example of what Marx calls 'false abstraction', that is abstractions which are not grounded concretely in history. Many Marxists also fall prey to this methodological error.

For example, Gramsci showed how Nicolai Bukharin's *Theory of Historical Materialism: A Popular Manual of Marxist Sociology* eliminated the dialectical standpoint and introduced a 'metaphysical materialism' or 'idealism upside down' (Gramsci 1971: 437). The search for single, last-instance causes reduced 'the philosophy of *praxis*' to something akin to the search for God, and the philosophical process to social mechanics:

> The philosophy implicit in the *Popular Manual* could be called a positivistic Aristotelianism, an adaptation of formal logic to the methods of physical and natural science. The historical dialectic is

replaced by the law of causality and the search for regularity, normality, and uniformity... In mechanical terms, the effect can never transcend the cause or the system of causes, and therefore can have no development other than the flat vulgar development of economism. (Gramsci 1971: 437)

Similar and quite fundamental criticisms can be made of the explanatory usefulness of the prevailing positivist approaches to the study of International Political Economy, such as its ahistorical nature; its lack of a dynamic, dialectical quality; the narrowness and incompleteness of its abstractions which are confined, almost tautologically, to the relations between theoretical abstractions (i.e. unitary rational actors called states); the tendency to extreme parsimony in explanation relative to the infinite complexity of its object of analysis, that is the international system.

Given the preceding arguments and observations, the persistence of the prevailing American approaches would appear to be surprising were we to live in a rational scientific world where, following the injunctions of Karl Popper, theories that are internally inconsistent and/or are refuted by the evidence should be consigned to the intellectual scrap heap (Popper 1976). I make this point simply because Popper has been very influential in the formulation of research programmes in American social science, not because I accept or advocate his positions. How then, do we explain the persistence of such a perspective? In my view, this can be explained in two ways. Despite its limitations it has a degree of *practical effectiveness* that partly stems from its parsimony and surface plausibility: it provides a framework for an instrumentalist social science to develop policy-frameworks. And, to a degree, its use has corresponded with the rise of American globalism, bound up with the tremendous dynamism of capitalist development in the USA. This is not to suggest that American policy-makers accept uncritically either its framework or its policy recommendations. Senior figures in the American political establishment are often more subtle and pragmatic. More important perhaps is that particular policies and initiatives can be articulated and justified through the use of these ideas, in so far as they correspond to 'common sense', and are reinforced by an appeal to 'authority' (in the sense of learning, wisdom) and to 'tradition' or the advocacy of a particular 'way of life'. There are at least two elements, which help to explain this practical effectiveness.

First, the plausibility of this approach at the policy level corresponds to the predominance of positivist and behaviourist traditions in Anglo-Saxon academia. These traditions have served to constitute the bulk of American social science, and are rooted deeply. They go back a long way in the short history of the USA. The resonance of this perspective is amplified by the substantial scope and weight of the largest and best-funded academic community in the world. Of course, many academics from other countries receive graduate training in the USA, which has many of the world's leading research universities and think tanks. The effect of this pattern of academic development is both to insulate the perspective from fundamental attack, especially within the USA itself, and to diffuse its impact on a global scale. This argument can be related to the social basis and funding of research in the USA, where there is widespread privatization of research initiatives and programmes. This filters into public debates and policy formulation. This is not to imply, however, that there is any simple input–output linear programming of policy. The American political system is one of the most complex in the world.

Second, and at a broader social level, as Enrico Augelli and Craig Murphy (1988) illustrate acutely, the abstract application of this discourse, with its substantive liberal capitalist and imperialist bias gains strength from and sits well with deep-rooted elements in America's Manichean political culture. Two aspects seem important here: American anti-intellectualism and pragmatism (that includes attraction to simple, parsimonious theories and to detailed empirical work) and, perhaps as fundamental, the pervasive metaphysics of denominational religion, with its ideas concerning Manifest Destiny, evangelism and vigilantism, that evoke a twin sense of mission and responsibility to save the rest of the world from itself. Moreover, I would add, the isolationist tradition, like its schizophrenic counterpart, messianic imperialism (both premised on the opposition between 'us' and 'them') parallels the radical separation of subject and object in positivist thought.

These then are aspects of both the practical effectiveness and the social myth of American liberalism. Here there is a correspondence with the pseudo-religion of Soviet Marxism. In both there is a tendency to protect a standard theorization, in a process that helps to constitute the limits of the possible in terms of academic innovation. In the US academic industry, at least in the fields of International Relations and International Political Economy, hundreds of PhD theses, and thus many careers, have been built around regime theory and the Theory of Hegemonic Stability. This is one instance of how the American positivist paradigm is consolidated. A process of social and intellectual enclosure ensures that adherents and their theorizations are insulated from critical dialogue with those of contending perspectives or paradigms. The dominant paradigm, for its adherents, assumes the mantle, as it were, of near, if not absolute, truth.

3
Transnational Historical Materialism and World Order

This chapter seeks to further develop a historical materialist perspective on political science and political economy that helps to identify moments or historical turning points that may serve to redefine the political 'limits of the possible' for collective action. Such an approach may be applied to explain very rapid political changes and transformations, such as the sudden collapse of communist rule in the former East Bloc in 1989–91. It is also useful for outlining fundamental, 'organic' crises (and their momentary conjunctures) that may last many decades, for example in seventeenth century England, or in the wider global context between 1919–45, involving two world wars.

In this context, we locate the method of analysis of a critical political science: the assessment of how political agency is constituted, empowered and constrained within political and civil society in any given world order.

To prepare the ground for this discussion the chapter begins with a short consideration of the dimensions of fundamental historical transformations in relation to the work of Fernand Braudel on historical time, and the ideas of Marx and Gramsci on the question of agency. This is followed by a review of the concept of socio-historical time both theoretically and in terms of moments of historical formation drawing on the examples of (1) early bourgeois state formation in England in the seventeenth century and (2) the transformation of key aspects of the post-1945 new world order from a hegemonic to a supremacist moment.

The limits of the possible and socio-historical time

Braudel, Gramsci and Marx all agreed that the emergence of industrial capitalism and the Enlightenment's 'epistemological break' were profound examples of rapid structural transformation in frameworks of thought and action. It is a moot point as to whether we are at the threshold of such a transformative process in the early twenty-first century. Indeed, in order to assess such a prospect requires us to assess what Braudel called 'the limits of the possible' or the conditions under which collective action is constituted and constrained. Braudel's method, like that of Gramsci and Marx was wide-ranging and specific as to time and place. This method encompassed all the ingredients of power, production and social reproduction: from the economy and social relations of the household to patterns of global trade, investment and the balance of power. It explored the co-ordinates of space and time and biological and ecological dimensions of social life. In doing so, he developed a differentiated social ontology, constructed for different regions of the world, between the fifteenth and eighteenth centuries. Braudel used this apparatus to sketch a three-dimensional model of society, economy and civilization, governed by three rhythms of social time in ways similar to Gramsci in the *Prison Notebooks*. It is the latter we focus on here.

The first rhythm of social time is 'events-time' (based on François Simiand's notion of *l'histoire événementielle*) and is the easiest notion to grasp. It refers to the continual flow and succession of actions and events in the movement of history. By contrast the *longue durée* involves sets of ideas, patterns of interaction, institutional forms and a structure of experience that may persist 'for an infinitude of generations'. A crucial example of this is the emergence of the exchange relations of capitalism since the late Middle Ages. As Marx pointed out, exchange relations constitute a 'mutual and universal dependence of individuals who remain indifferent to one another' in a 'social network that binds them together' (Marx 1973: 77). This network is reproduced through innumerable individual acts of exchange, mediated by money. Marx of course pointed out that under capitalism, this social network resulted in an alienated form of power: the subordination of people and communities to social relations that exist independently of them.

Thus the *longue durée* involves the patterning of habits and expectations in everyday life involving repeated actions that form regularities: *les gestes répétées de l'histoire*. Such *gestes répetés* form 'historical structures' that constitute and constrain the limits of what is politically possible for different classes and social groups at a certain moment in time: they are a form of power for some and constraints for others. Finally, the *longue durée* includes the persistence of philosophical and theological systems as well as conceptions of space and time (e.g. the concept of geometric pictorial space invented in the Renaissance). As Braudel notes:

> The Aristotelian conception of the universe persisted unchallenged, or virtually unchallenged, right up to the time of Galileo, Descartes and

Newton's system of thought; then it disappeared before the advent of a geometrised universe which in turn collapsed, though much later, in the face of the Einsteinian revolution. (Braudel 1980: 33)

Braudel points out that it is paradoxically more difficult to discern the *longue durée* in matters economic, since economic cycles, inter-cycles and structural crises tend to mask the longer-term regularities (Braudel 1980: 33). Nevertheless, as we have noted, here we could cite the spread of exchange relations involving monetization and commodification of social relations as aspects of the *longue durée* of the political economy of capitalism – a process that has its lineage in the laws of property in the Roman Empire. The spread of exchange relations began to accelerate in the nineteenth century with the consolidation and emergence of integral imperialist nation-states and were institutionalized in the world order by British hegemony, the international Gold Standard, and a balance of power system including, and not least, a proliferation of international organization (Murphy 1994).

Between events-time and the *longue durée* lies conjunctural time. This refers to the emergence and consolidation of social structures (e.g. mass culture, production and consumption) and institutions (e.g. forms of state) that may span several generations. An example is the conjuncture of the Cold War, a conjuncture that combined, amongst other things, a political economy of mass production and expanding consumption in the OECD with nuclear weapons and potentially mass annihilation (with its corresponding 'bomb culture'). Some date this conjuncture from 1947, lasting in Europe at least until the collapse of the Soviet Union in 1991 (the Cold War still continues in East Asia). Others, like Eric Hobsbawm, without minimizing the onset of weapons of mass annihilation, identify the origins of the Cold War in the Russian Revolution of 1917, lasting until 1991. These two dates are the bookends of the 'Age of Extremes', in which the Soviet Union and state socialism presented historical alternatives to capitalism (Hobsbawn 1994). In some ways, therefore, the apparent continuities of history are associated with the *longue durée* and with the embedding of social structures. These structures appear to have a *quasi-permanent* character, even though, of course, they are governed by transience, and by the shifting patterns of collective action.

So what is the role of political agency in this process? For Braudel, as for Gramsci and Marx, the answer is that structures are created through, and transformed by, collective action. They also agreed that such structures were institutionalized by repeated patterns of thought and action over time. Collective action is constituted by the interaction of human beings with their natural and social environment, driven in part by how they seek to secure the survival and reproduction of their communities and ways of life over time.

Thus the nature of social structures and political agents is part of the dialectic of historical transformation. This dialectic involves the making of one form of society with its patterns of social reproduction and its replacement by another. Braudel's most persuasive insights are in how he identified one aspect of this patterning of social relations and social reproduction: as a cumulative process involving the repetition of actions and predispositions across time and within and across particular spaces. His weakness perhaps lies in his reluctance to identify the actual and potential transformative power of collective action (other than that of elites and ruling classes) in restructuring social formations. By contrast, Marx and Gramsci stress the power of such agency much more, as well as what we have called transformative resistance, and both highlighted the role of organized violence in processes of transformation.

Some of these ideas may provide us with a set of meta-principles to help explain and interpret the ontology and constitution of historically specific configurations of world order. As we have intimated, ontology involves shared understandings and experience of the universe, the cosmic order and its origins, of time and space, and the interaction of social forces and nature. Social ontology rests upon the inter-subjective ('historically subjective') frameworks that help to objectify and constitute patterns social life, such as patterns of social reproduction, the political economy of production and destruction, of culture and civilization. One benefit of this approach is that it may enable us to go beyond the conventional ways social scientists define structure and agency – not as something separate or atomized but as constituted through collective thought and action in socio-historical time.

Event, conjuncture and *longue durée* in bourgeois state formation

With these methodological considerations in mind, let us now briefly explore in schematic fashion, the example of early bourgeois state formation in England to identify aspects of the *longue durée* of modern capitalist state forms. We relate this to how a historical situation is the appropriate object of analysis for Political Science and Political Economy and how this can be explored with reference to Gramsci's method of the 'relations of force'. The example of Britain is chosen because it was perhaps the first developed example of bourgeois nation-state formation (the other candidate is the Dutch Republic). Also, as noted earlier, because of its imperialist history, the British case is an exemplar for the globalization of political forms in capitalist modernity.

The seventeenth century in Britain was a period of unusual social upheaval, turbulence and political violence. A complex array of social forces – some conservative, some democratic and radical, served to constitute the century of revolution (1603–1714) (Hill 1980). It entailed a historical transformation away from a dynastic towards a modern bourgeois political and civil society, allowing for the emergence of British religious toleration, scientific progress and imperialist foreign policy. The politics of the era was characterized by a dialectic between the old and the new: that is, between the monarchy, bourgeois and more radical democratic forces, the latter for example in the form of the radical Diggers who wanted to see universal suffrage as the basis of the Constitution and the Generals and the somewhat more conservative Levellers who wanted to widen the franchise and system of representation to encompass larger numbers of 'men of property'.

In terms of events-history Britain experienced a civil war and, for the first time in its history England became a Republic under Cromwell's dictatorship (the Interregnum following the execution of the monarch) followed by a restoration in the form of the Settlement of 1689, again following a brief interregnum.

The century involved four overlapping political conjunctures/moments:

1. The despotism that failed: the collapse of the Tudor system 1603–42.
2. Great Rebellion and Interregnum, 1642–60. Here Civil War and Puritan Revolution were followed by a dictatorship that ultimately failed. Central to this process was the Puritan Revolt against Stuart despotism, where 'to be "old" became a weapon in the hands of a *new* class' (Rosenstock-Huessy 1969: 278). A unified opposition to the monarchy developed and it was based on the 'holy alliance of Puritanism and Capitalism' (Jones 1931: 55).
3. Restoration Settlement 1660–88. This period encompassed the King's Restoration, the threat of despotism; and failed effort at compromise. The Commons wished to restore *some* of the spirit of the Magna Carta – that is a law 'above' sovereigns – that had once terminated Angevin despotism. Specifically, the Common Law had to be rescued from the control of the King and Lord Chancellor so that constraints were placed on the King's ability to decree legislation, and in this way, to begin to separate the emerging economic interests from the political control of the Crown.

4. Glorious Revolution 1689–1714. This entailed an Anglican Restoration, the establishment of the constitutional supremacy of a parliament dominated by the emerging merchants and bourgeoisie, the creation of the United Kingdom, and the spread of its empire. In 1603 Britain was a second-class world power, by 1714 it was the greatest world power with an empire that had expanded from the early colonization of the Americas begun under Queen Elizabeth I. Thus the wider context for the revolution was the expansion of the world market and the growing political power of the emerging bourgeoisie. We focus on the latter aspect in this section.

Although this is well beyond the scope of this chapter, to fully understand this moment requires a longer historical perspective – one that places the question of revolution in both the national context (related to effort to create a centralized state and unified national market), as well as the international context. In this regard it is noteworthy that, ever since the Norman Conquest, political rule in England has always been internationalized. Except for the Tudors, no ruling dynasty has been English since 1066, and in the early sixteenth century, the upper levels of the Church, the War Lords and the Church Lords were foreigners. By contrast the Gentry (squires and merchants) were 'of English blood' and controlled and indeed became the socio-economic foundation and leading political agency – in conjunction with the Generals – of the new revolutionary system that emerged during the seventeenth century. In this revolutionary moment they were able to move from an awareness of corporate interests towards a more hegemonic form of political consciousness.

Thus the very first principle of the new constitutional structures that was to emerge was a limited monarchy. This meant removal of the Divine Right, as well as the absolute prerogatives of the King (e.g. control over finance and the army) whilst the King's duties of central administration continued. The King was made to work, not dictate. The Act of Settlement secured the independence of Parliament, and the alien King was checked by an independent House of Commons and an English Privy Council (1709–13) and the King was required by oath to preserve the Church of England. At the same time, Parliament established its supremacy, not only over the King, but also over the Church: 'The King's Church became the Parliament's Church, and instead of a Royal Parliament there was a Parliamentary King' (Jones 1931: 175).

With respect to the restructuring of the political economy, the prerogative of economic regulation was removed from the Crown. Now the state more directly served the interests of the emerging bourgeoisie.

Whilst industry was largely left to itself, Parliament intervened to promote the development of agriculture and commerce. In 1601 the East India Company was formed. By 1700 it was the most powerful company in Britain. Parliament removed remaining opposition to enclosures. Agricultural interests gained in power and influence. Capitalist agriculture was consolidated under what Deane Jones called the new protections of a 'capitalized constitution'. Jones shows how the supreme law locked in the victory of the property owners. The Constitution redefined the economic powers of the new state form, creating the institutions of the National Debt and the Bank of England in 1694. The latter had the effect of subordinating the Constitution to propertied interests, notably those of the Whig owners. By 1714 *laissez faire* had succeeded mercantilist regulation in most economic activities (Hill 1980: 3). The law of contracts was changed in favour of the wealthy classes in the mid-seventeenth century and 'clever safeguards against any confiscation of property by the Crown were established'. A personal debtor could be arrested without any preliminary proof, whereas Habeas Corpus was good against the Crown. Thus the 'producer mercilessly fell into the hands of the wealthy ... called a restoration of the Common Law' (Rosenstock-Huessey 1969: 280). In Polanyi's words: 'The government of the Crown gave way to government by a class – the class which led in industrial and commercial progress. The great principle of constitutionalism became wedded to the political revolution that dispossessed the Crown' (Polanyi 1975: 38).

And as Marx and Polanyi both showed, this revolution-restoration overthrew constraints on the flexibility of large property owners to accumulate capital and it initiated a process of primitive accumulation and commodification of land, labour and money. Of course it also institutionalized new individual freedoms and religious tolerance. However, from the viewpoint of the mass of the population, as E.P. Thompson put it, 'The commercial expansion, the enclosure movement, the early years of the Industrial Revolution – all took place within the shadow of the gallows'(Thompson 1980: 66). With respect to changes in world order, the revolution consolidated the power of an 'active oligarchy that governed and exploited the British Isles, India and America, at a time when European nobility were sinking into political paralysis and economic parasitism' (Jones 1931: 182). The glories of the new British Constitution became an export article of the mother country that covered the whole field of government: 'Christian spirit, democratic consent, authoritative government, royal independence of the courts, respect for the public opinion of those with property' (Rosenstock-Huessy 1969: 298) or what

Gramsci called a passive revolution for the settler colonies and dependencies (see below on passive revolution).

In terms of the *longue durée* we can note that there was not only a fundamental shift in British political economy and the onset of modern capitalism, but also a transition from pre-modern to modernist frameworks of thought and action. The revolutionary crisis of the seventeenth century in England took place amid a general transformation in European social and political experience – it was in Gramscian terms, an 'organic' crisis. For Gramsci an organic crisis involved a fundamental transformation from one civilization and political form to another. We can define organic crisis as an historical situation where the 'old' has exhausted its political potentials, and when the 'new' is struggling to emerge and consolidate a new order, and indeed a new form of political and civil society. Such struggles may involve political conjunctures that last for decades. *In the case of the seventeenth century the organic crisis entailed an epistemological and ontological shift away from an old, essentially metaphysical representation of being and of the political order towards a new, increasingly secular, gradually more modernist, more scientific, and materialist set of frameworks of thought and action.* For example, the post-medieval notion of the Divine Right of Kings (and with it the idea that subjects' property was at the disposal of the King) was not only contested but also supplanted during this period, at least in the Dutch Republic (by definition) and in Britain after the Tudor and Stuart order had been swept away in the successive waves of revolt and political renewal.

Indeed, in the earlier Elizabethan era, at least in drama, a new political actor (the possessive individual) made an appearance on the stage. This took a number of forms: in Christopher Marlowe's *Dr Faustus* where the new science posed the issue of how far human mastery of the material cosmos might be possible, albeit in a context where the price of mastery was Faustus' soul which he had pledged via Mephistopheles, to the Devil. In Shakespeare some of the issues characteristically involved the dialectic between the old and the new. In *King Lear* the early challenge of individualism, empiricism and secularism (e.g. Edgar) is counterpoised to an old hierarchical social order premised on a fixed chain of being with little or no social mobility. The legal basis of the emerging bourgeois order was explored in *The Merchant of Venice*. Here Shakespeare interrogated the way efforts to create absolute private property rights involved attempts to privatize rights over life itself through contract. Shylock's contract with Antonio specified that if the latter failed to pay his debts on time, Shylock could take a pound of flesh from any part of Antonio's body. When faced with Antonio's plea of mercy Shylock argues that contract right is supreme and that the property holder holds this right as a 'sovereign' power. So what was at issue in *The Merchant of Venice* was the degree to which private property involved rights to treat people as if they were simple commodities and whether this right should be central to the legal underpinning of the emerging modern state. Portia, in the guise of Justice, represented the position that such rights should be constrained and if need be, confiscated.[1] Thus the structural transformations of the century of revolution, in Hill's words 'embraced the whole of life'. By 1700 empiricism and atomism, and the new social and political perspective of possessive individualism, allied to a Newtonian view of the universe, began to hold increasing sway across Europe. In Europe this involved a dialectic of two conceptions of civilization: French absolutism as one model and the Dutch Republic (and implicitly therefore, the Glorious Revolution) as the other (Hill 1980: 4). This dialectic was, of course, also political, with issues of absolutism and capitalist constitutionalism counterpoised in an era when modern nation-states began to emerge in the century following the Thirty Years War (1618–48).

Twentieth century change and relations of force

Taking a longer historical view enables us to bring into relief some aspects of the important conjunctures in the twentieth century, with respect to the relations of force that involve aspects of structure, politics and strategy as Gramsci defined them.[2] Indeed, as indicated earlier, the 'structure' is subject to transformation from one conjuncture to the next. The nature of contemporary capitalism in Western Europe – in part because of the influence and power of the USA – is quite different to that in the 1930s. For example, despite the existence of mass unemployment in Europe today, the dislocations associated with contemporary capitalist development do not necessarily have the same material and political implications as in the 1930s. For example at the time of the Wall Street Crash in 1929 the service sector in Western Europe and North America comprised approximately one-third of all workers, whereas at the

1. I am grateful to Gibin Hong for highlighting the example of *The Merchant*.
2. Gramsci spoke of social forces 'closely linked to the structure' measured to estimate the formation of and alignment of 'groups in relation to production'. This enabled examination of whether 'the necessary and sufficient conditions exist in a society for its transformation' (Gramsci 1971: 179). A much-debated example is the conjunctural shift from Fordism to post-Fordism. The 'political' moment involved assessment of the homogeneity and consciousness of various groupings. The 'strategic' aspect primarily involved military relations.

beginning of the crash of 1987 two-thirds of all workers were in services, and half of those were within the public sector. In 1929 transfer incomes in Western Europe amounted to less than 4 per cent of GNP, whereas in 1987, because of unemployment benefits, pensions, family and social security allowances, transfer payments amounted to 30 per cent of GNP. Thus the scourge of mass unemployment today involves lower levels of social dislocation than in the 1930s, and despite the secular trend towards lower growth few speak today of a crisis of capitalism.

With respect to the *political* level of analysis, or the second moment in the relations of force, if we look at the situation in Europe today in contrast to the 1930s, once again the liberal democratic political form has been consolidated, and indeed has now become relatively universal in European politics in not only the European Union but also the former East Bloc, although its electoral democracy is not necessarily commensurate with the spread of substantive or direct democracy.

Indeed, in the West European context the main achievements of socialism and social democracy have been couched in terms of the *corporate* or *reformist* moments of consciousness, that is with welfare-nationalism understood primarily as a national project. The central goal of socialism and social democracy (and of some communist parties) was not the replacement of capitalism, but civilizing the capitalist mode of production, in effect conferring it with a *hegemonic* aura. Thus most of the institutional innovations associated with the post-war European welfare states, as well as the institutional order of the liberal international economic order that was restored after World War II, have been connected to the stabilization and legitimating of capitalism through the use of an expanding sphere of state regulation.

Indeed, if we survey the historical situation today, one hypothesis is that for most of the world, the central effective political reality of the early twenty-first century is the struggles connected to a new phase of the bourgeois revolution, albeit one that is on a more global scale than in the seventeenth century. I have elsewhere called this struggle the 'clash of globalizations' since it captures some of the key forces involved (Gill 2002). The lineages of this revolution lie in the early political and juridical forms of the Italian City States (e.g. Venice), the Dutch Republic, and, of course, subsequent to the Glorious Revolution, the American and French Revolutions. In the context of the early twenty-first century, with the decline of the traditional organized left (socialist and communist forces) we see on the one hand, an apparent consolidation of disciplinary neo-liberalism, whilst, on the other, we see a range of social and political forces, more or less interconnected globally and politically, arguing for alternatives to the rule of capital on a world scale. The forces of capital can be understood as combining the old with the radically new, in so far as the new involves extended and accelerated commodification of social life and the biosphere, including processes of work, leisure and political and cultural representation. This can be considered as part of the tendencies towards the development of a 'market civilization' in the early twenty-first century (see Chapter 7).

This poses the question: which other elements of the *longue durée* of capitalist political forms are significant specifically for the analysis of the historical situation of European integration today? Here we might cite at least three. The effective restoration of the political power of the propertied; the increasing subordination of state forms to capital (following some socialization and nationalization of the means of production between 1917 and 1991); and not least, the renewal of the process of primitive accumulation, for example privatization of public assets. Primitive accumulation was associated earlier in Britain with the enclosures in the seventeenth and eighteenth centuries and earlier still, with the dispossession of the monasteries under the Henry VIII in the sixteenth century that created many of the Whig fortunes that exercised growing influence in subsequent years.

Despite being accompanied today by a gradual extension of the franchise, liberal state forms are proliferating in the early twenty-first century. Today's social and political order, ultimately subordinated to the power of property (capital) has a long institutional and political lineage. Moreover, of course, communism in Europe, at least as a form of rule, has collapsed and as such really existing alternatives to capitalism are notable by their absence. This is not to say that alternatives to the dominant political orthodoxy do not exist, especially on the neo-fascist and racist right.

With respect to the *strategic* or *military* level of force, perhaps the central feature of the last two decades is how the power of the USA has increased. Here we understand the USA as a state–civil society complex, as a locus and model of accumulation. This situation – perhaps unprecedented since the Roman Empire – concentrates the bulk of the world's military power and power projection capabilities in the hands of a single state. This is despite the efforts of other nations, for example China and Russia, to counterbalance some of this strategic power; and despite efforts to countervail American economic and monetary power through the process of European integration, for example by developing a single currency for Europe. One indicator of this relates to the redefinition and extension of NATO and its use in the Balkans, most recently in the former Yugoslavia and Kosovo. Most of this has occurred on American terms, reflecting subordination of the European Union to American military supremacy, a fact reiterated after the September 11th attacks on New York and Washington in 2001.

The rest of the world is also subjected to American power projection and its capacity to sustain remote-controlled aerial warfare, irrespective of whether this power is sanctioned or legitimated by a UN mandate.

And what of other political alternatives to American dominance? If we think of this question in terms of regional rivalries we can see that penetration of European economic development by American power since 1945 has had a dialectical effect. On the one hand, it has meant that European integration is limited politically by the USA's relationship with each member state. On the other hand, the EU is creating autonomous institutional and political capacity such as the creation of a single currency, and it has become, along with the USA, the main player in world trade and investment negotiations (based upon the effective co-ordination of a common EU policy). So whilst in many ways each EU member state, albeit in differing degrees, necessarily responds to and is partly subordinate to American foreign policy (and especially military policy, e.g. the UK's adherence to the American line throughout the 1990s in Iraq and in the 2000s in Afghanistan), we should not underestimate the gradual construction of the EU as a potentially countervailing force to American power, although it seems unlikely that this challenge will change its subordinate position in terms of military/geopolitical matters.

Passive revolution and absence of hegemony: restructuring in the former East Bloc

So far we have largely discussed the dialectic between capitalist hegemony and the subordination of socialism and social democracy to that hegemony. However, as was noted earlier, a key concept in Gramsci's lexicon relates to a situation associated with the creation of a new form of state characterized by the absence of the hegemony of a leading class. Gramsci called this a situation of 'passive revolution'.

Generally for Gramsci, passive revolution refers to two sets of situations. The first is a revolution without mass participation that is often prompted by external forces. This type of revolution can often follow a 'war of movement' or a rapid overthrow of a regime. The second is a slower, more capillary or 'molecular' social transformation where the most progressive class must advance its position more cautiously through a long-term 'war of position'. The concept of passive revolution and its two related strategic concepts (wars of movement and position) are derived from what Gramsci calls 'two fundamental principles of political science':

1. No social formation disappears as long as the productive forces, which have developed within it, still find room for further forward movement.
2. A society does not set itself tasks for whose solution the necessary conditions have not already been incubated, etc. (Gramsci 1971: 106)

Passive revolution was used by Gramsci to characterize the relationship between the most dynamic form of productive power and political economy, that is Americanism and Fordism, on the one hand, and the backward forms of political economy in Europe, notably in Italy, on the other. In Italy, passive revolution involved efforts to introduce advanced methods of capitalist production in the absence of bourgeois hegemony. This occurred more generally in Europe, both before and immediately after World War II, the latter in the context of the American occupation and the Marshall Plan. Efforts were made to comprehensively introduce Fordist production under reformist conditions imposed from the outside, to both preserve European capitalism and to subordinate it to American dominance. Indeed, the American form of state, civil society and mode of capital accumulation have become models for passive revolution throughout the world in the latter part of the twentieth and early twenty-first centuries.

In sum, the revolution of capital (albeit with its new conditions of extended liberal freedoms in the sphere of exchange and in limited democratization through electoral politics) is experienced in the periphery of Western Europe today as a 'passive revolution'. Passive revolution, according to Gramsci, occurs when (transnational) bourgeois class formations increase their social power in locations where bourgeois hegemony has not been consolidated. Thus in the former communist states after political domestication of forces that propelled the revolutions to overthrow communist power in 1989 and 1990 a process developed that allowed a restoration of the power of capital. In the nineteenth century, British imperialism was the main vehicle for spreading the passive revolution of capital whereas, of course, in the twentieth century, the USA has been central and often decisive in this regard – that is it is the Piedmont, or leading state, in a constellation of states that are involved in the drive towards unification of the world market under the dominance of capital. Indeed, the USA's military dominance in Europe partly exercised through NATO since 1947 means that any discussion of

European integration has to be placed in the context of what Gramsci called the 'relations of force'.

Thus it is noteworthy that the reform programmes in the former East Bloc have been introduced very rapidly and imposed not only by domestic reformers but also by external forces drawn not only from Western Europe, but also from within the broader framework of the international institutional complexes of capitalism linked to the leadership of the United States in the G7. What these processes have in common is that they exemplify the introduction and/or imposition of new constitutional and political forms from above – in this case they serve the interest of advancing capitalism in the absence of a domestic capitalist class.

Here the EU and its G7 allies (what I call the 'G7 nexus') have acted to accelerate the transformation to restore the rule of capital and confer it with legitimacy and protection through liberal constitutional state forms, forms that have antecedents that date back to the early Dutch and British forms of state (see Chapter 9 for elaboration on the G7 and the globalizing elites of transnational capital).

The new situation in the former East Bloc can yield the following interpretation. On the one hand, the desire for freedom and equality before the law meant that Western political models held out considerable long-term appeal to the populations of the East. The constitutions that marked the settlements following the revolution thus served to institutionalize a moment of consent that redefined the political limits of the possible. They also served to lock in new property rights for capital. On the other hand, the conditionality that was imposed on the former East Bloc nations by the West left little choice. The consent of the populations was accompanied by coercive capacity since the former East Bloc either had to accept a Western liberal political and constitutional framework, with its absolute guarantees for private property rights, or Western aid would be denied and indeed, those who refused might be severely punished, for example Serbia. The tactics for this approach on the part of the West were established in restructuring programmes for not only Poland, but also and perhaps more importantly, the restructuring of the former East Germany (DDR) following its *de facto* annexation by West Germany.

Thus, the reforms were intended to domesticate radical-democratic impulses and allow both the restoration of capitalism in the East (moment of revolution-restoration as an aspect of passive revolution) and the further weakening and incorporation of the enemy. The strategic aim was to extend the boundaries and political basis of the Western bloc and incorporate a newly created and empowered bourgeoisie in the East, as well as subordinating or appropriating its military assets under NATO command. Indeed, the American interest was to prevent a purely European solution to the question of restructuring.

Today, a decade later, much of the evidence indicates that the restoration of capitalism has brought about a catastrophic decline in the standard of living and quality of life for the vast majority of the population in the former East Bloc, with women, children and the elderly particularly hard hit. Not only has there been a decrease in life expectancy, especially in Russia, but also there has been a precipitate drop in the birth rate, as women, like men, experienced greater anxiety and insecurity about the post-communist future. Since 1989, there has been a steep increase in murder, suicides, crime rates, domestic violence, and a rapid increase in income inequality.[3]

The new world order: between hegemony and passive revolution

When Gramsci addressed the question of Europe and the world in the 1930s the question posed was not of international and European integration but its opposite: the disintegration and destruction of civilizations. Gramsci argued that an 'organic' or fundamental crisis was manifest. An organic crisis was a moment where a civilization and political form was undergoing fundamental transformation, specifically involving the exhaustion of the old and its replacement by the new in a conjuncture that might last for decades. As we have noted earlier, what we might call the 'long seventeenth century' in Britain was probably a good example of organic crisis.

In a typically poetic way Gramsci noted in the 1930s that the period following World War I was one of organic crisis: at that time, as he put it, the old was dying and the new was struggling to be born, and 'in the interregnum' there arose 'many morbid symptoms'. Of course, writing from prison, Gramsci could not be certain exactly how this transformation was occurring and what new forces might precisely be produced in the struggle – in this sense the methodological distinctions between the different relations of force cannot be applied with any sense of historical determinacy – they involve situations in movement. Indeed, from the vantage point of the early twenty-first century we might still pose the issue in the same terms: the dialectic between old and new continues with

---

3. UNICEF documents much of the sorry evidence for this in a recent report: *Women in Transition*, New York: UN, 1999.

its particular morbid symptoms after the interregnum of state socialism and state capitalism posed temporary historical alternatives.

In the 1930s no solution to the crisis was evident. The crisis of the economic structure was a crisis of hegemony for capitalism as a system, a general crisis of the state and of political authority. 'Popular masses' no longer adhered to the orthodox political ideologies that legitimated the relationship between rulers and ruled. Thus the coercive face of power came to the fore and the ruling classes in many states were prepared to sacrifice constitutionalism and democracy at the altar of reaction and fascism.

Of course, it took the most destructive war in history for the organic crisis to be (perhaps temporarily) resolved. The struggle did not produce an authentic revolution against capital as such. In fact, in Western Europe, the defeat of fascism led to the restoration of capitalism and the rebirth of liberal democratic constitutional forms supplanted or obliterated by authoritarianism and fascism throughout much of the continent during the 1930s. The wartime alliance between Soviet Russia and the capitalist allies paradoxically allowed for the re-legitimation of capital in Western Europe under the aegis of the Marshall Plan. The geopolitical context was the emergence of the Cold War following the deterioration of US–Soviet relations after the use of atomic weapons by the USA in Japan. The symptoms of morbidity between 1939 and 1945 involved the deaths of perhaps 50 million people as a result of the war.

Nevertheless, in his analysis of the condition of political life in the inter-war years, Gramsci posed the question whether the advance of Americanism and Fordism constituted the beginnings of a new historical epoch, or simply a combination of particular events that had no long-term significance. Indeed, he posed the question relative to the forms of state and class structures of the old and new worlds to ask whether emergent American productive power in the inter-war period was provoking a 'transformation of the material bases of European civilization' (Gramsci 1971: 317). Well before his incarceration Gramsci thought that the revolution in production in the new urban centres of industrial capitalism clarified the class struggle and symbolized the fundamental political issue for the future of Europe.

The dialectic between hegemony and passive revolution is a central theme of *Americanism and Fordism*. For Gramsci, Fordism and Americanism represented an acceleration of a new social form based upon a deep organic link between form of state, civil society and mode of production, and as such, represented a new form of planned economy where hegemony was based in the forces of production and 'was born in the factory'. By contrast the European class structure involved many parasitic elements. This was not unique to Italy since it was found throughout 'Old Europe' and in an even more extreme form in India and China. As such the bourgeoisie were not hegemonic in these societies, and the transformations took the form of 'passive revolution'. Often political dominance was manifested by a regressive Caesarism where order is imposed from above in a situation of deadlock between contending old and new social and political forces, sometimes by dictatorship (e.g. when Cromwell ruled England during the Interregnum). In the situation of the 1930s in Italy the productive apparatus of society was not shaped by the hegemony of capital in civil society but from control from above by the authoritarian state apparatus, mobilizing the *petit bourgeoisie* and repressing the working class as in fascism.

Fordism had triumphed in the USA by a combination of *force* (destroying working-class unionism and solidarity) and *persuasion* (high wages, social benefits, ideological and political propaganda) to create a new form of worker subjected to intense and 'Puritanical' moral and social regulation (requiring monogamy and freedom from alcoholism). However, Gramsci considered each of these weapons of exploitation as a doubled-edged sword: workers resist the imposition of moral regimentation and identify the hypocrisy of the ruling classes with respect to sexual relations; the workers gain 'a state of complete [mental] freedom' after the worker has 'overcome the crisis of adaptation' associated with repetitive mechanical work, so that he has 'greater opportunities for thinking' (Gramsci 1971: 310).

Americanism and Fordism required a particular form of state and social structure, namely a liberal state based on free initiative and economic individualism and a corresponding form of civil society, but the very development of a planned economy and the need for social and moral regulation meant an increase in state intervention. Thus, according to Gramsci, the capitalist state can never be the same as before. The state increasingly intervenes in the process of production, even reorganizing productive processes according to plans and, when necessary, assuming the nationalization and socialization of risk. Thus the formal character of the liberal state is preserved within civil society at the level of freedom of initiative and enterprise but with its fundamental meaning reconfigured by statism, industrial concentration and monopoly.

Historical blocs and International Relations

The central critical question today concerning the future of Europe – and indeed for world order more generally – can be posed as follows: how to create a new transnational political community, and how to construct radical-democratic hegemony within that space.

In this context, the concept of a historical bloc helps to describe the basis of a form of state and its capacity for rule and leadership. An historical bloc is not simply the creation of leaders, since this must be based on collective action of political groups as they seek to forge their own personality in ways that combine material capacities and potentials with persuasive ideas and a sense of direction in an organic way. Indeed, as Gramsci shows, the historical bloc is not something that depends upon a specific 'state' for its existence as such. *The Modern Prince* principally explores the case of modern Italy, which was a nation *before* it had a state, and as such, the formation of a *blocco storico* preceded the unification of Italy in the nineteenth century under Garibaldi.

An historical bloc refers to an historical congruence between material forces, institutions and ideologies, or broadly, an alliance of different class forces politically organized around a set of hegemonic ideas that gave strategic direction and coherence to its constituent elements. Moreover, for a new historic bloc to emerge, its leaders must engage in 'conscious, planned struggle'. Any new historic bloc must have not only power within the civil society and economy, it also needs persuasive ideas, arguments and initiatives that build on, catalyse and develop its political networks and organization – not political parties as such.

As we have seen, twentieth century economic development and political identity have been over-determined by American globalism and Soviet communism. The result for the European Union is that the national state–society formations are penetrated by, or interpenetrated with, those of other nations and by international organizations. Of course, the USA is the imperial sun in this respect with its power radiating across the political universe of less powerful states. Indeed, after World War II, in the context of the Marshall Plan, NATO and the emergence of the EEC, the *pax Americana* involved an *international historical bloc* built on Fordist foundations, and on the internationalization of aspects of the American New Deal state form, modified by wartime mobilization and the subsequent establishment of the military-industrial complex. The new political settlements included moderate organized labour and big capital – as well as leaders from civil society for example in the media, centrist and political parties and churches – in a series of European and transatlantic political settlements under American leadership. It thus combined coercion and consent with Fordist accumulation and the legitimating of the material basis of the system through mass-consumption. Its ideological banners included the concepts of liberty, modernity, affluence, welfare and the 'end of ideology', fused into a concept of 'the West' and an anti-communist alliance. The bloc balanced national and transnational capital, organized labour and the state. This transatlantic bloc was constructed during the late 1940s and 1950s, and lasted until at least the late 1960s (Gill 1990: 49). With respect to this, intellectuals like Jean Monnet, who, because of their transatlantic activities and connections, shared with the American leaders the norms of liberal internationalism, played a strategic leadership function, such that they qualify for Gramsci's nomenclature as 'organic intellectuals', that is those close to the dominant elements in the bourgeois class formations.

Recently, political change and economic globalization have undermined this integral hegemony. For example, there has been an ideological shift towards neo-conservatism in politics and neo-liberalism in economics. Finance has taken the place of production as the main determinant of capitalist accumulation strategies. A political shift occurred which marginalized labour and social democratic parties from the inner circles of power (less so in some countries, such as Germany, than in others, e.g. the USA, UK and Japan). What I call the 'terrain of political contestability' has shifted to the right in the OECD countries since the early 1970s and it has moved further in a neo-liberal direction during the 1990s period of American triumphalism.

Here the institutions and collective agency of large-scale capital have been important both within international political life and in transnational class formations, taking initiatives, forging compromises and searching for a synthesis of positions in a long-term war of movement to restore the supremacy, if not the hegemony of the power of capital worldwide. This involved political initiatives designed to promote internationaliza-tion and liberalization of production, capital and exchange markets, complex communications grids, rapid innovation and diffusion of technology, with American capital at the vanguard.

In time, therefore, with the emergence of a more integrated global political economy, the former *international historic bloc* was transformed into an American-centred and -led *transnational historic bloc*, where organized labour has been virtually marginalized. At its apex are elements in the leading states in the G7 and capital linked to advanced sectors in international investment, production and finance. Increasingly in the 1990s these have been American firms.[4]

4. In the 1999 *Financial Times Global 500 Survey* of the world's largest corpor-ations by country, the USA ranks highest with 244 American owned and controlled firms (up from 222 in 1998) with a market capitalization of $7.3 trillion; the UK is next with 53 firms valued at $1.2 trillion; Japan comes third

By contrast, one of the most salient features of the 1990s is an unprecedented increase in social inequality, and an intensification of exploitation of both people and nature in an increasingly naked pursuit of profit, a development that is particularly noticeable in the USA.[5] At the same time, the neo-liberal shift in government policies has tended to subject the majority of the population (most workers, small businesses) to the power of market forces whilst preserving social protection for the strong (e.g. highly skilled workers, oligopolistic corporate capital, those with inherited wealth). In this context neo-liberal forms of accumulation are associated increasingly with a politics of supremacy, rather than hegemony (see Chapter 7 for further elaboration). By a situation of supremacy we mean rule by a non-hegemonic bloc of forces that exercises dominance for a period over apparently fragmented populations until a coherent form of opposition emerges, for example relative to the social disintegration in the former East Bloc and the divide between the employed and unemployed, 'locals' and immigrants, in Western Europe. The supremacist bloc is based on giant oligopolistic firms that operate politically both 'outside' and 'inside' the state and form part of the 'local' and 'global' political structures. The central purpose of this bloc is the intensification of the discipline of capital within state and civil society in order to increase the rate of exploitation and profit flows. Much of what this entails – both in terms of its contradictions and its connection to patterns of collective action and transformative resistance – is discussed in Parts II and III.

---

with 46 companies valued at $866 billion; then Germany with 23 firms at $654 billion, and France with 27 firms at $490 billion. Nine of the top ten corporations were American. The most noticeable trend was that banking, finance, insurance, business services, telecommunications, computer software, high technology and pharmaceuticals were now the largest sectors, with Microsoft the world's largest company.

5. The UNDP's *Human Development Report 1997* indicated that the world's 225 billionaires had a combined wealth of over $1 trillion, equal to the annual income of the poorest 47 per cent of the world's people (2.5 billion). Indeed, the three richest people in the world had assets greater than the combined annual output of the 48 least developed countries. One billion people had no access to safe drinking water; 842 million adults were illiterate; 158 million children under 5 were malnourished. In 1996 there were 1.3 billion people (or 20 per cent of the world's population) living below the income poverty line. At the same time, unemployment has been rising throughout the world. The ILO estimated that in 1996 about 1 billion people were unemployed. They note that this global unemployment crisis began in the early 1980s. See International Labour Organization, *World Employment Report, 1998–99*. Geneva: ILO.

4
Hegemony, Culture and Imperialism

This chapter draws links between organized violence, interventionism, hegemony, culture and imperialism. It focuses on the important case of Chile, immediately preceding and following the *coup d'état* of 11 September 1973, when the democratically elected government was overthrown by a military coup and a repressive dictatorship was installed. The coup inaugurated, for the first time anywhere, what we have called the historical project of disciplinary neo-liberalism, although under unconstitutional conditions of authoritarian dictatorship (see Chapter 7 for discussion of new constitutionalism and neo-liberalism). This reflected the political formula 'freedom of enterprise under a strong state'. The coup in Chile therefore served to highlight the real strategic framework for progressive politics in Latin America during the latter part of the Cold War, and how this framework was determined by the relations of force – and specifically how covert action and military power in a transnational framework was immediately decisive in the massacre of the left (see Chapter 3).

In many respects, the Chilean question is salutary for not only the understanding of the relations of force, but also for how, in a post-Cold War era, global politics involves questions of collective action and political identity in the context of a dialectic of violence, hegemony and counter-hegemony. In part, this dialectic can be understood through analysis of cultural struggles, including representations in popular culture as well as in poetry and art more generally. Indeed we might suggest that greatness in art depends in part on intellectual and moral resistance to conventional, hegemonic or supremacist ways of seeing and interpreting the world. Innovation in art, and in the social order can thus be related to cultural transformations that entail critical discovery and reconstruction of the self in alternative projects of society, founded on constructive critique of the limits and contradictions of everyday life.

In sum, problems of hegemony involve not only questions of power, authority, credibility and the prestige of a system of rule; they also involve the political economy and aesthetics of its representation in culture and its media. Systems of cultural meaning and signification are the complex products of the making of history, a process that also generates forms of state and civil society. In this context, any understanding of hegemony and indeed cultural imperialism also means consideration and analysis of the roles of education and other key cultural institutions, such as churches, political parties, trades unions, and of course, the activities of intellectuals, and artists, poets and entertainers. Cultural hegemony involves political struggles to constitute what Gramsci called the 'common sense of an epoch' and the identity of social forces in and across complexes of civilizations.

Cultural resistance after the Chilean coup, 1973

Matt Davies' book, *International Political Economy and Mass Communications in Chile: Transnational Hegemony and National Intellectuals*, focuses on specific aspects of these questions. Its focus is on how Chilean-based media intellectuals, many of whom were working in leading universities, sought to make sense of national cultural development in the context of the global political economy (Davies 1999).[1] Often these intellectuals developed the concept of (American) cultural imperialism as a critical tool, and applied it in a series of studies of media texts and communication forms. These intellectuals of the left sought to find ways to extend a democratic-popular culture both *horizontally* across Chilean society, and *vertically* within the media industries or complexes. Some of these intellectuals were inspired by the way in which Gramsci consistently emphasized that counter-hegemonic struggles involve cultural dimensions of social life. For Gramsci, to found a new type of society required the foundation of a new democratic form of culture. So the issues raised in this book – a scholarly monograph on media intellectuals in Chilean society – are also general ones. They are important for understanding the constitution of world order and the problem of hegemony. And indeed, Davies' book shows how the achievement of hegemony is complex, contested, contradictory and necessarily incomplete.

From the vantage point of both right and left in Chile in the 1960s and 1970s, the media was seen as a crucial site of hegemonic struggle, and a set of agencies and processes of domination and subordination, resistance and emancipation.

1967 was a key turning point, and Chilean politics swung to the left. Also the period of 1967–73 was one of great creativity in Media Studies in Chile, and important initiatives were taken to try to mobilize democratic

---

1. The original version of this chapter was the preface for Davies' book.

media and communication projects. Indeed, prior to 1973 American cultural and politico-economic imperialism was resisted from within Chilean society. The political struggles were reflected in scholarship concerning the mass media, often involving foreign intellectuals, such as Armand and Michele Mattelart (from France) and Mabel Piccini (from Argentina). For example Armand Mattelart used Roland Barthes' notion of mythology to develop an ideological analysis to unmask the system of bourgeois rationality. And Mattelart argued that bourgeois ideology is at its most effective in areas which appear to be politically neutral. So Mattelart's work, which was widely read and appreciated throughout Latin America, identified the cultural imperialism in Disney products sold in Latin America (for example Donald Duck comics). He linked this to the penetration of foreign capital, publications, movies, television programmes and other cultural products in the region. Mattelart also argued that freedom of the press, which is usually defended by the owners, has in fact little to do with freedom of expression, since the expression of universal values is structurally precluded under conditions of transnational oligopoly and monopoly.

This type of intellectual critique and creativity came to an abrupt end with the *coup d'état* on 11 September 1973. The Chilean left was crushed and critical theory was removed from the universities.

Davies is careful to point out that although the military took control in Chile, there were also divisions within the ranks of the officers, as well as within the ranks of the bourgeoisie. Some officers and members of the bourgeoisie wanted a swift return to civilian rule, and to a national, state capitalist development project. Many were hostile to the combination of neo-liberalism and authoritarianism represented by Pinochet. Nevertheless, following the military coup, left-wing democratic forces were killed, exiled or imprisoned, and critical university media institutes were closed down. The political economy of the Chicago Boys (neo-classical economists trained at the University of Chicago) was brutally imposed in Chile by Pinochet, with considerable help from the US government and from IT&T. (The CIA had for many years invested much time, money and effort in developing its media and political 'assets' in the country, in particular the most powerful newspaper, *El Mercurio*, which consistently produced editorials in favour of neo-liberal economics.) In this context it is worthwhile to remember one of the last and most stark visions of the great Chilean poet laureate of the masses, Pablo Neruda (who was the official Communist Party candidate for the presidency in 1969 before a coalition agreed to nominate Allende). Neruda published a collection in early 1973 just before he died and before the coup actually occurred.

Incitement to Nixoncide and Celebration of the Chilean Revolution was written as if the poet was anticipating the approach of barbarism. And his final poems included images such as the poet's expulsion from his house and garden by an army of corpses, and a terrifying vision of the world flooded by 'a great urinator'.

Needless to say, the traumatic moment of the coup gave rise to very different cultural and political conditions in Chile. Everything was framed by brutal repression. Under Pinochet there was a shift from broad popular and intellectual cultural resistance to gradual cultural incorporation (*trasformismo*) along with a shift from authoritarian rule to a newly dominant discourse of formal democracy and market civilization – that is the discourse of US power and transnational capital (involving amongst other things, what Davies calls the victory of Donald Duck and Teenage Mutant Ninja Turtles in Chile). So, on the one hand, Davies suggests that this seems to have produced a domestication of radicalism. On other hand, the author notes that subordinated classes in Chile were not simply passive victims of these processes of repression and incorporation. Indeed opposition to the Pinochet regime began to regroup and this led to protest movements in the 1980s, indicating a continued potential for counter-hegemonic projects. In fact, given that these protests and their communications strategies were emerging whilst Chile was still under military rule shows how, as with the Correspondence Societies in England during the repression of the 1790s (that are discussed by E.P. Thompson in *The Making of the English Working Class*), popular-democratic forces in Chile (and indeed elsewhere) can always create the cultural and political resources, not only to resist, but also to challenge the rationality of dominant forces.

The Chilean question and global politics

Thus one way to read Davies' book is in terms of the ways that American and Chilean ruling class strategies have been framed in a struggle to consolidate power. Indeed, although the USA has from time to time largely succeed in supporting or indeed forging a 'national' (sic) historical bloc to rule in Chile, the evidence that is presented by Davies suggests to me that the USA never achieved hegemony in the sense of an active and broad-based endorsement of the central tenets of its rationality and civilizational form amongst a majority of the citizens of Chile. Of course, American attempts to promote the hegemony of (transnational) capital in Latin America have always had a cultural dimension as well as political economy forms: from the Monroe Doctrine of the nineteenth century to modernization theory in the 1950s and 1960s (for example both involving different concepts of the civilizing mission of the USA); from the early forms of the structural adjustment and stabilization policies in the 1960s to those practised today by the IMF and World Bank; from covert action and manipulation of the media and politics in the 1960s and 1970s to the strategy of the normalization of market rationality, commodification and limited democratization today. Nevertheless, Davies is right to conclude that neo-liberal hegemony in Chile is fragile particularly since struggles for representation and democracy continue and because of the weaknesses of the neo-liberal model of accumulation despite the fact that it has some popular appeal in a more commodified and televisual cultural universe.

In conclusion, we might suggest that the present condition of global politics is reflected in the Chilean case. On the one hand, US leaders are at the apex of a transnational historic bloc of neo-liberal forces that is anchored in the state apparatuses of the G7. This bloc has achieved supremacy over apparently fragmented and subordinate forces in the new context of globalization. One central characteristic of supremacist strategy is the way that it involves the coercive imposition of power over apparently fragmented populations in a situation of extreme class inequality and political impasse. On the other hand, this supremacy is being challenged. Many are calling into question the rationality of the neo-liberal form of accumulation under the dominance of the giant oligopolies and monopolies of transnational capital. The vulnerabilities of the system are being increasingly exposed, for example in the series of intense financial crises in the Americas and in East Asia in the 1990s. Now we are on the threshold of the new millennium, and in similar ways to the 1930s, dominant forces are being challenged politically, not only from the left but also from the right, which comes in various stripes: authoritarian, dictatorial, fundamentalist and of course nationalist (cf. Nazism and fascism in the 1930s). A central question for world politics is therefore, whether this American-centred, neo-liberal form of supremacy is sustainable. This is a question that will be posed on the terrain of culture and politics, as well as political economy.

Part II

The Political Economy of World Order

Part II outlines some of the key aspects of global power and resistance that constitute the new world order: American dominance and imperialism; the power of capital; disciplinary neo-liberalism and new constitutionalism as programmes of global restructuring and politico-juridical reform; the extension of an emergent market civilization; and finally, intensifying and cascading global economic crises during the 1990s and related geopolitical and regional responses.

Whilst it is by now quite clear that the geopolitical structures of the new world order are dominated by the USA, it is worth reminding the reader that American power was severely underestimated by many theorists in the 1970s and 1980s. Indeed many expected American power to decline further with the likely result of increased global conflict, based on traditional forms of inter-state resistance (to both superpowers). This would produce re-alignments within the balance of power. By contrast, in the 1990s the issue debated by most international relations theorists did not concern America's relative decline, but the wider implications of renewed US dominance, imperialism and hegemony in an era of intensified globalization. In this context Chapters 5–8 call for attention to the major geopolitical and deeper structural changes that have shaped and are reshaping new world order, and how this creates new sets of limits and possibilities for political forces.

Indeed, as is noted in Chapters 5 and 6, one way that these structural changes can be linked to world order questions is through the concept of a 'crisis of hegemony'. This crisis is not to be understood as a decline of American state power as was suggested by a range of predominantly US-based authors, such as those drawn from the Realist and World-Systems traditions, but as a transformation in the structures of power, hegemony, dominance and resistance that constitute world order. Since the early 1990s, the capitalist system has become more universal and as such, the historical structures of the new world order – in politics, law and culture – are being transformed, partly by virtue of the growing power and mobility of transnational capital and associated neo-liberal ideas, ideologies and theories. This has produced a movements towards a market civilization configured by disciplinary neo-liberalism, new constitutionalism, and extensive and often coercive methods of discipline and surveillance.

Nevertheless, as Chapters 7 and 8 indicate, these developments can be interpreted as part of a wider, organic crisis, which should be understood not simply as a crisis of political economy, but also as a profound cultural and civilizational crisis. As the Chinese have long pointed out, crises provide dangers and opportunities for political actors. Thus in the case of the regional Asian crisis of 1997–98, which rapidly became a global crisis, one response was to seek to consolidate elements of a regional bloc, led by Japan. Japanese leaders sought (unsuccessfully) to resist restructuring of the regional political economy along the lines of disciplinary neo-liberalism. The crisis in fact gave rise to diverse forms of resistance, for example from workers movements as well as nationalists in several countries.

In this context, the late 1990s can be interpreted as a new phase of struggle between different projects of capitalist restructuring. The Asian crisis shows the interplay between geopolitics as conventionally understood by the strategists, and the new terrain of political economy with its associated relations of force. Thus, by the start of the twenty-first century, the problem of hegemony could be redefined as one involving struggles between historical blocs. The dominant forces were connected to a politics of supremacy, whereas the subordinate forces struggled to create a new politics of resistance. Indeed, there were signs that the project of disciplinary neo-liberalism was increasingly resisted both by states as well as by diverse social forces on the left and the right; some were progressive, some were reactionary. Many of the new forms of resistance were associated with struggles for identity, community and survival as well as, potentially, alternative projects of political economy, or what we have called transformative resistance.

Thus Chapter 5 sets the scene for these discussions by linking questions of power and hegemony to general transformations in the post-war new world order and provides a critique of the conventional wisdom that surrounded the question of American power and its supposedly relative decline in the 1970s and 1980s. Chapter 5 argues that orthodox perspectives, for example those of Realist and World-Systems schools have limited theorization of important transformative processes in the global political economy, with the result that assessments of the nature and prospects for hegemony in world order can be queried. More to the point, hegemony is not to be understood as simply a relation of dominance between states in the inter-state system; it involves the construction of a relatively consensual form of politics within its sphere of reference, with its combination of power and leadership giving due weight to subordinate forces in a series of institutionalized political settlements. Hegemony is forged in a complex set of historical blocs that link public and private power within and across nations in transnational political networks that seek to sustain, regulate and rule an increasingly global capitalist order.

Thus the issue is not so much the decline of American hegemony; rather the question is how far and in what ways hegemony is being reconstituted, in a historical process that involves continuity and discontinuity, limits and contradictions. Indeed the argument of the chapter is based upon the proposition that not only is US power unparalleled in comparison to earlier hegemonies, but also, and perhaps more importantly, it combines material and normative capacities and potentials in a new, modernist cultural and institutional framework that serves to channel and direct changes in identification and practice across territorial jurisdictions – often in ways that promote the interests of large corporate capital, and the interests of American corporations in particular. Thus the power and influence of elements in American political and civil society have been significant in shaping and reshaping the post-war international economy, which has become increasingly globalized. Reminiscent of the Roman Empire, the USA has used a 'mixed strategy' that combines unilateralism, bilateralism and multilateralism to promote and to consolidate a new global political and economic order congenial to American state interests, and to the extension and reach of its own firms. This mixed strategy has been central to the constitution of the post-World War II, 'new world order'. The USA has employed a combination of coercive and consensual means and succeeded in encouraging (and often forcing) other states to liberalize their economies. The policies of the Reagan Administration are interpreted in this context: as attempting to reconstitute US national power under a qualitatively different, transnational regime of accumulation. The deeper question posed in this essay anticipates many of the debates of the 1990s and the early twenty-first century: whether a transnational hegemony under US leadership is possible in a more liberalized global economy.

Chapter 6, co-authored with David Law, directly relates to the debates of Chapter 5 through a theorization of the power of capital. Working from a transnational historical materialist perspective, the article introduces a distinction between structural and direct forms of the power of capital in an attempt to overcome the structure–agency debate in social and international theory. In a more concrete historical sense, what is analysed is the shift that involves the increasing power of capital that coincides with the emergence of a 'disciplinary neo-liberal' project of transnational accumulation. More specifically, during the 1980s and 1990s, there was a shift towards more 'flexible' transnational forms of accumulation associated in part with 'large-scale' and 'internationally mobile' elements of capital. Such transformations should be understood as aspects of a broader accumulation strategy that encompasses conscious efforts by organic intellectuals to steer state strategies and market forces so that they might shape expectations in material life. This is a process that is simultaneously cultural, political and material, since it involves the deepening of 'market values' and perhaps more importantly, rethinking and redefinition of the role of the state in a more liberalized global political economy. At the same time, the question of the state is linked to the issue of resistance: for example, around the question of whether a transnational hegemony is possible and how social forces contribute to its establishment or resist such an enterprise.

With such issues in mind, Chapter 7 is central to Part II since it seeks to bring together key aspects of the emerging world order to explain some of its fundamental contradictions as well as limits and potentials for further transformations. The chapter identifies and conceptualizes some of main historical structures identified as serving to constitute globalization: (1) market civilization; (2) disciplinary neo-liberalism; (3) new constitutionalism; and the articulation of each of these with strategies of discipline and surveillance ('panopticism').

The concept of market civilization is presented, on the one hand, as an oxymoron – a contradiction in terms. It is however, on the other hand, a referent for restructuring in world order, understood as a set of contradictory, yet nevertheless fundamental transformative practices. These practices are reshaping the structure and language of social relations, so that they become more commercialized, marketized and commodified. At the same time, in an era of globalization, in contrast to the neo-liberal ideologies that seek to legitimate the dominance of capital, the emergent market civilization can also be interpreted as part of a wide-ranging 'organic crisis' (see also Chapter 3). In this crisis, there is a transformation of not only basic social institutions and traditions, but also of forms of state and world order. In effect, market civilization is the cultural terrain of struggle between the old and new. To fully interpret the struggle requires the analysis of new social forms emerging within the broader framework of neo-liberal restructuring. It also requires a critical understanding of power and knowledge in order to soberly assess the opportunities and challenges that social forces confront. In the mid-1990s, the dominant forces can be described as a 'supremacist bloc': social forces exercising a transient dominance over global society until a coherent programme of resistance emerges to challenge it, and to offer an alternative. The supremacist bloc is transnational in form, associated with elements of the G7, transnational capital, and other privileged members of an unfolding market civilization, and it is linked to policies and governing frameworks that expand the role and protection for free enterprise and market forces on the one hand, and restrict democratic control and accountability on the other.

Most scholarly literature on the Asian financial and economic crisis tended to focus rather narrowly on its economic aspects. By contrast Chapter 8 seeks to understand the crisis of 1997–98 in a global context and to link it to geopolitics. Thus this short chapter first argues that the Asian economic crisis should not be considered as 'simply a matter of movements in the global markets', but more importantly, as part of a wider process of economic restructuring. It illustrates contradictions between free market theory and the reality of a system that is built to support investor interests; the class based nature of restructuring; and popular struggles and mobilization of worker interests. It also highlights the role of political agency, and especially the 'organic intellectuals' that make recommendations as to how to deal with the crisis: called here 'the usual suspects'.

Second, Chapter 8 illustrates links between the financial meltdown in East Asia and US geopolitical interests in the Pacific region and in the wider new world order. Thus one of the elements at issue during the crisis was whether the appropriate policy response involved the implementation of restructuring along the lines of the American model of 'capital-market' based free enterprise where owners make all the key decisions, in contrast to the variants of the East Asia model in which the interests of not only owners, but also workers and the wider community are often taken into account in situations of crisis. Thus efforts were made by Japan to institutionalize a regional response to maintain its own and the region's social structures of accumulation, although in the first instance, these efforts have been defeated by the USA. Other forms of resistance to US strategy in the region varied and included reinforcing nationalist projects of state capitalism.

Indeed the efforts by the USA and the IMF to implement a neo-liberal response to the East Asian crisis can be viewed as the third phase in a longer strategy that has sought to incorporate different regions more comprehensively into neo-liberal globalization, that is to liberalize domestic social and economic structures so that they are more amenable to penetration, ownership and exploitation by US and other foreign corporate interests. The previous phases were (1) 'structural adjustment' programmes implemented following debt crises in the Third World since the early 1980s; and (2) rapidly implemented reform programmes to promote the transition from communism to liberal capitalism in Eastern Europe and the former Soviet Union during the 1990s. We are now in the phase of the universalization of disciplinary neo-liberalism, and the globalization of resistance to it (see Part III).

5
US Hegemony in the 1980s: Limits and Prospects[1]

Mark Twain did die eventually, and so will American hegemony. But in both cases early reports of their demise have been greatly exaggerated. (Russett 1985: 231)

This chapter criticizes a conventional wisdom of both right and left that assumes there has been a substantial relative decline in American power and hegemony. Indeed the conventional wisdom has significantly underestimated the capacity of the USA to engage in a strategy to reconstitute its international dominance, notably in the international economy, and as such obscures significant changes in the nature of US and capitalist hegemony. After making my critique, I will show how by using a Gramscian approach, important light can be shed on these changes. Indeed although material aggregates of US power indicate relative decline in the US position, the sheer scale of the USA in the global political economy means that it has wielded (perhaps since the 1930s), and continues to wield, substantial structural power. From a Gramscian perspective that focuses on national and transnational class and political formations, and on changes in forms of state, I argue there has been a re-constitution or 'crisis' of hegemony, both internal and external since the late 1970s. I also argue that the form and coherence of the post-war US-centred world capitalist system have changed in ways increasingly congruent with material interests of the most dynamic, transnational fractions of capital, a process which US policies can be said to have encouraged.

Theories of hegemonic decline and the conventional wisdom

Realist and World-Systems theorists are remarkably alike in terms of the theorization of the rise and fall of hegemonies, and use similar concepts

1. © *Millennium: Journal of International Studies*. The original version of this chapter first appeared in *Millennium*, 15 (3) 1986: 311–36. Excerpts are reproduced with the permission of the publisher.

of power and a shared cyclical view of history. They arrive at similar conclusions and together they help form what I have called the conventional wisdom on the American case.

Realists define hegemony in terms of the preponderance of one state over others in the inter-state system. This view tends to equate hegemony with dominance, and so I will use the term 'dominance' when referring to the Realist concept in this chapter. For Realists, dominance is anchored in unequal distribution of material capabilities, that is economic capacity and military strength. Sometimes it is seen that the mobilization of these capabilities is difficult, so that a distinction between realized and potential state power is necessary. Thus American Realists often lament the fact that certain forces in domestic politics (what I will call civil society) act as strong constraints on the autonomy of the US state to rationally pursue the 'national interest'. Often cited is the inability of the US state to effectively establish a national energy policy without its coherence being undermined by the power of 'vested interests'.

Realists use a Weberian concept of power as a basis for their understanding of hegemony. Hegemony is equated with 'power over', the power of one state to enforce its will over others. This view of power – be it overt or covert – is useful for explaining some aspects of interstate relations (and foreign policy). However it is weak in explaining the social basis of power relations. It also tends to underestimate the development (and policy-making role) of non-state organizations such as transnational corporations, and other social forces that transcend national boundaries, including culture and ideology.

With respect to world order, for Realists, political order – national or international – is inherently problematic. Stable, peaceful and predictable relations between actors do not arise naturally (in what Hobbes called 'the state of nature') but require continuing actual and/or threatened use of sanctions by powerful actors: the state (in domestic politics) and a hegemonic state (in international relations). This notion of the state is narrow, in so far as it refers primarily to an institutional arrangement of coercive and leadership capacities which produce order and discipline in a situation that would otherwise tend towards anarchy. The post-war bipolar structure of power is seen as involving two competing hegemonies. Thus it is unstable, but less unstable than when many states of roughly equal power resources compete to gain power over each other. Several Realists associate the creation and maintenance of the post-war liberal international economic order (LIEO) with a high concentration of military and economic power resources in American hands. Since aggregate measures of these resources (e.g. GNP, foreign exchange reserves, number of military bases and size of armed forces) show a relative decline in US capabilities, theorists of hegemonic stability such as Stephen Krasner have been driven to conclude that more disorderly relations are likely and that the LIEO tends to 'self-destruct' (Krasner 1983). Realists have had great difficulty, therefore, in reconciling what they see as a substantial relative decline in US power with the fact that the LIEO has not collapsed, and indeed has remained in essence intact through the recessions of the 1970s and 1980s. Also, the Realist view that failing economic growth might promote the development of neo-mercantilist economic blocs, as in the 1930s, is difficult to reconcile with the increased liberalization of significant aspects of the international economy.

Both Realists, like Robert Keohane, and World-Systems theorists, like Immanuel Wallerstein and Christopher Chase-Dunn, come to similar conclusions concerning the rise and decline of hegemonies. For example based upon a reading of the case of Dutch hegemony in the seventeenth century, Wallerstein argues that superiority in agriculture and industry leads to dominance in commerce and invisibles such as transport, communications and insurance. Commercial primacy leads to control in the financial sector of banking and investment. Successive superiorities acquired by the dominant power are followed by a similar pattern involving loss of advantage as contender states seek to catch up. First productive leadership declines, then commercial and financial. Wallerstein generalizes this sequence to the nineteenth century British and twentieth century American cases (Wallerstein 1974). Gilpin, from a Realist perspective, has sought to apply a similar framework to 'the governance of international systems ... provided by empires, hegemonies, and great powers that have risen and fallen over the millennia' (Gilpin 1981: 156).

At some point in the evolution of hegemony, the costs and benefits of expansion reach equilibrium, and thereafter a tendency emerges for the costs of maintaining the *status quo* to rise faster than the capacity of the dominant state to finance its maintenance. In the pre-modern era, this process of growth and eventual decline of hegemony took several centuries, whereas in the modern period of rapid economic and technological change this process is accelerated. The *pax Americana* is, according to Gilpin, no exception, and it is under threat of decline after only some 40 years. Gilpin cites a range of internal and external factors that contribute to erosion of hegemony. First, structural changes in the state's economy undermine its long-term capacity to finance its military strength: its economy reaches a 'climacteric' and begins to stagnate and lose its dynamism, whilst other 'latecomer economics' innovate and grow more rapidly (Gilpin 1981: 156–7). The burden of military commitments linked with loss of economic growth produces a fiscal crisis, wherein the hegemonic state (e.g. the USA) begins to amass budget deficits and faces a choice between investment, warfare and welfare. Underpinning this fiscal crisis are a loss of technological dynamism and the fact that military innovations become diffused. A further internal change, one that resembles the shifts in the structure of economic activity noted by Wallerstein, is closely related to the preceding changes, that is there is a movement from agriculture through manufacture and into services. Moreover, Gilpin stresses the 'corrupting influence of affluence' (such as decay of values conducive to economic growth). Key external factors involve two related developments: 'the increase in costs of political dominance and the loss of technological and economic leadership'. Gilpin applies the theory of public goods to suggest that dominant states are bedevilled by the 'free-rider problem' in the provision of international security. (Although it can be argued that security is not necessarily a public good, since the concept of a public good implies non-excludability; military alliances are not designed to provide collective security for non-members.) In any event, the costs of the provision of security come to outweigh the benefits. This is particularly the case when military expenditures are being financed when growth rates are in decline, a symptom of declining international competitiveness as well as, more fundamentally, a loss of productivity lead in key (high-tech) sectors. Other countries take advantage of military and economic innovations, despite attempts by the hegemonic power to prevent their diffusion. Thus the challenge from late developers is likely to undermine the hegemony of the USA, as British hegemony was undermined by the 'catch-up mercantilisms' of Germany, the USA, France and Japan at the turn of the century.

Common to World-Systems and Realist perspectives is a cyclical view of history, where national dynamism and power resources propel a state to hegemony, particularly in the aftermath of a major war that weakens potential rivals. In the long term, a combination of loss of the state's economic primacy and the rise of new centres of economic and military power are inevitable. Hegemony is a temporary, and increasingly short-term condition in the 'world system'. Thus the issue concerning US hegemony is not whether it will decline with the result that the USA becomes 'like an ordinary country', but rather which point in its inevitable decline the USA has currently reached. A consensus seems to have emerged: US decline is inevitable, and US hegemony is bound to erode. This consensus is reflected in the critical acclaim given to Robert Keohane's book, *After Hegemony*, the major premise of which, our being in a period that follows the end of US hegemony, has yet to be fully challenged in the literature. Keohane thus argues that US policy in the 1980s must reflect the constraints of interdependence and its relative loss of international autonomy since the high point of US international power in the 1950s. In the face of this interpretation, how do such theorists envisage the development of US strategies to cope with hegemonic decline and to maintain the LIEO? Christopher Chase-Dunn, from a World-Systems perspective, argues that the USA will rationally seek to organize a 'core-wide' approach to the management of the world economy to maintain its political and economic centrality. This means the USA would have to accept a 'collective capitalist' approach to world order and avoid unilateral policies particularly vis-à-vis its major capitalist rivals. This 'collective capitalist' perspective is similar to the Kautskian, early Marxist notion of ultra-imperialism (Chase-Dunn 1982). In accordance with this view, and using a rational choice variant of Realism, Robert Keohane is arguing for a similar strategy. Indeed, Keohane's frequent co-author Joseph Nye is a member of the North American–West European–Japanese Trilateral Commission, which Chase-Dunn refers to as the exemplar of such a strategy. In the early 1980s Nye contrasted long-term (irreversible) and short-term (reversible) causes of US relative decline. Long-run causes were related, first, to the process of dispersion of world economic growth, a process shared by the major US allies (Nye 1982). (The latter can be interpreted both as a challenge to American hegemony and as an extension of it, in so far as US transnational corporations have benefited enormously from such economic growth.) A second long-run cause was the breakdown of the bipolar security system, as other powers gained military capacity. (On the other hand, it can be argued that US military power has been effectively extended by the development of its alliances, surpassing those of its Soviet bloc adversaries.) Short-run, and possible reversible causes listed by Nye included 'the Vietnam syndrome' (i.e. the unwillingness of the US public to permit Third World interventions by the US government, which was tested by the Grenada intervention, and by the bombing of Tripoli), Soviet military growth since Vietnam, US energy vulnerability (still significantly less than most of Western Europe and of Japan), and relative decline in US productivity growth. Nye noted the latter was conceivably a long-term problem.

Nye, like Keohane argues that the US can maintain its position via a strategy which involves 'careful alliance maintenance and development', 'flexibility' in coping with change in the Third World, and strengthening international rules and regimes. This position combines features of the Realist and Liberal Rational Choice perspectives in its dual stress on the re-consolidation of US national power and the imperatives of interdependence providing rational grounds for co-operation. In a more recent article, Keohane and Nye criticized the first Reagan Administration for too much unilateralism with respect to its allies, for consistent repudiation of many important international organizations, and for the primacy it gave to domestic revitalization, often at the expense of US long-term interests abroad. They restated their earlier argument that the second Reagan Administration should thus pay much more attention to the long-term construction and development of international regimes, and to co-ordinating policies with allies (Keohane and Nye 1985).

A critique of the conventional wisdom

The above arguments underestimate the capacity of the USA to adopt a mixed strategy involving some multilateral co-operation, some unilateralism, and the increasing use of bilateralism to maintain US leadership. Even at the height of relative US dominance, the USA engaged in co-operative strategies with key capitalist allies. The USA invested significant power resources in the construction of its alliances, and in particular, it made concessions, such as opening its market to the Japanese. It could be argued that the USA is rather less co-operative today than it was in the 1950s. More fundamentally, the premise of a necessary form of 'ultra-imperialism' of the 'core' begs more questions than it answers. It fails to compare and contrast the costs and benefits of bilateral and multilateral co-operation for US dominance. For much of the last five years this question has been hotly debated, both within the Reagan Administration and the Congress, the administration tending to opt for a generally multilateral approach to trade (focused on the EEC and Japan), whilst accepting the need for some bilateralism (e.g. Mexico, Israel). The administration has taken care not to overplay its bilateralism in order not to risk the break-up of the GATT system. However, Susan Strange has suggested that the maintenance and strengthening of bilateral trade links can, and has, contributed to a high and growing level of world trade (Strange 1985). Through its stress on reciprocity, the GATT may be viewed as building on, and extending, bilateral trade links. Thus bilateralism, allied to the investment and production strategies of big corporations, may be a significant element in the growing transnationalization of the post-war global political economy. Moreover, it is not self-evident that the USA really wants a much closer relationship between the EEC and Japan: from a Realist perspective it would be better for the USA to both incorporate and divide its allies, so as to retain unchallenged leadership within its alliances. The 'golden triangle' of US–EEC–Japan relations is highly unbalanced, with trade tensions and cultural differences between the EEC and Japan making closeness between them unlikely in the short term. The USA would, from a Realist and neo-classical perspective, seek to take advantage of the high level of Japanese savings, rather than enabling the EEC to use them. There is a strong material basis for this type of strategy in that Japan is highly dependent on the US market. Both the USA and Japan are 'Pacific' countries, and this is the fastest-growing region in the world. It would be logical, therefore, for the USA to develop stronger bilateral links with countries in this region, although tensions remain, for example with South Korea over liberalization of trade and services. US interests in the Atlantic are likely to continue to be important, but possibly less so in the long term than its Pacific interests.

.Certain forms of bilateralism, as is noted in the Roman case discussed below, may contribute to the establishment of hegemony and acceptability of the hegemonic power's leadership: *pax romana, pax americana*. However, bilateralism may have major limitations in certain issue-areas, such as money and 'the debt crisis' which helps to explain the increasing importance the second Reagan Administration has paid to the Group of Five (G5) capitalist nations. This is illustrated in the September 1985 Baker initiatives on exchange rates and lending to heavily indebted Third World countries. From Wallerstein's perspective, US dominance would be seen at its greatest in the monetary sphere, whereas, as a result of the increased mobility of capital, economic interdependence and the distribution of monetary power, the contrary would appear to be the case.

A further major criticism which can be made of the Realist and World-Systems perspectives relates to what might be called their underlying 'inevitability thesis' concerning the decline of hegemony. This problem is bound up with the tacit assumption, central to Realist theory, that identity and interests are constructed on a relatively fixed, primarily national basis; and, as such, any hegemonic power is likely to be met with the inevitable challenge of rival interests and identities, which, in the long term will serve to erode its position (this shortcoming may also be seen to apply in much Marxist writing). As a result of the assumption of inflexible identities, these perspectives pay little attention to the possibility of changes in identification and interest in ways that might effectively extend the power resources of the hegemonic power, facilitate co-operation and mitigate certain conflicts. This also tends to lead Realists to underestimate the importance of the spread of liberal economic ideas and international institutions in the development of US post-war hegemony.

An example from antiquity may help to illustrate this point. Ancient Rome built up an 'Italian Alliance' by means of bilateral treaties with dozens of Italian states, without the terms being unduly onerous on the allies. The basis for a sense of Italian solidarity was gradually developed to the point where most allies stayed loyal to Rome and made considerable sacrifices, for example at the time of Hannibal's invasion, which lasted well over a decade. The extension of Roman citizenship, first within, and then beyond Italy, facilitated the extension and consolidation of a huge empire that lasted for centuries (the final collapse of its eastern 'Byzantine' half, was not until 1453).[2] In the US case, the forging of special bilateral (as well as multilateral) relationships with Canada, Britain, Israel, West Germany and Japan facilitates the mobilization of military power and the spread of US influence. Seen from this angle, the forging of transatlantic links with the UK and West Germany to develop the Strategic Defense Initiative (SDI), and the forging of free trade links with Israel under the 1984 Trade Act (and prospectively also with Canada) can be interpreted as extending US power resources, and possibly *vice versa*.

The Gilpin/Wallerstein thesis is plausible if the rate of economic and military change (in turn related to the pace of technological change) is much greater than the rate at which the social, cultural and political resources of the hegemonic power are developed and extended. In Roman times, the pace of technological change and diffusion was very slow, whereas today it is rapid. However, one aspect of changing technology in the twentieth century has been a dramatic improvement in transport and communications, which facilitates the activities of transnational corporations and the attempts of the US government to develop worldwide alliances. This is not simply the 'Coca-colonization' of the world (or Pepsi-colonization in the USSR), since it involves the construction, development and maintenance of institutions, ideas and contracts across a range of national boundaries.

In the sphere of security, the USA, particularly with respect to the SDI, has used its 'special' (bilateral) relationships, especially with Germany and the UK, to reassert its leadership of the NATO alliance, and to put pressure on the USSR. Thus any assessment of US strategy must take into account a complex mix of tactical possibilities, involving combinations of unilateralism, bilateralism and multilateralism. Some unilateralist measures may be needed to prevent other countries from assuming that the hegemonic power will always be co-operative, for example willing to

2. I am grateful to David Law for pointing out this example.

provide contributions to international regimes and tolerate 'free-riding'. Unilateral measures may be viewed as necessary to obtain co-operation from other countries, such as the so-called 'Nixon shocks' of August 1971, where the USA unilaterally broke IMF rules in order to force other countries to permit a realignment of exchange rates (Calleo 1982). From a Realist perspective such a 'mixed' strategy may, in fact, be the most rational one.

A final point to be made in this section relates to what might be termed hierarchy of structures. Although US power resources may, in economic terms, have been in relative decline, this is less the case with respect to military power, partly because of the greater ability of the USA to mobilize resources for military spending – in sharp contrast to the inter-war period. The 'security structure' is, however, the most fundamental to the maintenance of hegemony since, as the Realists (and all Soviet leaders since Lenin) argue, of state objectives, security (internal as well as external) has the highest priority. Here US capacity has been re-constituted since the mid-1970s, in the context of the 'Second Cold War' (Halliday 1984). This should be seen against the wider strategic background. The unity of the communist world has been undermined since the Sino-Soviet split and, since the early 1970s, China has moved gradually toward the USA and Japan, and further away from the USSR. As Bruce Russet has argued, the Soviet 'loss' of China, once its foremost ally, more than outweighs any 'gains' it may have made in Afghanistan, Vietnam, and parts of Africa. Thus the USA has a strong interest in China's development – up to a point – as an economic and military power. The USA needs to be involved in the promotion of Chinese development, not only to balance Soviet military power in the region, but also to offset Japan's economic power in the region whilst enabling US corporations to make profits in a rapidly growing country with the world's largest population.

To add extra weight to this point, it should he noted that the US worldwide system of alliances effectively extends its military power resources, such that, for example, combined NATO forces exceed those of the Warsaw Pact. However, US military alliances and pacts are worldwide in scope, providing the USA with greater overall military capacity than its Soviet rival. Since 1975, almost all NATO countries have increased military expenditures, and the Reagan Administration has engaged in massive rearmament and increased military research and development. This is occurring at a time when Soviet economic growth is faltering, and the USSR seems increasingly unable to innovate, absorb or effectively diffuse high technology within its highly bureaucratic, centrally planned economy. In addition US private companies account for nearly 50 per cent of the total research and development (R&D) spending of all OECD countries. Since US military R&D is 28 per cent of the US total, the USA accounts for over 60 per cent of the OECD total. US spending as a percentage of GNP is greater than in Japan or Germany by a ratio of more than 3:1, and is rising. This amounts to a 'military-industrial' policy for the USA, with the Pentagon the main co-ordinating and spending agency.[3] ...

Decline or continuity?

Even when material power resources are used to assess the question it is easy to underestimate the absolute scale of US power when compared to previous hegemonies. The key question is, however, how far the USA has lost control over 'outcomes'. Russett argues that the major post-war achievement of the USA was historically unprecedented; whilst America was not so overwhelmingly powerful so as to be able to set all the rules for the post-war international economic order, it was able to establish the basic principles of a capitalist system which involved more than four-fifths of the world economy, as well as organizing a system of collective security to maintain political and economic control over that system. It thus achieved both security (defined in terms of peace amongst the major capitalist states), and prosperity. Further, with the decolonization of much of the Third World, the USA was able (or more accurately its transnational corporations were able) to enter previously closed markets and assure supplies of raw materials, as well as enabling the transnational corporations and banks to invest. Thus the USA was able to accelerate the introduction of advanced capitalism into the Third World, and the USA 'was the most efficient capitalist'. The USA also succeeded in gaining 'an open door' to foreign investment in the advanced capitalist countries (although Japan was somewhat of an exception), as well as converting the former Axis powers into allied liberal democracies and avoiding retrenchment into fascist reaction or their movement towards socialism. Russett also notes, although perhaps with some exaggeration, that the USA developed a pervasive cultural influence in these countries after World War II, when 'authoritarian political cultures

---

3. J.L. Badaracco Jr., and D.B. Yoffie, 'Industrial Policy: It Can't Happen Here', *Harvard Business Review* 6, 1983: 100; military figures are from P. Marsh, 'A Disturbing Outlook', *Financial Times*, 3 December 1985.

... were utterly discredited, and liberal democratic elements ... revivified' (Russett 1985: 213–18).

Some Marxists, such as Mike Davis and Giovanni Arrighi, also stress the continuity and interdependence of this post-war neo-imperialist order that unified accumulation, legitimation and repression on a world scale. Davis stresses that the US 'national security state' was central to maintaining this order (Davis 1984). However, Keohane and Nye seem correct in stressing that military power was generally only indirectly useful to the USA with respect to its relations with its allies in Western Europe and Japan. Their post-war relations increasingly approximated a condition of 'complex interdependence', although this interdependence was often asymmetrical, and balanced in favour of the USA (Keohane and Nye 1977). As a result of the interweaving of their economies, and the binding together of their security systems, it can be proposed that the USA was at the centre of an *organic alliance* structure, stronger and more stable than World War II 'tactical alliance' between the USA, the UK and the USSR. The latter broke down in the Cold War of the late 1940s.

Thus the USA succeeded in creating a political framework for world capitalism, as well as promoting its growth through trade and investment. Russett does not mention, however, that this framework facilitated the pursuit of the material interests of the emerging transnational corporations, mostly headquartered in the USA, nor that US strategy helped to promote the growth of the US military-industrial complex (MIC), which became embedded within the US state and economy. Both the MIC and transnational capital came to constitute powerful vested interests. These interests subsequently tended to undermine the persuasiveness of the US liberal democratic model, as US capitalism came to be viewed by many as oligopolistic and militarist, and US foreign policy became associated with the support of authoritarian political systems in Latin American and South East Asia.

Analyses that stress continuity of American hegemony rest upon the claim that the post-war order is historically unique and qualitatively different from its predecessors. The Gramscian metaphor of an organic alliance implies that US post-war policies have produced a structural change in international relations, one that has a great deal of permanence and continuity. This organic alliance was itself based upon the congruence or 'fit' between interpenetrating political, economic and military structures. Central to this was the compromise between the gradual liberalization of the world capitalist economy and the interventionist imperatives of domestic social democracy, and a general military commitment to contain the spread of Soviet communism. This congruence enabled the institutionalization of US hegemony, and the careful construction and maintenance of international regimes embodying principles and values favourable to the USA. It did not, however, extend to the capacity for mobilizing resources for military purposes. What in fact may help to explain the security 'regime' is a hierarchy of 'force activation', or capacity to mobilize resources. In this hierarchy, the USA was predominant, followed by the former imperial powers of Britain and France, and with West Germany, Japan and the smaller European countries mobilizing a relatively small part of their GNP for military spending. The key contrasts are between the USA, the biggest capitalist economy and military power, and Japan and West Germany. The latter are the second and third largest capitalist economies, but both are third-rank military powers.

US hegemony and transnational capitalism

An innovative development in the political economy literature has been an attempt to utilize and develop certain ideas of Gramsci to explain patterns of historical change in the political economy, and in particular, to explain shifts from periods of global stability to instability or from 'hegemonic' to 'non-hegemonic' world orders. ... In this perspective, hegemony forms the basis of the supremacy of a class, or faction of a class, and is manifested as both material and cultural domination and intellectual and moral leadership. ...

In this perspective, the state can be viewed as both 'restricted' (state as formal governmental institutions and legal-coercive apparatus) and 'extended'. The 'extended state' comprises both 'political society' and 'civil society' or 'hegemony' armoured by 'coercion', although of course, the use of coercion by the armed forces and police implies their consent (Gramsci 1971: 262). Political society refers to the state in the restricted sense (i.e. similar to the Realist view of the state). The idea of civil society ... refers to social forces normally considered to be private, and which rely on 'indirect domination' (for example through the use of market power) and consent (through the use of periodic elections in a parliamentary or liberal democratic system). Hegemony implies that the coercive face of power recedes, and the consensual face becomes more prominent. Thus the hegemony of a particular class, or faction of a class, requires continuing success in persuading other classes and groups in civil society to accept its leadership as well as most of its key values. Hegemony is exercised through the development and mobilization of a trans-class politico-economic formation or coalition of forces in an historical bloc.

This Gramscian concept is thus both theoretical and historical and refers to a congruent 'fit' between the major social forces in a national and transnational context. Gramsci advanced the proposition that some societies appeared to display a strong compatibility between these social forces. Others did not. In those which did, the state could be viewed as being 'organically' rooted in, and protected by, the 'fortresses and earthworks' of the institutions and practices of civil society. For example, in the countries of Northern and Western Europe and the USA in the 1920s and 1930s, this capitalist hegemony had been largely attained. Here there was a strong 'fit' between the dominant ideas, social institutions and the dominant mode of production. Thus the severe economic crisis did not generate fundamental challenges to the prevailing order, in contrast with the more brittle Weimar order in Germany. Such 'hegemonic' social formations contrast with 'non-hegemonic' ones, for example Tsarist Russia, where civil society was relatively underdeveloped or 'primordial', and largely 'separated' from, and dominated by, the (centralized) state.

Gramsci also stressed how the ideological formation of classes (the nature of their self-consciousness as a class) took place within what he called the 'people-nation'. Class consciousness, and forms of social identification, are not simply reflections of the economic organization of production, but are culturally produced in complex ways, for example 'pre-capitalist' cultural institutions live on and permeate civil society; Gramsci paid particular attention to Catholicism in Italy to illustrate this point. The importance of culture and nationalism as mobilizing forces can be seen in these terms, not simply for the hegemony of a class but for the dominance of a nation relative to other nations.

The Gramscian perspective can help to explain how the 'mixed strategy' I have discussed above, allied to forms of national and transnational mobilization, is essential for understanding US power and hegemony. For example, the domestic strength of US (capitalist) hegemony is currently linked to the mobilizing capacities of the charismatic President Reagan. The administration has sought to revitalize many sectors of US capital as well as re-constituting a sense of national purpose in the 'US people-nation'. In so far as the symbolic elements in the Reagan Administration have any central meaning it is that they have helped to re-create a sense of national purpose, self-confidence and reassertiveness, particularly in the wake of President Carter's recriminations about an American 'crisis of confidence' in the 1970s. Also, and perhaps most fundamentally, the virtues of the market, rugged individualism and the capacity of Americans to use their skills and vitality to reach and to expand the 'highest frontiers' of technological development, have all been stressed by Reagan. Reagan contributed to attempts to reconstruct belief in 'American exceptionalism'; a belief that Daniel Bell claimed had come to an end in the mid-1970s (Bell 1975). ...

Whereas Gramsci tended to focus almost entirely on the processes of class formation and the achievement of hegemony at the national level, Robert Cox has suggested that a transnational capitalist class, with its centre in the USA, is developing (Cox 1983). Kees van der Pijl has documented the transatlantic basis of this class formation and shows that its US origins lie in the early inter-war period (Pijl 1984: 35–75). Global production, exchange and capital flows have widened the basis of this class formation beyond the Atlantic circuits of capital, as industrialization of many parts of the Third World has developed, and as Japan and East Asia have become much more powerful economically. At this 'transnational' stage in the development of capitalism, the developing transnational capitalist class or 'international establishment' can be said to comprise the segments of the national bourgeoisies and state bureaucracies of a range of countries who have material interests in the relatively free flow of capital, goods and services within the world economy. This class can, in sum, be said to be at the core of an emerging transnational historical bloc, whose material interests and key ideas are bound up with the progressive transnationalization of the global political economy. Its key members include top owners and managers of transnational corporations; central and other international bankers; and many, though not all, leading politicians and civil servants in most advanced capitalist countries, and those in some less-developed countries. The growth of this class has been facilitated by improved transport and communications, and increasingly by 'private' as well as 'public' institutions fostering dialogue and interaction between elites.

The strengthening of some of these links and associated networks has gone with what Cox has called 'the internationalization of the state', although I prefer the term 'transnationalization' since the social forces implied relate to the hegemony of transnational capital.

For Cox, the consciousness ('framework of thought'), of these people is crucial to the determination of their class membership. The achievement of hegemony implies the development of ideas and policies conducive to the promotion of transnational forces within a range of government bureaucracies (e.g. foreign, finance, economics ministries) and international organizations established since 1945 (e.g. IMF, IBRD or World Bank) and the private Trilateral Commission. These international organizations tend to express liberal economic discourses and promote associated liberal policies. Thus they tend to give priority to market efficiency, and in particular the virtues of free trade, foreign investment and free foreign exchange markets; the control of inflation and public expenditure; and the private sector relative to the public. Increasing attention has been paid by these international organizations, and others (for example the OECD and certain 'think tanks') to the virtues of labour market flexibility and the dangers of trade union monopoly power which may obstruct the introduction of new technology and hold up real wages at a level incompatible with full employment. These connected ideas can be said to make up a 'framework of thought' which, first, helps orientate the actions of 'the transnational capitalist class'; second, serves to legitimate its leadership: and third, restricts the ability of subordinate classes to analyse the nature of the political economy, and to construct an alternative to this form of 'hegemonic rationality'.

The key material forces associated with these ideas and institutions are the internationalization of production and growing economic interdependence manifested in the post-war growth of transnational corporations and of world trade relative to world output. I would add the internationalization of financial markets to this list. What is crucial here is that transnational capital relates not only to transnational corporations but also to internationally mobile capital in general. It can be argued that the power of these forms of capital, *vis-à-vis* certain states and *vis-à-vis* labour has increased considerably in the post-war period. Moreover, in the Reagan years, this shift in relative power has arguably accelerated.

The forces of transnational capital have developed in the post-war context of what John Ruggie called the compromise of 'embedded liberalism', or what Kees van der Pijl calls the Atlantic format of 'corporate liberalism'. This post-war settlement amongst the major interests in the capitalist world corresponded to an internationalization of the basic ideas of the New Deal: it was a negotiated compromise between the various factions of capital and labour in a range of capitalist states. This compromise was congruent with the structural properties of the emerging post-war capitalist system, although it was shaped by US initiatives and the creation of US-dominated international institutions such as the IMF. Central to this compromise were the ideological notions of the 'mixed economy' and a liberalizing international economy. The compromise allowed for a range of national policies to be practised in a relatively expansionist, stable structure. It was related to a set of Keynesian-mercantilist frameworks of thought, themselves premised on the idea that the market had been discredited as the major steering mechanism for the contemporary capitalist system. These 'frameworks of thought' were themselves related to a structure which had, to a large extent, identifiably separate 'national capitals' which were not significantly interpenetrated. This post-war structure was also premised on what Gramsci called a 'Fordist' pattern of accumulation, namely a mass-production and mass-consumption system that rewarded and incorporated (organized) labour. Binding this together was the US-centred security structure with its ideology of anti-communism and the defence of the free world.

Thus, certain frameworks of thought, sets of institutions, and a range of key material forces may converge at a given historical moment. It is in this sense that one might refer to the post-war settlement as hegemonic, with the USA and its dominant class elements at the core of the post-war historical bloc of forces. In so far as it is possible to speak of a 'crisis of hegemony', it is that the forces of transnationalization and capitalist development have increasingly tended to undermine the coherence of this type of historically specific hegemonic order, and have promoted a movement to a more fully transnationalized, and more liberalized order. This involves a shift away from the Fordist pattern of accumulation and labour processes in many of the major capitalist states, away from mass industrial employment towards services. This shift also involves the discrediting of Keynesian ideas across a range of states and the relative rise in importance of monetarist/pro-market frameworks of thought, which I have associated with institutions such as the IMF. They are also very important in understanding the foreign economic policies of the Reagan Administration.

With respect to the previously relatively self-sufficient USA, this process has led to the recent rapid transnationalization of the US domestic economy. US Federal Reserve economists have recently estimated that there has been a sevenfold increase in the nominal value of US international activity (defined in terms of net transactions and transfers by the US government and US residents abroad and by foreigners to the USA) in the period 1970–85, from $146 billion to $1 trillion, such that international transactions now amount to roughly a quarter of total US GNP. Moreover, this process of internationalization is growing faster than the growth of GDP. During this same period, nominal GNP rose on average by 9.5 per cent a year, whilst international activity rose on average by 14 per cent.[4] Whilst this development has been interpreted as creating major constraints for the USA, it can also be interpreted as providing US interests with major new opportunities to promote the

4. J.L. Harvey, 'The Internationalization of Uncle Sam', *Economic Perspectives*, Federal Reserve Bank of Chicago, 10 (3) 1986: 4.

government's long-term aim of a more liberal global political economy, that is one which is much more congruent with the more dynamic and most competitive elements within the domestic structure of US capitalism, its giant transnational corporations.

Towards a more liberal and transnational hegemony

The 1970s and 1980s have been characterized not only by a crisis of the old post-war hegemony, in terms of structural economic changes involving the US and world political economies, but also by a series of recessions and rising unemployment in a range of countries. It can be argued that these recessions have in fact contributed to the increasing liberalization of important elements within the global political economy, which is a key characteristic of what I have termed 'the crisis of hegemony'. This is because these recessions have led to a widely based reappraisal about the role of governments and of the public sector in capitalist economies, that is about the appropriate 'mix' of intervention and market. These recessions have also lead to changes in expectations about international relations, for example, the likelihood of concessions by the developed countries to less developed countries and the viability of commodity agreements and cartels such as OPEC. Indeed, the pressure of recession coupled with high real interest rates in the late 1970s led many indebted nations to turn to the IMF, which in turn has pressed these countries to liberalize their economies as well as to cut back on the size and growth of the public sector. In addition, since 1981, the USSR has been weakened relative to the other major capitalist states because of the rapid fall in the price of oil, its major source of foreign exchange. The drop in world oil prices is not simply caused by recession (there is massive surplus capacity within the oil industry), but recession has led to the closure of many heavy industrial users of oil, as well as a range of energy conservation programmes. Thus demand today is lower than in the late 1970s.

There is, however, a remarkable degree of interdependence between the economic, ideological and military aspects of global restructuring in the late 1970s and early 1980s. Together, they constitute a resurgence of cold war liberalism in certain capitalist states, although the degree of political commitment to this stance and the policies it entails is highly variable. In many ways the recession of the early 1980s can be seen as facilitating the material and ideological refurbishing of US hegemony. This might be seen as ironic given that the recession was more severe in the USA than in Japan, West Germany or the USSR, the main competitors and rivals of the USA. Further the US Federal Reserve did much to precipitate and worsen the recession with its tight monetary policy (1979–82), although the rise in oil prices following the fall of the Shah of Iran was also a significant factor. Thereafter, the Reagan 'boom' took off, with a combination of fiscal stimulus (through vastly increased military expenditures in particular), resulting in a spiralling budget deficit, supply-side measures designed to stimulate investments and improve productivity and the competitiveness of certain sectors of the US economy, as well as tax cuts (such as the 1981 Economic Recovery Tax Act). The capacity of the USA to expand out of recession in this way contrasts with the other major capitalist states that by and large, have tended to exercise very strict controls on the growth in public spending. ...

How far there has been a real basis to the US recovery in the 1980s rests upon whether the long-term trend of US productivity growth has improved. This is still an open question. However, foreign based transnational corporations are becoming much more dependent upon the US market at the same time as US manufacturing capital has shifted its assets towards high-profit sectors like energy reserves, financial services, real estate, emergent technology and defence. These developments can be interpreted as having the effect of generally strengthening a possible transnational historic bloc (since they are bound up with the interpenetration of capital across national boundaries), strengthening the power of internationally mobile (finance) capital *vis-à-vis* labour and some states.

The 1980s have been characterized by a substantial shift in the balance of power between labour and capital, a shift partly caused by the threat of unemployment and closures in the context of recession ... The US experience in terms of this power shift since 1983 is noteworthy. In the midst of a very rapid upturn in the economy, important sectors in organized labour have accepted real wage reductions, and much lower pay levels for new employees, in the emerging two-tier wage structure (i.e. new employees accepting much lower wages that the rest of the workers in certain firms). Moreover, union membership has continued to decline. This shows the continuing defensiveness of US labour, such that unions may have jeopardized their long-term solidarity and strength.[5] This should be interpreted in a context where, in the US, there is no strong socialist movement to challenge capitalist hegemony. In this sense, US capitalism is perhaps more stable and domestically 'hegemonic' than its West European and (to a lesser extent) Japanese counterparts. Although

5. T. Dodsworth, 'The Wage Deal that Bucked a Trend', *Financial Times*, 5 October 1983; and 'Unions Bow to Management's New Found Strength', *Financial Times*, 14 May 1985.

Japan has a sizeable socialist party and a smaller, but still significant communist party, its challenge has not been as strong as that of the left-wing parties in Europe. In this respect, Japan may be closer to the US than the West European countries as its once powerful trade union movement is now rapidly losing influence as its membership declines. In the 1940s, over half the workforce in Japan was unionized, whilst in 1983 this had fallen to less than 30 per cent. In 1986, 28.9 per cent were unionized, and in 1985 the number of working days lost through strikes (already very low by US and West European standards) fell to its lowest level since the war. Also, since 1980 manufacturing sector efficiency has risen by 30 per cent, whilst wages have risen by only 10 per cent.[6]

Davis argues that the upturn in the US economy has 'dramatically speeded up the transformation of American hegemony away from a "Fordist" or mass accumulation pattern'. He notes three trends that are important. First, there was a shift in profit distribution towards interest incomes, thus strengthening a 'neo-rentier bloc reminiscent of the speculative capitalism of the 1920s'. Second, US industrial corporations have begun to shift away from consumer durables towards 'volatile high-profit sectors like military production and financial services'. Third, a shift in trade relations and capital flows as the focus of accumulation in new technologies has been displaced from Atlantic to Pacific circuits of capital' (Davis 1985: 47). Also, the Reagan boom has been accompanied by a flood of cheap imports, encouraged by the 'super dollar' sustained by unprecedented real interest rates of 8 per cent or more. This has allowed the administration to 'internationalize the financing of its $500 billion in cumulative new debt. The Bank of International Settlements estimates that one-third of the aggregate US credit demand ... is now supplied by foreign capital inflow.' For the first time since World War I, US foreign liabilities exceed its assets, that is the rest of the world (and notably Japan because of its high level of savings) is helping to finance the re-industrialization of the US economy, as well as funding the $130 billion trade deficit (a recent estimate suggested half of this is financed directly by Japanese savers).[7] Much of the trade deficit is accounted for by capital goods and high technology, although a number of LDCs have benefited from increased exports to the USA. While imports grew by 28 per cent in 1983, foreign investment also rose by 17 per cent (Davis 1985: 48–55). This US dynamism is in stark contrast to the stagnation of the West European economies. The major challenge to the USA comes from the

---

6. Robert Whymant, 'Unions Lose Their Fighting Spirit', *Guardian*, 1 July 1986.
7. Robert Whymant, 'Out Tele-coming Telecom', *Guardian*, 15 July 1986.

Pacific economies. The USA has a substantial trade deficit with East Asian countries, but this is more or less balanced by an equivalent surplus with Europe. Europe on the other hand is in deficit to both the USA and Japan. Pacific capitalism has grown much faster than that of Western Europe during the 1970s, and there has been a consistent shift in high-tech industries to the US Pacific Coast and Japan during the 1970s and 1980s. It should be noted that the USA might threaten denial of access to its markets to discipline East Asian countries if the political need ever arises. Nonetheless, this threat has not been sufficient to significantly open up the Japanese market, although some progress appears to have been made in the last two years in opening the potentially lucrative Japanese money and capital markets.

6
The Power of Capital: Direct and Structural

(*with David Law*)

This chapter concerns the theory of power and it elaborates direct and structural forms of power within present-day capitalism. It argues that power and hegemony involve normative and material, structural and existential (behavioural, relational) dimensions of social relations.

Indeed, by developing our concepts of power in conjunction with Gramscian concepts of hegemony, historic bloc and the 'extended' state, we seek to meet two major challenges in the study of Political Economy. The first is to integrate better 'domestic' and 'international' levels of analysis. A second, related challenge is to theorize the complementary and contradictory relations between the power of states and the power of capital. In meeting these challenges we also think a possible key to the resolution of the structure–action problem in social theory and international relations may be through the development of mediating concepts such as structural power and historic bloc outlined here and elsewhere in this book. ...

Historic blocs and social structures of accumulation

Recent writers have suggested that capitalism is entering into a transnational, post-Fordist stage, which differs from the imperialist/welfare nationalist (national capitalist), Fordist stage analysed by classical Marxists. This includes shifts from one type of *social structure of accumulation* to another within the broader confines of a particular mode of production (Cox 1987). Cox's concept of social structure of accumulation is paralleled by that of a *regime of accumulation*, used by the French Regulationist School. We assume that such a regime must be social since it involves class and intra-class relations. It must also be cultural and political. This is because accumulation involves not only composition of the labour force, the nature of the labour process (in its technical, organizational and human

93

aspects) and the legal regulation of production. It also encompasses the modes of everyday life and of the political organization of workers. A regime also involves regulation that concerns the scope of markets and freedom of enterprise at both national and global levels. More broadly a regime may encompass forms of social *reproduction* that together constitute conditions of existence for development in a particular historical period. ...

Two regimes of accumulation have been identified in modern capitalism (De Vroey 1984). The first, 'extensive regime' (roughly encompassing the first three-quarters of the nineteenth century) was associated with relatively competitive industrial structures and less capital-intensive forms of production than in the later, 'intensive' regime, which more fully emerged in the twentieth century. The first regime was associated with a rather narrow domain of state intervention and, to a certain extent, a doctrine of economic liberalism. Moreover, political democracy and workers' organizations were very underdeveloped. The second, somewhat more democratic regime was characterized by more capital-intensive, mass-production systems and a gradual rise in real wages. It was accompanied by wide-ranging state intervention, especially as regards monetary and macroeconomic management, and the promotion of education, training, research and development. It was also associated with the widespread growth of trade unionism, left-wing political parties, corporatist planning, and the consolidation of the welfare state – a complex of policies and class compromises that has been called the 'politics of productivity' (Maier 1987). At the international level, these two regimes of accumulation coincided, respectively, with a period of British hegemony and the Gold Standard and an international balance of power, and the second after 1945 with American globalism, integral or organic alliances between the USA and the other major metropolitan capitalist states, and the Bretton Woods system, counterposed to the Soviet bloc of 'existing socialism' and China.

What were the key international elements in the post-1945 regime of accumulation that generated uniquely rapid economic growth throughout the industrialized capitalist world? We would suggest at least four. The first was the construction of a US-centred economic, security and political structure for the non-communist world, ensuring peaceful conditions at the capitalist core (in sharp contrast to the 1914–45 years). The second, closely related element, was the ability of the USA to maintain the growth of global aggregate demand through its balance of payments deficits, partly generated by heavy overseas military expenditures. The third element was the substantial congruence of ideas, institutions and policies among the leading capitalist nations, in a system of 'embedded liberalism' (Ruggie 1982). This involved the emergence and consolidation of ideology of the 'mixed economy'. Along with the rise of the Cold War, this was important in the re-constitution (or creation) of the legitimacy of the liberal-democratic form of rule in the West and in Japan. A fourth element was the cheap and plentiful supply of raw materials, especially oil.

Cementing this order was a new *international historic bloc* of social forces, centred in the USA, which came to be the socio-political centrepiece of the post-war organic alliance in the 'West'. This bloc originated in the outward expansion of emerging social forces within the USA. The leading elements in this constellation sought to internationalize New Deal principles and associated forms of Fordist capital-intensive, mass-consumption accumulation, and to extend opportunities for exports and/or foreign direct investment, both in manufacturing and extractive industries, notably in oil. The bloc also encompassed financial interests on Wall Street that sought wider investment opportunities overseas and a more comprehensive international role for the dollar. However, this bloc brought together not only fractions of productive and financial capital, but also elements in the state apparatuses, centrist political parties and non-communist organized labour in the major capitalist nations. Forces associated with the bloc in the USA were able to forge links consciously with counterparts in Europe, to form a concept of a transatlantic political community. ...

Viewed from this perspective, the post-war mix of social democracy, and the 'mixed economy' incorporated a range of class interests that sustained the emerging liberal international economic order. This maintained its coherence and continuity for approximately 25 years after 1945, although the appearance of continuity in this period can be considered to be deceptive, since certain contradictory forces were at work that would, in the long term, erode the basis of the regime of accumulation and the integral nature of the associated international historic bloc. Examples of such forces were the growing knowledge-intensive nature of production and organizational systems and the related gradual rise in the importance of transnational capital, especially financial capital, highlighted in the growth of the Euromarkets since the 1960s. At the same time, the scale and scope of welfare expenditures was also growing, as were state expenditures as a proportion of GNP.

In a structural sense, what was occurring in the post-war period was the emergence of a globally integrated economy whilst political regulation at the domestic level was becoming ever-more comprehensive. We discuss this below, in terms of the simultaneous and in some ways contradictory growth in the 'power' of both states and market forces.

States, markets and the power of capital

Both markets and states long preceded industrial capitalism. However, the latter was historically associated with the growth of integrated capital markets. Whilst Marxist writers have typically stressed the emergence of wage labour markets as a defining feature of capitalism we suggest that the emergence of elaborate capital markets is at least as important, and we concentrate on this below.

Markets have normally required some form of political organization and protection, normally provided by the state. By the same token, governmental institutions require finance. This need creates an added interest in both facilitating and regulating markets, for example to obtain taxes. However, extensive regulations and restrictions often lower profits and breed forms of evasion (e.g. smuggling, black markets, financial 'innovation'). The incentive for capital to evade controls is greater if national regulations vary, especially if technical obstacles in transport and communications are reduced, that is as capital becomes more mobile. The growth in the Euromarkets since the 1960s is an important example of this, one that we relate below to the structural power of capital. Just as capital seeks the most propitious conditions for investment, states compete to attract capital flows and direct investments. Under the recessionary conditions of the 1980s, this gave rise to *competitive deregulation* of different national capital markets. Competitive deregulation is a misnomer however, since it went with attempts to redefine market rules under new conditions. However, most crucial was that the process progressively reduced the barriers to the international mobility of financial capital, creating a more integrated and global capital market.

An evolving dialectical relationship exists between the nature and scope of markets, and the forms of state regulation, especially as knowledge, technology and transportation change. The dialectic involves both domestic and international dimensions of state activity, which seek to reconcile the potentially global reach of economic activity with the socially and territorially specific aspects of political rule. The latter is circumscribed by the problems of legitimation, mobilization and communication in political time and space. Thus *capital as a social relation depends on the power of the state to define, shape and be part of a regime of accumulation.* By capital as a social relation we have in mind the contrast between those with a substantial or even privileged ownership, control or access to both financial and/or physical assets, in contrast to the bulk of the remainder of society (most of labour and their dependents).

The form of different regimes of accumulation provides the wider context for our discussion of contemporary state–capital relations and the question of the structural power of markets. We will argue that the widening of the scope of the market along with certain changes in technology and communications, contributes to the rising structural power of internationally mobile capital. By contrast, the state (as an institutional and social entity) also creates the possibility for the limitation of such structural power. This is partly because of the political goods and services it supplies to capitalists and because of the institutional autonomy it possesses. The stance of the state towards freedom of enterprise, in a given regime of accumulation, is at the heart of this issue.

At the domestic level, the distinction between direct and structural forms of the power of capital or of 'business' has already been well developed (Lindblom 1977). Direct aspects of business power and influence, relative to labour, include its financial resources, expertise, contacts with government and control over much of the media. Business has a privileged ability to influence governments, for example through lobbying. Moreover, in oligopolistic industries, large firms possess some *market power* over prices and perhaps wages. This can be contrasted with the case of highly competitive markets where both buyers and sellers are subject to the *power of the market*. An instance of the latter case is the behaviour of highly competitive financial markets (in which governments borrow regularly). In this type of conceptualization ... business (and capital) is viewed as a type of privileged vested interest in a more-or-less pluralist political system. By contrast, Marxists associate business with capital as a class. As such, analysis of its power implies a deeper, socio-structural dimension, inherent in the capitalist system. Nonetheless, the power of capital in general needs to be distinguished from the power and influence of particular fractions of capital.

Here, our chief concern is to analyse the power of those fractions of capital, which are both large scale, and internationally mobile. This category includes both some fractions of 'productive capital' (in manufacturing and extraction) and 'financial capital' (e.g. financial services, such as banking, insurance and stock-broking). The power of capital in general partly rests upon the degree of division between different fractions of capital, or different sections of business. At the same time, of course, competitive pressure may mean that co-operation between capitalists within different fractions is difficult or even impossible to achieve. Nonetheless, in virtually all analysis of the conflicts and divisions between capitalists, the concept of power used is a behavioural one. Thus the focus is on the way a given group of capitalists seeks to exert direct power and influence over others or the state apparatus. Whilst this dimension is essential, it needs to be combined with an investigation of structural power. Indeed, the more striking are the divisions within its ranks, the more crucial the structural aspect of capital's power becomes.

This structural aspect is associated with both material and normative dimensions of society (such as market structures and the role of ideology). These may or may not be mutually reinforcing. The tenacity of normative structures is illustrated by how, in modern economies, consistently higher priority is given to economic growth relative to other goals (such as conservation). Another illustration concerns the assumptions and claims made about the conditions for the achievement of growth, for example that it is fundamentally dependent on investment and innovation by private enterprise.

Acceptance of these assumptions and claims by politicians and the public means that governments have to be concerned with the cultivation of an appropriate 'business climate', or else investment might be postponed, and a recession might be precipitated. An elected socialist party, with a radical programme, would therefore be constrained in its policy choices by the nature of the 'business climate', not least because it would need tax revenue (and/or loans) to finance its ambitious spending plans. An assumption behind these arguments is that there is a market for capital, enterprise and inventiveness, and the supply of these will be reduced by higher taxation. Indeed, such arguments are the essence of so-called 'supply-side' economics influential in the USA in the 1980s.

There is a striking contrast between the ability of capital and labour to shape policy in the long term under capitalist conditions. Whereas an 'investment strike' by business may occur spontaneously if the business climate deteriorates, labour, in order to exert corresponding influence, would have to directly organize a wide-ranging or even general strike. The example of an investment strike is a case of structural power, uniquely available to business. This power works primarily through the market mechanism in capitalist economies. Whereas a reduced willingness to invest for productive purposes usually comes about gradually, the supply of finance to governments through the purchase of government bonds and bills may decline very rapidly. This might result in the government being unable to finance its current activity unless it resorted to monetary inflation. Such inflation would, from the point of view of business, cause the 'investment climate' to further deteriorate, so prolonging the investment strike. Thus capital, and particularly the financial fractions of capital, may have the power to indirectly discipline the state. In so far as many of the top financiers have access to the government leaders, this indirect power may be supplemented by direct use of power, such as lobbying, and 'gentlemanly' arm-twisting. However, such arm-twisting is secondary to what can be termed the power of markets, notably the financial markets. This power constrains the participants in the market, including the government when it needs to raise finance.

Some of the points made above fit in with the notion of a hegemonic ideology, which serves the class interests of capital relative to those of labour. At the heart of this are the ideas that private property and accumulation are sacrosanct, and that without the private sector growth would be endangered. A specific case of the force of such ideas was the way in which monetarist ideas about the need to control inflation became widely accepted and embodied in deflationary policies in the Western countries during the late 1970s and early 1980s. This commitment was reflected, for example, in discussions during and *communiqués* of the seven-power Economic Summits. The late 1970s was, of course, before conservative governments were in power in most of the Summit nations. Nonetheless, monetary targets rapidly became commonplace, mandating discipline in goods and labour markets. Either wages had to be restrained, or, according to the logic of these policies, workers would 'price themselves out of jobs'.

In Britain, Thatcherism involved not just a change in policies but a conscious effort to change ideas and expectations about the appropriate role of government, the importance of private enterprise and the virtues of markets. The aim has been to convince voters that 'there is no alternative' to Thatcherism (if they wish to grow steadily more prosperous). It can thus be argued that a Gramscian form of hegemony favouring capital was being reconstructed. However, this polarized labour-capital analysis can itself be criticized as over-simplified, particularly as it fails to distinguish between transnational and national fractions of capital, and says little about the political and ideological contradictions associated with Thatcherism, which entailed jingoism and racism whilst encouraging Japanese foreign direct investment, and the use of economic and physical violence to defeat selected political opponents (as in the 1984–85 miners strike) whilst the bulk of the mainstream of the Conservative Party still spoke in terms of 'one nation' Toryism.

The direct power of capital

Turning now to the world level, given the rise of transnational corporations and of international capital mobility, monetary and information flows and communications links, a *global* analysis of the power of capital is essential. Realist analysis is backward here, although some writers on interdependence have shown an awareness of international capital mobility. Neo-classical economists have examined the bargaining power of transnational corporations, and the determinants and policy consequences of short-term capital flows, but have neglected the institutional and ideological aspects of power. This shortcoming also applies to many Marxists.

With respect to direct, behavioural forms of power, while Lindblom distinguished between authority (associated with governments) and markets (associated with private enterprise) at the national level, it is also the case that transnational corporations exert authority across national boundaries when they allocate resources internationally. Corporate headquarters often decide on the geographical location of production. Transnationals make investment decisions on a global scale, shifting funds from one country to another. Certain subsidiaries are kept from exporting their production, since others are allocated that function. Different subsidiaries engage in intra-firm trading at 'transfer', rather than 'arms length' prices. This means that, to some extent, the output of their subsidiaries (which may be vast, and collectively perhaps greater than the GNP of many countries) is taken out of the market-place, and is allocated, in Charles Lindblom's terms 'authoritatively' within a single transnational firm. This implies that it is allocated consciously, and politically. A dramatic instance of this intra-firm power is when a factory is opened in one country, at the same time as one performing the same functions is closed or not built in another. Of course, the scope for the use of this type of power is constrained by political pressures and competition from other firms. The fewer the number of competitors, the less the constraints are likely to be. Indeed, if there are only a few firms, oligopolistic collusion is much more likely, producing similar patterns of behaviour on the part of several firms.

The market power of oligopolistic firms in certain industries operates at an international level. The classic case is that of the so-called 'Seven Sisters' in the international oil industry. The seven oil 'majors' (five American-owned, one British, and one Anglo-Dutch) dominated the world oil industry from the 1920s until the end of the 1960s. Posted prices were fixed at agreed levels between the companies. This meant that differences in marginal and transport costs were not consistently reflected in prices and the oil companies were able to exert power over many parts of the Third World. This case also illustrates the interrelatedness of direct forms of economic and military power. Inroads of Western, especially

British, oil firms in the Middle East between 1900–40 were built upon British military power in the region. Profit-making interests of British Petroleum and Shell, and the security interests of the British Empire went hand in hand. BP lobbied the British government for military action when its Iranian assets were nationalized in 1953. The British government then turned to the US CIA to secure the return to power of the Shah. Denationalization followed with BP regaining some of its former stake, the rest going to American majors (Blair 1976).

So far we have referred to transnational corporations lobbying their parent governments to obtain policies favourable to their operations overseas. Such lobbying also takes place with regard to host governments, as well as international organizations, such as the World Bank. Transnational financial networks are particularly well-developed, and links between commercial banks, central banks, the IMF and World Bank are illustrated in a number of international forums: for example, the Bank for International Settlements.

International patterns of elite interaction – between business, state officials, bureaucrats, and members of international organizations – and the networks they generate, have not been thoroughly researched or understood, at least in comparison with domestic networks. However, some organizations such as the Bilderberg meetings (which began in 1954), and the Trilateral Commission (formed in 1973) are explicitly concerned to foster social interaction, networks and a shared outlook amongst the international establishments of the major capitalist countries. Similar interaction is found within inter-governmental organizations such as the OECD, which organizes conferences and research initiatives. What is crucial to note is that there are elements of a common perspective, at least with respect to the role of international business and private enterprise, which cuts across all of these institutional forums. Whilst research on aspects of strategic consciousness and ideology-formation at the elite level is in its infancy, some work has identified the way in which the business and government leaders of different countries seek to develop a common outlook on the general conditions of existence of the international order, although not one which is homogeneous on all issues. There is much debate over a number of key questions, such as the welfare state, East–West relations and the regulation of global capital and exchange markets. What we are suggesting is that during the 1970s and 1980s, the emphasis, certainly with regard to economic policy, has shifted towards a definition of questions and concepts more congruent with the interests of large-scale, transnational capital (Gill 1990).

People active in transnational networks are increasingly well-served by a range of international periodicals, such as the *Financial Times, The Economist, Far Eastern Economic Review* and the *Wall Street Journal*. Elite interaction and network-building helps to shape the agenda for those state policies that affect the operation of transnational capital. In so far as international organizations accept a framework of thought that serves the interests of capital, they are likely to exert influence and sometimes even pressure (for example in IMF loan conditions) on national governments of a sort which is congruent with that exerted by business. Several writers have suggested that the elements mentioned above are coming together to produce a 'transnational' capitalist class or class fraction, with a 'strategic' consciousness of its own. This involves a long-term time horizon, and consideration of the general conditions under which transnational capital operates, as well as of more specific, immediate and 'crisis management' issues. However, time horizons of fractions of transnational capital vary, with private financial capital often displaying a more short-term outlook, one which is perhaps less 'strategic'. A plausible example of the latter was the way in which leading commercial banks, in their efforts to recycle surplus petrodollars, rushed into making loans to less-developed countries in the mid-1970s. However, it is questionable whether governments of the leading capitalist countries were much more aware of the dangers of such loans than were the banks (Frieden 1987).

The structural power of capital

We noted earlier the importance of the business or investment climate and the concept of business confidence. Today, capital is so internationally mobile, especially between the major capitalist economies, that the 'investment climate' of one country will be judged by business with reference to the climate that prevails elsewhere. Transnational corporations routinely appraise the legal freedoms (e.g. to remit profits), production costs, labour relations, political stability, and financial concessions offered by many different countries. This is popularly known as 'political risk analysis'. They also examine the size and growth potential of a country's market. As a result, governments are increasingly constrained in their freedom of manoeuvre by the economic policies of other states, as well as the investment decisions of internationally mobile capital. Indeed, such appraisals are made daily or even hourly by market analysts and investors in the financial sectors.

For example French attitudes to foreign investment have tended to be highly nationalist, especially under de Gaulle (e.g. they feared American and other foreign corporations would be like a Trojan horse, undermining French economic sovereignty). Nonetheless exclusion of such firms from France simply resulted in them locating in a neighbouring member of the European Community (EC), from where they could avoid tariff barriers and supply the French market. Thus under the Socialist government of President Mitterrand in the 1980s, French attitudes became more 'flexible', even welcoming some Japanese firms, after years of complaining of Japanese inroads. Similar flexibility was also shown in a range of other nationalist, mercantilist, and even communist countries, such as in China, and in much of the developing world.

Such flexibility makes it all the easier for corporations to play off one government against another in their search for concessions. Indeed, within some countries, different regions often compete to win such foreign investment. This phenomenon is visible in countries as diverse in character as the USA, Britain and China. At the national level, a key question for research is how far can, and will, the central government regulate the competition for foreign investment by different regions (and their state or local administrations). For example, in the US case the institution of federalism makes the creation and implementation of a unified nation-wide policy very difficult. In turn, this situation makes it easier for foreign (as well as domestic) capital to play off one state against another and increase its relative bargaining power.

At the international level, the bargaining power of transnational corporations would be reduced if most national governments were able to co-ordinate their regulations and financial concessions. However, even supposedly like-minded, and wealthy countries, bound together in a collective economic organization like the EC have not been able to seriously discuss, let alone achieve this goal. Even if governments of some member states were so inclined, given the EC voting rules, there would almost certainly be others (such as Britain) who would oppose such measures, and veto any such policy initiative. It remains to be seen whether the process of EC political and economic union will change this situation. In an age of transnational firms, states may be forced to adopt neo-mercantilist policies in order to compete better to attract foreign direct investment, in order to obtain the sinews of power (skills, capital and technology). This reinforces the structural power of transnational corporations, in contrast to national firms, a power that owes much to the division of the world into many states. Thus the threat of nationalization is less crushing to a transnational company, since it is likely that any single country would expropriate a small proportion of its assets. The purely national firm is more at the mercy of its own government.

We have already seen how business confidence in a government may depend on its economic policies, including its macroeconomic policies. Ideas about 'sound finance' and 'fighting inflation' constrain governments. Such ideas may spread from one country to another. The pursuit of such policies is likely to attract more foreign investment (other things being equal). The response of firms to such policies and other determinants of the investment climate is often gradual, and spread over a number of years. As has been noted, financial capital can react to government policies, or expected policies, much more rapidly than productive capital. With the liberalization of capital flows between the major capitalist economies (and some less-developed countries) the reaction of financial capital need not be one of postponement of investment (as in an 'investment strike'). Instead, huge sums of money can quickly flow out of a country to more attractive havens. The result of this can be a balance of payments crisis under fixed exchange rates, or a foreign exchange crisis (fall in the exchange rate), under floating exchange rates. A falling exchange rate brings increased risks of rising inflation, especially for a small, open economy. Hence the international mobility of financial capital can swiftly force governments that deviate from policies seen as suitable by the 'market', to change course. For example, governments may be driven to raise interest rates, tighten monetary policy, and thus create a rise in unemployment to offset a currency, or payments crisis. This is in fact precisely what occurred in Britain in 1976, although in this case, the Labour government was able to blame the IMF (the media generally blamed the unions) for imposing its austerity policies. The point was, however, that against a background of high inflation, Britain would have had to change its policies in this direction anyway or there would have been a further collapse in the international value of sterling. The Socialist French government changed course after 1981 because of the same types of international pressures.

From the above example, it is tempting to reinterpret the Thatcher slogan, so that it would become 'there is no alternative', in the long-term to providing a business climate, attractive by international standards. In other words the conquest of inflation would be just one aspect of a wider doctrine. We have already noted how the major capitalist states adopted macroeconomic policies premised on the 'war on inflation' from the late 1970s to the mid-1980s. One explanation of the adoption of such policies is, of course, because of the power of markets. However, there is nothing inevitable or automatic about a particular policy response to changes in market conditions, or to the business climate. What may have been crucial in the adoption of monetarist policies was the growing acceptance of a policy outlook amongst political leaders, as well as central and private bankers, which meant that no significant alternative (to market monetarism) was actually contemplated, except in one or two major capitalist states, such as France. Where such policies are adopted, with little reflection on, or more realistically, belief in the credibility of possible alternatives, the power of capital attains a hegemonic status.

We are not suggesting that a transnational hegemony has been attained, or is likely to be in this century. However, the social forces making for such hegemony, based on free enterprise and open markets, have become more prominent in the 1980s. At this point, however, the question arises, who would benefit from such hegemony?

The impact of increased capital mobility, and also of recessions, has worked to the advantage of large-scale transnational capital, relative to national capital. Transnational capital is not entirely dependent on the business conditions of one country, in the way that purely national firms obviously are. When a recession in one country occurs, it will be easier for transnational corporations to survive or prosper than it is for national firms. A notable example of this was the ability of Ford Motor Company to survive large losses in its US operations during the recession of the early 1980s through drawing on the profits of overseas subsidiaries, a trend which has continued. Indeed, the process of restructuring, whereby weak firms are either made bankrupt, or else taken over by the stronger survivors, is likely to work systematically to the advantage of transnational capital, particularly in the manufacturing sector.

While the structural power of transnational capital has risen relative to that of governments since World War II (except perhaps in primary industries), it has also risen relative to that of organized labour. Transnational, but not national, firms can threaten unions with plant closures and relocation of investment to other countries. Countries with relatively weak, or politically controlled labour movements, will, other things being equal, tend to attract investment at the expense of countries with strong, independent labour movements. For example, part of the American electronics industry shifted to Asian countries like Singapore and Taiwan in the 1960s. Such tendencies have also been at work *within* particular capitalist countries. ... The wider point to be made here is that the 'new international division of labour', where some manufacturing has been selectively located in the Newly Industrializing Countries (NICs), is merely one of various manifestations of the rising power of transnational capital, relative to national capital, and to labour, especially in the core capitalist states. On the other hand, it might be noted that some of the most successful firms from the NICs have themselves gone transnational and invested in the core capitalist countries. It is important not to overstate the exodus of manufacturing from the core: there has been some internationalization, but it has frequently been exaggerated. This may be because much potential foreign direct investment is discouraged by adverse political, as well as economic conditions. There is also recent evidence that changes in communications, production technologies and organizational systems, as well as a need for a base in each of the three largest market areas are causing production to shift back to the USA, the EC and the Pacific Rim. The general point is not that capital will flee to the NICs in the face of labour militancy, but that it will move to other countries, even ones within the capitalist core.

In the past, the power of capital implied in the 'new international division of labour' might have been countervailed to a certain extent. In the 1950s and 1960s organized labour was relatively stronger in the core states and appeared to have the potential to organize internationally. By the 1980s, such a potential was undermined substantially. Unionized workers of different states found themselves in a similar position to that of their national governments: that is, competing to attract foreign investment. Much higher levels of unemployment put them on the defensive. ...

With regard to the structural power of capital, the key contrast at the international level is the relative mobility of capital, and the relative immobility of labour in most sectors of activity. However, it is important to qualify this point in respect of skilled, knowledge-intensive labour. This is often internationally mobile, at least between capitalist countries. In certain high-technology industries (where transnational corporations often predominate), the USA has been able to draw talent (scientists, engineers, managers) from many other countries. The same applies to that most knowledge-intensive 'industry', education. Such skilled labour is crucial to the economic strength of both countries and transnational firms. To date, the most knowledge-intensive activities (e.g. research and development) have tended to be carried out mainly in the parent country of the transnational company. As a result, some national characteristics have continued to feature in the corporate culture of many of these firms. ...

Although the position of traditional organized labour appears reduced in the emerging transnational historic bloc, this may not necessarily imply a much narrower bloc than that of the post-war boom years. The decline of unions in the last 20 years has been associated, not just with the internationalization of production, but also with a shift away from 'traditional' manufacturing towards services. … Whilst this shift and the international transformation it is linked to would appear to have set back the prospects for international trade unionism based upon traditional workers' organizations, it opens up the prospect of a wider incorporation of workers and other interests, including foreign governments, into a transnational historic bloc. This is for four main reasons. First, many service subsidiaries, because of the intangible and perishable nature of service activity, carry out similar activities to those of the parent company and often offer higher rates of pay than their national competitors, that is skill levels are not centralized in parent companies. Second, skill levels spread to host countries and represent a considerable transfer of skills and technology. Third, transnationals are rapidly building affiliate networks. Finally, these activities appear to offer considerable growth in employment opportunities for the future. At the same time the proportion of female workers in the labour force has drastically increased. Apart from highly skilled labour, these and many other manufacturing workers may yet be incorporated into the new bloc. This can happen, for example, through their links to, or involvement in, small family businesses and home-based contractual work in a new type of putting-out system. Control over such a system if facilitated by new communications and information technologies, can be linked to the use of Just-In-Time (JIT) inventory systems, pioneered by Japanese automobile producers.

At the ideological level, a struggle is under way for 'the hearts and minds' of the growing numbers of non-traditional members of the working class: they may see themselves as middle class, even though most of their current income comes from the application of their labour-power, rather than from property and financial assets. An implication of the above points is that far more needs to be known about the political impact of changes in industrial structure, the labour process, and the degree of labour mobility. These changes need to be related to the consolidation of an individualist consumer culture and the possibilities for collective action on the part of workers and consumers. Specifically, it seems likely that the emerging regime of accumulation will be dominated by information- and knowledge-intensive industries. Thus the organization of the labour process, geographical location and ideological outlook of key workers in these fields is crucial to any kind of major change. Any successful transnational historic bloc would need to have comprehensively incorporated these relatively privileged workers.

Therefore, to conceive of historic blocs in purely material terms would be a fundamental mistake, since the broad contours of any new regime of accumulation will be partly shaped by the ideological climate at the national and global levels. Hence developments in the media and in education may prove to be of major long-term importance. Apart from allowing for the generation of technologies and knowledge which allow for the co-ordination of economic and political activity, these sectors of activity also embody both ideological and material structures which operate increasingly on a worldwide basis, such as in advertising and sponsorship, which involves both professional and amateur sporting and cultural pursuits.

In media and education, institutions have usually been under national control. Indeed, many centres of higher education, as well as telecommunication and radio and television companies have historically been in the public sector. However, given new technological developments (e.g. satellites, cable links for information processing), these sectors are likely to develop much more globally. Economies of scale in the production of television programmes, have put Western, especially American media corporations, at a competitive advantage to such a degree that US soap operas are shown in a majority of nations worldwide. The importance of such scale economies may increase with the growth of satellite broadcasting … breaking down national attempts to control foreign media access and output. In this context, transnational media companies have significant market power over their national competitors, power which is likely to increase if, as seems likely, more and more nations turn to the widespread use of English as either their first or second language. … Scope for these trends to develop is widened by a movement towards a more internationally competitive market in higher education, as well as the media. …

The power of capital: limits and contradictions

There are a variety of social forces that may run counter to the interests of capital in general. While we examine some of these, we are particularly interested in those that serve to limit the rise in the power of transnational capital. Essential to the analysis of these social forces are contradictions that affect the state–civil society relationship at both domestic and global levels.

There is neither stasis nor uniformity in capitalism. In order for capital to reproduce itself it needs to use labour-power profitably: capital is in a dialectical class relationship with labour. As has been noted, this relationship develops within a regime of accumulation that provides broader conditions that establish the scope and opportunities for investment and growth. In this sense, the form and character of state institutions, in the narrow or extended sense, are a central component of any regime of accumulation. As was noted implicitly in our previous discussion of Lindblom, this raises the issue of the relative autonomy of the state. Lindblom suggests that in a 'polyarchical' (pluralist) capitalist system, the state will tend to serve the interests of capital. At issue, therefore, are the dimensions along which this relationship may vary, so as to place limits on the power of capital. One axis of variation is the state's orientation towards national and transnational capital. That is, what is the balance of forces between nationalists and internationalists within the ensemble of state institutions? Which institutions are most associated with internationalist, and which with mercantilist ideas and policies? A state apparatus may be internally divided so that it lacks both cohesion and consistency in its foreign economic policies. This was the case for the USA in the 1920s and 1930s (Kindleberger 1973).

The logical corollary of this from the viewpoint of economic liberals who seek to increase the power of capital is to change the orientations and outlook of the bureaucracy, whilst simultaneously dismantling supports for declining industries. For example, incentives encouraging efficiency, elements of competition within the public sector, and a reduction in social and job security would serve to weaken the forces that support the forms of welfarist Mercantilism we have noted above. ... For example, in some developing countries constellations of state and industrial interests have emerged. These have often coalesced around a concept of 'strategic industries' under national control, sometimes, as in India, based on the Soviet planning model. ... One outcome of the experience of gaining independence, in countries like India, was an entrenched suspicion of foreign capital, and a determination to develop national capital (private or public), if need be, at very high investment outlays, and costs to consumers. Thus historical experience and the form and quality of the state–civil society relationship are thus major considerations in understanding how far limits to the power of capital, especially transnational capital, will vary between countries. It would be unrealistic to expect the same range and degree of limitations to the power of capital to exist in each country; this is ultimately an empirical question, depending upon the relationship between state and civil society. For example, countries with high concentrations of world mineral reserves are special cases. Sooner or later, transnational firms will seek accommodation with the rulers of such nations, whose direct power to control access to indigenous resources has increased since decolonization. Good examples of this are Libya and Saudi Arabia. The apparent paradox here is that whilst the direct (market) power of some, relatively unusual,

Third World states in the minerals sector has tended to rise with political independence, the structural power of transnational capital, relative to Third World states more generally, has become more pronounced. Such structural power affects all Third World states with regard to the bulk of manufacturing.

At the global level, limits to the power of transnational capital are grounded in contradictions in what, in Gramscian terms, would be called an embryonic international political society, and a still underdeveloped, but more discernible, internationalized civil society. International and domestic aspects of the limits to the power of capital are closely knit. For example, with regard to the political society, the strength of nationalism, concern with security, and of the military/public sector interests are directly related to the intensity of inter-state conflicts. As we have noted, the 1930s saw economic nationalism, militarism, and a pronounced shift towards regional economic blocs. This heightened the tendency towards an international political economy of rival national capitals. By contrast, the more 'orderly' periods of what Realists call hegemonic leadership (Britain in the mid-nineteenth century, the USA in the 25 years after World War II), gave more scope to 'liberal internationalist' elements in domestic political coalitions, and therefore, some extension of domestic civil society at the international level. In these more liberal periods, there was a rise in the relative and structural power of internationally mobile capital. In contrast, such structural power declined between the two world wars, as the form of the state–civil society relationship was more nationally circumscribed.

However, the significance of hegemonic leadership for the power of capital depends crucially on the nature of the political economy of the dominant states, and the domestic coalitions that control international economic policy. Both Britain and the USA were not only capitalist, but also in favour of liberal international economic policies. If the hegemonic state after World War II had been the USSR, then the power of capital would have been severely circumscribed, as it came to be in Eastern Europe. The enlargement of the communist sphere with the 1949 Chinese communist victory extended the political constraints on the international mobility of capital. It also made communist ideas more appealing, particularly in the Third World. Changes in the policies pursued in the communist states in the 1980s, notably in the Soviet Union, Eastern Europe and China towards a more liberal approach to private enterprise, markets and international trade were, therefore, major enhancements of the power of capital. This is because they gave more scope and potential for foreign investment, and increased the number of states and regions competing to attract foreign capital.

While the power of internationally mobile capital may be weakened when inter-state rivalries are intense (especially among the major powers as in 1914–45), the structural aspect of its power owes much to the division of the world into competing states. Indeed, the relationship between transnational capital and the state has a contradictory character. Perhaps the power of internationally mobile capital would be maximized by a world confederation, with states competing to attract foreign investment (as they do within the EC and the USA), and as the successor states to the Soviet Union in the Commonwealth of Independent States (CIS) are likely to do. Co-operation in such a confederation would be easier, the smaller the number of states, since communication would be simplified and the 'free-rider' temptation less pronounced, provided that the leaders in question shared a set of defining concepts of how the world works and a vision of the future. Given the latter, for a large number of states, substantial co-operation is easier if power resources are concentrated in the hands of relatively few states. This point has been developed with respect to the provision of international 'public goods'. What is crucial, therefore, is which forces influence and shape state policy in the small number of key states in the capitalist system: are they 'internationalist' or 'nationalist' in outlook? With respect to the successors to the states of 'existing socialism', are dominant political groups in favour of participation in the structures of global capitalism, or do they wish to pursue autarkic development strategies?

From the viewpoint of capital, the question of the optimal number of states is a dialectical one. It involves tensions between both 'political' and 'economic' dimensions, and direct and structural forms of power, at the domestic and global levels. As has been noted, capital needs the state to provide public goods, including law and order, that is coercive activity by the state. Thus, for capital, structural power is insufficient to sustain its hegemony – direct power is also needed. At the global level, the precise ways in which these public goods (or, more accurately, quasi-public goods) are provided is a matter for debate: are they to be provided by a hegemonic state, acting, as it were, as a substitute for a global *Leviathan*? Or are there other, emerging forms of international political authority that perform similar, and perhaps more legitimate functions? This is why, although the structural power of internationally mobile capital would be enhanced by having a large number of relatively small states, the problem of political and social order at the global level might be left unsolved.

However, the number of states, large or small, in any historical configuration is only one factor influencing the degree to which international co-operation and order is possible. As fundamental is the degree and type of international congruence between different state–civil society complexes. Another factor, alluded to above, is the adequacy of theorizations and models of the global political economy, and the degree to which these can form the basis for a 'practical consensus' on the directions of policy amongst key states in the system. Even if all these conditions were to be met, successful co-operation would still require massive amounts of accurate, up-to-date information, much of which is not publicly available: it is either controlled by private institutions or by public agencies operating under conditions of secrecy; also much information is notoriously imperfect.

The general point to be made here is that there is no clear-cut ideal international political society that would promote transnational hegemony globally, since any of the alternatives involves contradictory elements. Moreover, the question is a dynamic and historical one, since the conditions for the creation of hegemonic structures may be very different to those for its maintenance and development. As Cox has noted, the need for political consent within such structures is most crucial at the heart of the system, where capitalist hegemony is at its most intense (Cox 1983). What is still an open question is how far this core can be expanded to incorporate more states and interests from the periphery within an emerging transnational historic bloc. ... In the conditions of the late twentieth century, perhaps the best possible situation (for transnational capital) is the one which more-or-less exists in practice for the West, that is where the bulk of transnational capital is headquartered in a small number of economically large nations, ones in which capitalist hegemony is firmly embedded. However, this situation would only be ideal if a restructured USSR were to become a member of the capitalist inner-group, and was to do so with a reasonably broad-based political support at the domestic level for the types of (painful) economic and political restructuring which would go with the transition to capitalism ... . Change in the former Soviet Union and China (in the sense of adopting a more welcoming attitude to foreign capital) is therefore of the first importance in this respect. Alternatively, the break-up of a large, relatively autarkic state, particularly one reluctant to liberalize its economy, would result in an increase in the structural power of transnational capital. India is a possible case, and some limited liberalization occurred in the 1980s. However, another key consideration for capital is the maintenance of orderly conditions for capital accumulation. Therefore, unrest in a country like India would need to be weighed against the possibility of regional wars in a sub-continent that might be divided into many states.

In addition, the proliferation of new states since 1947 has tended to increase the level of global militarisation partly generated by a growing, quasi-capitalist international arms trade and by a more limited spread of arms production. Indeed, these two elements have combined to make possible a more competitive arms market, which is, as a consequence, now much less amenable to the control of the superpowers. Whilst militarisation has gone with the development of the internal security apparatuses of new states, it has also raised the possibility of severe wars, particularly in the Third World. The growth in terrorism is another aspect of these structural changes. One implication is that interests within the state apparatus that prioritize national security (even at the expense of civil liberties and democracy) are strengthened. They may ally with other statist and nationalist forces and reinforce a nationalist bloc, often protected by a veil of secrecy and other forms of political insulation. In this sense, the need of capital for stable political conditions for accumulation may be at the expense of substantial freedom of enterprise. Thus, whilst the structural power of capital is enhanced by a world of many states, its political conditions of operation may, in some ways, be weakened. Put another way, we are far from a situation in which a global political society is truly in prospect. The persistence of nationalist blocs and security complexes is mainly a problem, in this context, for transnational capital, since concepts of national security are likely to mean that such firms are denied equal access and treatment, when compared with national firms. This is most often the case in the sphere of military production.

The limits and contradictions that affect the formation of a transnational historic bloc and the attainment of transnational hegemony also arise with respect to market structures and economic policy. The inter-nationalization of production and finance and the spread of consumerism have resulted in an increasingly integrated world economy, as former social structures/regimes of accumulation and forms of state either disintegrate or are reconfigured. This means that it is becoming more plausible to apply Gramsci's concept of civil society to world orders. However, financial instability and policy perversity associated with what economists call 'fallacies of composition', pose both problems and opportunities for transnational capital. This is not to suggest that such composition effects are confined to economic matters: the search for security by each individual state may generate more insecurity for the world as a whole. In the monetary sphere, this fallacy may be manifested in the macroeconomic policies of governments, and the lending policies of banks. Other spheres where this fallacy can apply are in trade policy and with regard to the environment and ecosphere, as well as in the issue of global migration, which is related intimately to the restructuring of production and widening economic disparities, as well as political violence and instability.

More specifically, a transnational hegemony, involving banks, manufacturing firms, highly skilled labour and governments, particularly if it is reflected in policies of 'market monetarism', is invested with contradictions. If all countries compete to prove their 'monetary soundness' their deflationary policies will have negative multiplier effects. World recession is the natural outcome, if all deflate simultaneously. The dangers of the hegemony of a strict financial orthodoxy were illustrated during the 1930s, particularly in the USA and the UK. In these countries a commitment to balanced budgets and monetary discipline made it difficult to reverse the slide into recession. Other countries more rapidly abandoned this orthodoxy, to the point where some capitalist states actively pursued policies to constrain the power of markets. One extreme example of this was Nazi Germany. The wider macroeconomic issue is that what may appear to be 'rational' policy from the point of view of one country, may, if replicated elsewhere, add up to 'collective irrationality' in a single, highly integrated world capitalist economy. This fallacy of composition was involved in the attempts by countries to export their unemployment through competitive depreciation and the restriction of imports during the 1930s. This led to a fall in the level of world trade, exchange rate instability, and a growing climate of international uncertainty which some writers claimed not only discouraged investment, but was one of the conditions which led to the outbreak of World War II. ... By contrast ... the internationalized policy-process noted above managed, at least by the mid-1980s, to produce an extraordinary amount of cooperation amongst governments and banks in the G7, to manage the crisis, so avoiding the large-scale defaults that occurred in the 1930s. ...

Whilst the developments discussed above (and those in communications and education) may well appear to favour dominant agents in the global political economy, they also open up possibilities for counter-hegemonic forces, particularly at what Gramsci called the ethico-political level. An effective counter-hegemonic challenge requires access to large financial resources, knowledge and information, and a degree of control over production and distribution processes. Thus, counter-hegemonic challenges imply that these groups would need to become much larger, forge more comprehensive transnational links between themselves and mobilize significant support from unions and other producer interests and perhaps from political parties (old and new) who might be sympathetic to these alternatives. Organizations and movements which might form part of a counter-hegemonic bloc include Amnesty International, Green parties and ecological groups, socialist think tanks like the Transnational Institute, peace groups such as European Nuclear Disarmament, development agencies such as Oxfam, and religious organizations like the World Council of Churches. Given its size and potential as a vehicle for popular discontent in a range of less-developed countries, Islamic participation in a counter-hegemonic bloc is likely to be essential, although unlikely. One way in which the collective power of such groups could be brought to bear is through the mobilization of funds at the expense of orthodox capital, for example in the form of 'ethical' investment trusts. In some Muslim countries, such as Egypt, Islamic funds (mutual funds/investment trusts) have been established, to the embarrassment of the authorities, especially since they have gained large numbers of depositors. Much more research needs to be done on the ways in which such coalitions might form and become better organized and represented.

7
Globalization, Market Civilization and Disciplinary Neo-Liberalism[1]

This synthetic, somewhat complex chapter is an effort to sketch some of main frameworks of political economy, governance and culture that characterize world order in the late twentieth century. Its specific aims are threefold.

First, it situates world order problems in the context of the emergence of an organic crisis that is both civilizational and encompassing the global political economy (see Chapter 3 for an elaboration of organic crisis). To help explain this crisis the chapter outlines some of the principal social forces serving to re-constitute power, authority, accumulation and legitimation, as well as culture, life-chances and consciousness. The chapter then seeks to identify contradictions associated with the liberalization of capitalism, and to deconstruct and critique some of its ideological and mythic representations.

Second, the chapter seeks to link global transformations to changes in the ontology of the new world order. It is argued that this is partly constituted by three dominant historical structures – structures that need to be understood not as something abstract but as the product of collective action (see Chapters 2 and 3). These historical structures are disciplinary neo-liberalism, new constitutionalism and market civilization. They relate, respectively to political economy, to law, constitutionalism and governance, including that relating to control over ownership of the means of production and destruction, and to culture and civil society.

Third, Chapter 7 relates changes in ontology to shifts in political culture and specifically to the emergent 'market civilization'. Contradictions in the three historical structures are associated a new politics of supremacy (as opposed to hegemony). Such changes are bound up with a more globalized regime of accumulation that has reinforced

---

1. © *Millennium: Journal of International Studies*. The original version of this chapter first appeared in *Millennium*, 24 (3) 1995: 399–423. Excerpts are reproduced with the permission of the publisher.

the power of capital (see Chapter 6 on how this was emerging in the 1980s). In particular, the ontological shift involves cultural transformation, and new, although discordant, forms of 'common sense' (shared perceptions and experience of the world). New common sense expresses, for many, the emergence of a more self-regarding, individualistic, commercial, immediate although more insecure consciousness of and perspective on the world. Thus 'market civilization' refers to cultural transformation, in particular changes in the structure and language of social relations, a language that has become more marketized, individualized and linked to commodity logic.

Each moment in the constitution of historical structures involves intensified forms of discipline and surveillance ('panopticism'). This is partly because many aspects of power and discipline in the new world order are built into the everyday lives of workers, consumers and citizens – particularly those normalized and incorporated into what is called a 'supremacist bloc' of affluent structures of globalizing capitalism. As such, they provoke resistance, partly from within the supremacist bloc (by elements threatened by the new disciplines), as well as from social forces outside it (see Chapter 11).

Introduction

The present world order involves a more 'liberalized' and commodified set of historical structures, driven by the restructuring of capital and a shift politically, to the right. This process involves the spatial expansion and social deepening of economic liberal definitions of social purpose and possessively individualist patterns of action and politics. Current transformations can be related to Fernand Braudel's concept of the *longue durée*, in so far as the structure and language of social relations is now more conditioned by the long-term commodity logic of capital. Capitalist norms and practices pervade the *gestes répétés* of everyday life in a more systematic way than in the era of welfare-nationalism and state capitalism (e.g. from the 1930s to the 1960s), so that it may be apposite to speak of the emergence of what I call a 'market civilization'.

By market civilization, I mean a contradictory movement or set of transformative practices that entail, on the one hand, cultural, ideological and mythic forms understood broadly as an ideology or myth of capitalist progress. These representations are associated with the cumulative aspects of market integration and increasingly expansive structures of accumulation, legitimation, consumption and work, largely configured by the power of transnational capital. On the other hand, market civilization involves patterns of social disintegration and particular, exclusionary and hierarchical patterns of social relations. Indeed, whilst the concept of the *longue durée* suggests the lineage and depth of market practices, it can be suggested that a disturbing feature of the emerging market civilization form is that it tends to generate a perspective on the world that is ahistorical, economistic and materialistic, me-oriented, short-term, and ecologically myopic. Whilst the governance of this market civilization is primarily framed by the discourse of globalizing neo-liberalism, and expressed through the interaction of free enterprise and the state, its co-ordination is achieved through a combination of market discipline and the direct application of political power.

In this sense, there has been a globalization of liberalism, involving the emergence of a market civilization: neo-liberal globalization is the latest phase in a process that originated before the dawning of the Enlightenment in Europe, and accelerated in the nineteenth century with the onset of industrial capitalism and the consolidation of the integral nation-state.

The purpose of this chapter, is to probe aspects of this situation which, following Gramsci, we call one of organic crisis. This crisis involves restructuring of prevailing ideas, institutions and material capacities that constitute historical structures of world order. As Gramsci put it:

> In every country the process is different, although the content is the same. And the content is the crisis of the ruling class' hegemony ... A 'crisis of authority' is spoken of ... this is precisely ... a general crisis of the state. (Gramsci 1971)

When we introduce the issues of power and justice into our examination of neo-liberal forms of globalization, what is emerging is a politics of supremacy, rather than a politics of justice or hegemony. By a situation of supremacy I mean rule by a non-hegemonic bloc of forces that exercises dominance for a period over apparently fragmented populations until a coherent form of opposition emerges. For example, bourgeois hegemony implies the construction of an historical bloc that transcends social classes and fuses their direction into an active and largely legitimate system of rule. This implies a fusion of both economic, political and cultural elements of society (state and civil society) into a political alliance or coalition that combines coercion and consent, that is the creation of such a bloc presupposes opposition and a means for incorporating or defeating it in a process of struggle. Whilst there is no compromise by the leading class fraction on the fundamentals of the mode of production, there is nevertheless an inclusion politically of a significant range of interests. Subordinate classes thus carry weight within the formulation of state policy.

In the present era, this supremacist bloc can be conceptualized as commensurate with the emergence of a market-based transnational free enterprise system dependent for its conditions of existence on a range of state–civil society complexes. It is both 'outside' and 'inside' the state: it forms part of the 'local' political structures as well as serving to constitute a 'global' political and civil society. Thus, in my sketch of power structures of contemporary global politics, with significant local variations, a transnational historical bloc is formed, with its nucleus largely comprising elements of the G7 state apparatuses and transnational capital (in manufacturing, finance and services), and associated privileged workers and smaller firms (e.g. small and middle-sized businesses linked as contractors or suppliers, import–export businesses, service companies such as stockbrokers, accountants, consultancies, lobbyists, educational entrepreneurs, architects, designers).

One vehicle for the emergence of this situation has been policies that tend to subject the majority to market forces whilst preserving social protection for the strong (e.g. highly skilled workers, corporate capital, those with inherited wealth). These policies are cast within a neo-liberal discourse of governance that stresses the efficiency, welfare and freedom of the market and the actualization of self through the process of consumption. However, the effects of these policies are hierarchical and contradictory in their result so that it is also possible to say that the neo-liberal turn can itself be interpreted as partly a manifestation of a crisis of governmental authority and credibility, indeed of governability, within and across a range of societies: it represents what Gramsci called 'a rift between popular masses and ruling ideologies' expressed in widespread 'skepticism with regard to all theories and general formulae ... and to a form of politics which is not simply realistic in fact ... but which is cynical in its immediate manifestation' (Gramsci 1971: 276).

Indeed, partly because aspects of this political-civilization pattern provoke resistance and political counter-movements, many associated political forms are 'illiberal', authoritarian and anti-democratic in nature. Here, prevailing class forces of transnational capital seek to stabilize their dominance, in a global situation that approximates passive revolution, a situation characterized by 'dominance without leadership', or 'dictatorship without hegemony' (Gramsci 1971: 105–14). Where necessary this may entail limited formal democratization, in a strategy that involves either *transformism* (the 'formation of an ever-more extensive ruling class' through incorporation and absorption of rival elites, often leading to their 'annihilation or decapitation', e.g. Salinas' Mexico), or *Ceasarism*, such as 'where the forces in conflict balance each other in a catastrophic manner' a dictatorial tendency prevails, perhaps as in Yeltsin's Russia (Gramsci 1971: 219–23).

Thus, the statement that we are in a situation of organic crisis suggests that whilst there has been a growth in the structural power of capital, its contradictory consequences mean that neo-liberalism has failed to gain more than temporary dominance over our societies. To investigate this proposition further, the article begins with a brief methodological statement, and then examines the precise form of the politics of supremacy embodied in contemporary globalization and disciplinary neo-liberalism.

Analysing power and knowledge in the global political economy

The dominant forces of contemporary globalization are constituted by a neo-liberal historical bloc that practises a politics of supremacy within and across nations. The idea of an historical bloc – a concept which is one of the most fundamental innovations of Gramsci's political theory – is consistent in some ways with what Foucault called a 'discursive formation', that is a set of ideas and practices with particular conditions of existence and that are more or less institutionalized but which may be only partially understood by those that they encompass (Foucault 1972: 31–40). Both concepts allow us to make sense of the way that practices, understandings (and styles) come to pervade a wide range of social and political life but do so in complex, perhaps unpredictable and contested ways.

Marx's concept of commodity-fetishism (the ways that the exchange of commodities in the form of money masks the conditions and struggles associated with their production) can also be related to the content of the prevailing cultural discourse, in so far as it enables us to identify the basic social form that it presupposes: the way in which capitalist commercialization shapes outlooks, identities, time-horizons and conceptions of social space. The increasingly widespread commodification of social relations is partly reflected in the growing preoccupation with an aesthetic of surface textures and symbols rather than historical depth and with architectural collage and immediacy that characterizes some forms of postmodernism.[2] David Harvey notes (perhaps forgetting the potential impact of new technologies) that for Foucault the only irreducible element is the human body, the particular 'site' at which discursive repression is ultimately experienced and localized (Harvey 1989: 39–65). For Foucault, nevertheless, this very individualized and localized 'moment' is also where 'resistance' to repressive discourse can occur.[3]

Foucault's approach is useful in the way that it highlights the constitution and constraints of particular discursive forms and for its emphasis on the way in which certain forms of power and knowledge serve to constitute particular aspects of civilization. What is often missing from the Foucauldian view, however, despite its preoccupation with localized, capillary forms of power/knowledge, is a convincing way of linking these forms of power to macro-structures and to a theory of social transformation. For example, Foucault identifies a 'great transformation' at the start of the nineteenth century that produced a new 'historical, comparative grammar', an 'archaeological rupture' in modes of thought so general that it came to bear on 'the general rules of one or several discursive formations', including, as he notes, both Ricardian and Marxian Political Economy (Foucault and Gordon 1980: 176–7). Yet how does Foucault explain this transformation? He speaks elusively of multiple determinations, but strangely missing from his explanation of this epistemological revolution is any sustained analysis of the rise of capital as a social relation, and indeed any attempt to speak of its power either specifically or in general. Missing also is a discussion of historical struggle over the modalities of power and knowledge.

Thus despite the Foucauldian preoccupation with the problematic of power/knowledge as localized and institutionalized by discourse, with

2. Examples of this tendency include the British 'heritage' industry and theme parks, theme-park casinos and wax museums in the USA and elsewhere, as well as architectural forms that create collage fantasies that annihilate any meaningful sense of history. They nevertheless constitute a particular sense of collective identity in a period of widespread economic and social insecurity, *anomie* and rapid social transformation. Many of these innovations are financed and controlled by large corporations. An excellent analysis of the attempt, by the government in concert with corporate Japan, to create this form of middle class 'leisure society' is McCormack (1991).
3. 'It's true that during these extraordinary events [May 1968, at the Sorbonne] I often asked: but why isn't Foucault here? Thus granting him his power of attraction and underscoring the empty place he should have been occupying.' Maurice Blanchot, 'Michel Foucault as I Imagine Him' (Blanchot and Foucault 1990: 63).

localized resistance through interventions in the systems of power/knowledge – in a political economy where knowledge is viewed as the principal form of production and power resource – there is little by way of an emancipatory dimension to this perspective in so far as there is no adequate link between macro- and micro-structures of power in the approach. Even in a world where we might accept the postulate of multiple identities and a radical sense of discontinuity in forms of representation and human consciousness, unless our social perspective is one of the ostrich it seems difficult to ignore the overwhelming evidence of tremendous growth of inequality over the past two decades: income has been radically redistributed between labour and capital in an era of stagnating growth in most of the OECD nations. Indeed, the concentration of capital has proceeded very much along the lines anticipated by Marx and thus must be central to any explanation of the present global transformation, just as the incipient forms of capitalist industrialization were central to the epistemological changes in the nineteenth century, and to the new representations of political economy, that were revealed by Foucault's archaeological excavations.

My approach, then, uses certain Foucauldian ideas but repositions them within an historical materialist framework to sketch a model of power that is able to account for those who are included and those who are excluded or marginalized in the global political economy. Whereas Foucault tends to depict power relations in an all-encompassing way, perhaps the usefulness of his concepts of discursive formation and panopticism is more specific: they apply mainly to some members of the 'culture of contentment' (Galbraith 1992): people who are exemplars of the commodified and normalized society *par excellence*. These people are simultaneously Foucault's willing victims that hold credit cards and who willingly provide or call for the wider provision of personal information that can be manipulated in the 'panoptic' databases. By contrast, the marginalized are both within the societies of the culture of consumption and elsewhere in the world and they may have forms of knowledge that are not amenable to rationalization and discipline in the sense of Foucault, and they may not necessarily co-operate with normalizing practices. They may actively seek to develop counter-hegemonic forms of power/knowledge, for example in that archetypal 'panoptic' society, apartheid South Africa, a society that incarcerated Nelson Mandela and other ANC leaders for decades. Here, state violence and surveillance could not prevent change. Thus where Foucault represents a cry of outrage at the taming of the individual and a purely defensive strategy of localized resistance, historical materialism goes much further in an attempt to theorize and to promote collective action to create an alternative form of society – even from within a prison (where Gramsci sketched his notebooks). This is why it is necessary to theorize the problem of change in local and global dimensions and to look beyond the currently fragmented forms of opposition to neo-liberal supremacy.

The meaning of 'globalization'

In this section I ask the question: what is meant by the concept of 'globalization' as used in conventional political discourse in the OECD? We need to ask, 'globalization of what, where, and for whom?'

In their post-1945 phase, contemporary processes of globalization are unparalleled, at least in terms of their scale and extension: there have been massive increases in productive power and compressions of time and space. This has occurred in the context of tremendous and unprecedented population growth that began to rise significantly, again from the late eighteenth century onwards (Braudel 1981). Indeed, according to Eric Hobsbawm, globalization is one counterpart to an unprecedented social and cultural revolution, at least in the OECD nations. In the OECD, at least, the peasantry as a class have effectively been eliminated – thus bringing to an end the seven or eight millennia of human history in a major portion of the world, as well as consolidating the trend towards a more urbanized, rationalized and marketized form of world economy.[4] For the first time in history there is 'a single, increasingly integrated and universal world economy largely operating across state frontiers ("transnationally") and therefore increasingly across the frontiers of state ideology' (Hobsbawm 1994: 287–343).

Thus globalization is part of a broad process of restructuring of the state and civil society, and of the political economy and culture. It is also an ideology largely consistent with the world-view and political priorities of large-scale, internationally mobile forms of capital. Politically, it is consistent with the outlook of affluent minorities in the OECD and in the urban elites and new middle classes in the Third World. The current phase of economic globalization has come to be characterized increasingly not by free competition idealized in neo-classical theory, but by *oligopolistic neo-liberalism*: oligopoly and protection for the strong and a socialization of their risks, market discipline for the weak.

---

4. Of course this has to be qualified somewhat. As the landless peasants' movement in Brazil has shown, as have the Zapatistas, the political agency of the peasantry remains significant in the Third World.

Of course, 'globalization' as a process is not amenable to reductionist forms of explanation, because it is many-faceted and multidimensional and involves ideas, images, symbols, music, fashions, and a variety of tastes and representations of identity and community. Nevertheless, in its present, mythic and ideological representations, the concept serves to reify a global economic system dominated by large institutional investors and transnational firms that control the bulk of the world's productive assets, and that are the principal influences in world trade and financial markets. For example, in 1992, the 300 largest transnational firms controlled about 25 per cent of the world's $20 trillion stock of productive assets; the top 600 corporations with annual sales over $1 billion accounted for over 20 per cent of the world's total value-added in manufacturing and agriculture.[5] There were about 37,000 transnational corporations by 1992, with 170,000 affiliates (up from 7,000 in the early 1970s). These firms had cumulative foreign direct investment of about $2 trillion, one-third controlled by the 100 largest corporations. The top 100 had global sales of $5.5 trillion, a sum roughly equal to the GNP of the USA. The 1992 value of world exports of goods and non-factor services was around $4 trillion, of which a third was intra-firm trade, between parents and affiliates of transnationals.[6] Transnationals are large capital- and knowledge-intensive firms that together employ about 72 million people, of whom 15 million are in developing countries. Most workers of transnational corporations are well paid, and tend to enjoy better working conditions than those in local firms. Directly and indirectly transnationals perhaps account for 5 per cent of the global work force, although they control over 33 per cent of global assets. In the financial markets, by 1994 the daily flow of foreign exchange transactions worldwide may have exceeded $1 trillion, roughly equal to the foreign exchange holdings of all the central banks in the OECD (UNRISD 1995). This is despite the fact that perhaps no more than 10 per cent of all financial transactions are related to real economic activity (that is to finance trade flows or capital movements). Much of the rest is related to speculative activity, money laundering and tax evasion, as well as the offsetting of risk.

In this context, partly as a consequence of the global decline of the left and the rising power of transnational capital, political life in many parts of the world has come to be configured, to a degree, by 'neo-liberal' economic and political principles over the past two decades, a process

5. 'A Survey of Multinationals', *The Economist*, 27 March 1993.
6. UNCTAD, *World Investment Report*, UN: Geneva, 1993.

hastened by the collapse of communist rule and articulated in different ways mainly by conservative political leaders such as Margaret Thatcher and Ronald Reagan. What seems to be emerging in present-day globalization is an intensification of the *longue durée* of commodification (the shaping of social relations by making labour and nature into exchangeable commodities) in ways commensurate with not only the new right and neo-liberal ideologues, but also among elites and emerging middle classes in the Third World.

With respect to the dominant discursive formation of our time, the neo-liberal concept of 'globalization' suggests that privatization and transnationalization of capital are either inevitable or desirable from a broad social viewpoint. In this sense, the concept of globalization exhibits positive and negative forms of ideology. A positive aspect is the equation of free competition and free exchange (global capital mobility) with economic efficiency, welfare and democracy, and a myth of virtually unlimited social progress, as represented in TV advertising and other media, and in World Bank and IMF reports. A negative aspect is how neo-liberal market forces are often said to have marginalized non-market alternatives, especially from the political left. Thus some equate globalization with the unfolding of a business Hegelian myth of the capitalist market ('the global information standard') as the Absolute Idea: global financial markets are said to be 'civilizing' although implacable and gigantic forces for good government (Wriston 1992). Some equate neo-liberal globalization with the 'end of history', although, as implied in his invocation of Nietzsche's dispirited and pathetic 'Last Man', for Francis Fukuyama the victory of liberalism is a hollow one, since the post-communist Last Man (where liberalism is the only global alternative) is doomed to boredom: a morbid repetitiveness simulates death; a condition that may be palliated by satellite TV showing World Cup soccer (Fukuyama 1992: 319).

Nonetheless, the privileges of the politically powerful and economically strong have been reinforced in the OECD nations since the late 1960s, often to the detriment of the vast majority of the population (Galbraith 1992). The neo-liberal shift in government policies has tended to subject the majority of the population to the power of market forces (most workers, small businesses) whilst preserving social protection for the strong (e.g. highly skilled workers, oligopolistic corporate capital, those with inherited wealth). In the Third World, the counterpart to Galbraith's 'culture of contentment' are urban elites and ruling and emerging middle classes that benefit from the consumption patterns and incorporation into transnational financial and production circuits of capital.[7] Recent growth in enclave residential development, private provision of security (e.g. the massive growth of private police relative to public law officers), and private insurance and healthcare suggests that access to what were often considered to be public goods under socialized provision is now increasingly privatized, individualized and hierarchical in nature. More broadly, there has been a transformation of the socialization of risk towards privatization and individualization of risk assessment and insurance provision. Nevertheless, this process is hierarchical, not only because some people can have platinum credit cards and others only green ones (the former provide cheaper credit to higher income earners and *vice versa*) but also in so far the burdens of risk are redistributed, marketized and individualized (e.g. associated with illness, old age, pensions) as opposed to being fully socialized through collective and public provision.[8]

Despite enormous increases in global output and population since World War II, central to the restructuring process of the last 20 years has been a significant polarization of income and of life chances: for the 800 million or so affluent consumers in the OECD, there is a counterpart number starving in the Third World, with 1 billion more that have no clean drinking water or sufficient food to provide basic nutrition.[9] More than half Africa's population lives in absolute poverty. In the 1980s, the

---

7. On Latin America, see Celso Furtado, 'Transnationalization and Monetarism', *International Journal of Political Economy*, 17 (1) 1987: 15–44; on Africa, see Fantu Cheru, *The Silent Revolution*, London: Zed Books, 1989. On the somewhat different conditions in East Asia, see Frederic C. Deyo, *The Political Economy of the New Asian Industrialism*, Ithaca: Cornell University Press, 1987.
8. The IMF and World Bank have pressed recently for privatization of public pension provision, especially in the Third World, to create larger local capital markets.
9. There has been, of course, substantial improvement in basic living conditions. The UNDP showed that nearly 70 per cent of world population lived in 'abysmal' conditions in 1960; by 1992, only 32 per cent suffered such conditions. Global GNP rose seven-fold since 1945 from $3 trillion to $22 trillion. World population more than doubled from 2.5 billion to 5.5 billion, per capita income more than tripled (UNDP 1994). UNDP adds, 'we still live in a world where a fifth of the developing world's population goes hungry every night ... and a third lives in abject poverty – at such a margin of human existence that words simply fail to describe it ... the richest billion people command 60 times the income of the poorest billion ... Poor nations and rich are afflicted by growing human distress ... food production must triple if people are to be adequately fed, but the resource base for sustainable agriculture is eroding' (UNDP 1994: 1–2).

income of two-thirds of African workers fell below the poverty line. A disproportionate burden of adjustment to harsher circumstances has fallen on women and children, and weaker members of society – the old and the disabled. Many of these people also live in war-torn societies, where huge quantities of cheap mass-produced conventional weapons have accumulated, including 'weapons that never miss': over 100 million landmines. One million landmines exploded under Third World victims in the last 15 years (UNRISD 1995).

A re-emergence of serious global public health problems may be indicated by the growth in contagious diseases once thought conquered in the march of medical progress (e.g. cholera, anthrax), as well as in diseases associated with environmental degradation and pollution (e.g. asthma among children, allergies, and new viruses such as AIDS). During the decades since World War II life expectancy increased steadily throughout the world. This process has now apparently gone into reverse in a number of countries (notably in the former communist-ruled nations of Eastern Europe):

> The resurgence of epidemics is a crucial indicator of the state of our world, not only in terms of human suffering, but also in terms of development more generally. It implies the breakdown of the social controls that usually prevent such diseases – hygiene, nutrition, resistance to infection, immunization programmes, housing. (UNRISD 1995: 26)

Prices of many medical products marketed by transnational pharmaceuticals firms have risen and the relaxation of trade barriers and other market forms of restriction and regulation has made it simpler to dump expired or unsafe medicines in parts of the Third World (UNRISD 1995). Globally, public health and educational provisions have been reduced, partly because of the neo-liberal structural adjustment pressures on most governments to exercise monetary restraint, cut budgets, repay debts, balance their international trade, devalue their currencies, remove subsidies and trade and investment barriers and, in so doing, restore international credit-worthiness and thereby extend the market civilization globally. Such pressures emanate from agents in the global financial markets and from international organizations such as the World Bank and IMF, and from within these societies. Thus in many parts of the Third World and in the former Soviet Union, economic liberalization has been welcomed as a means of reforming the old, unaccountable political order.

From a socio-historical perspective, then, a remarkable feature of world society is how more and more aspects of everyday life in OECD nations have come to be premised upon or pervaded by market values, representations and symbols, as time and distance are apparently shrunk by scientific-technological innovation, the hyper-mobility of financial capital and some types of information flows. Commercialization has configured more aspects of family life, religious practice, leisure pursuits and aspects of nature. Indeed, processes of commodification have progressively encompassed aspects of life previously viewed as inalienable. Increasingly, corporations routinely obtain patent rights over human genes and pharmaceuticals and tissue, plants, seeds and animal hybrids. This includes the DNA of 'endangered peoples' that is aboriginal or native peoples. Such private 'intellectual' property rights are being internationalized and extended into the legal regimes of the world through the new World Trade Organization. Such developments are taking place when, in much of the OECD, there has been little political debate over the repercussions of biotechnology and genetic innovation, to say nothing of the privatization of life forms. At the same time large numbers of people are almost totally marginalized from enjoyment of the fruits of global production.

In this sense, the 'social question' is posed anew today, and, as in the nineteenth century, it is posed locally and globally. Indeed, this tendency is inherent in the expansion of capital that serves to disintegrate and to transform the existing social order. Capital tends to supplant the old with an order that is radically new and historically unprecedented. Thus, social taboos are overcome and capital exerts growing influence over the most sensitive rituals of different civilizations (provided that they offer opportunities for profit):

The American way of death has cast its pall over Europe. Service Corporation International, the US's largest burial business, spent £306m on buying 15 per cent of the UK market last year and is now paying FFr2.05bn to take a 30 per cent share of French funerals. But there is sound business strategy behind this apparent megalomania. Funeral parlours offer vast potential economies of scale. Centrally locating hearses, embalmers and attendants ... and there are added benefits from bulk buying ... Tax and accounting differentials mean the deal will enhance earnings even before operating improvements ... Competition and monopolies issues have restricted further US acquisitions while a flat death rate has constrained organic growth. A fragmented European market provides a vast new customer base. There is the risk that xenophobia might provide the kiss of death for such deals. But its Australian operations have demonstrated few barriers to international undertaking.[10]

In this quintessential representation of the ideology of global neo-liberalism, even the rites of death and burial are associated with profit. Megalomania is conflated with sound business strategy and equated with the maximization of efficiency through the exploitation of economies of scale that have been inhibited in the USA because of the government's anti-monopoly legislation; and, not least, because people are not dying in sufficient numbers. Nevertheless, the author worries at the risk to the venture posed by cultural particularities of other countries, which are viewed as xenophobic barriers to the expansion of capital.

To recapitulate: the current phase of globalization is part of a social and cultural transformation in which links between work, effort, and savings, and life-chances (and death) more generally are reified through ideological representations commensurate with a growth in the power of capital. Social interaction, work patterns, and leisure become increasingly monetized, marketized and abstracted; but not necessarily in ways that ordinary people cannot understand. At the most obvious transactional level, for example, most citizens in Latin America and Asia can calculate complex financial transactions (e.g. the interplay between commodity prices, inflation rates, exchange rates and the nominal rate of interest). In principle such calculations are no more complex than those made in financial dealing rooms in London, Singapore, Tokyo and New York, although the calculations of the former are more likely to be matters of immediate survival – indeed of life or death – for the individuals concerned, and not linked to extravagant bonuses. In this way, the health/sickness/death of the 'market' is globally incorporated, at the micro-level of the individual, as it were, into popular consciousness and action, into 'the structures of everyday life' (Braudel 1981).

By implication, this situation involves methods by which patterns of privilege can be defended from encroachment and possible expropriation by those subordinated and marginalized. In the terminology of Fred Hirsch, privileged consumption and production patterns of a small section of the world's population are, in effect, the 'positional goods' of the global political economy that contemporary systems of policing and military power, used in the 1991 Gulf War, are designed increasingly to protect (Hirsch 1976).

10. 'Fatal attraction', Lex Column. *Financial Times*, 11 July 1995.

The following two sections elaborate other dimensions of power associated with the globalization of neo-liberal politico-economic forms.

'Disciplinary' neo-liberalism

Max Weber defined the concept of discipline as follows: 'Those who obey are not necessarily obedient or an especially large mass, nor are they necessarily united in a specific locality. What is decisive for discipline is that obedience of a plurality of men is rationally uniform' (Weber 1963). For Weber, classes, status groups and political parties are phenomena of the distribution of power in society, and 'discipline' is a form of its exercise in social organizations. For Weber, a status order is the reverse of a market order that 'knows no personal distinctions' and which generates the process of class formation (Mills 1961). For Emile Durkheim, (self) discipline, or the restraint of one's inclinations, is a means to develop reasoned behaviour and to foster the moral growth of the healthy personality: unregulated emotions can produce *anomie* (Pearce 1989). For Michel Foucault 'discipline' is sometimes used in ways that approximate Weber and Durkheim but generally the term is used in a more encompassing way as both a modernist framework of understanding that underpins a terrain of knowledge and a system of social and individual control: 'The Enlightenment, which discovered the liberties, also invented the disciplines' (Foucault 1979: 222).[11]

The concept of discipline advanced here combines macro- and micro-dimensions of power: the structural power of capital (including the broad capacity to shape expectations, material constraints and incentives); an ability to promote uniformity and obedience within parties, cadres and organizations, especially in class formations associated with transnational capital (perhaps involving self-discipline in the Durkheimian sense), and particular instances of disciplinary practice in a Foucauldian sense. Thus 'disciplinary neo-liberalism' is a concrete form of structural and behavioural power, combining the structural power of capital with 'capillary power' and 'panopticism' (Foucault and Gordon 1980).[12] In other

11. As Blanchot notes, 'This is perhaps exaggerated: the disciplines go back to prehistoric times, when, for example, a bear was transformed, through successful training, into what would be later a watchdog or a courageous policeman' (Blanchot and Foucault 1990: 87).
12. Foucault believed that he had discovered the origin of 'structuralism' in the administration of measures to map out and contain the spread of plagues, to which humans had learned to submit in a docile manner so as to function as interchangeable units: 'In a discipline, the elements are interchangeable,

words, neo-liberal forms of discipline are not necessarily universal nor consistent, but they are bureaucratized and institutionalized, and operate with different degrees of intensity across a range of 'public' and 'private' spheres, in various state and civil society complexes. Discipline in this sense is both transnational and a local dimension of power. That is to say, these dimensions of discipline are part of the discursive formation of global power associated with the interests and forces of the supremacist transnational historical bloc that I have sketched in the previous section of this chapter.

New constitutionalism and global governance

Disciplinary neo-liberalism is institutionalized at the macro-level of power in the quasi-legal restructuring of state and international political forms: the 'new constitutionalism'. This discourse of global economic governance is reflected in the policies of the Bretton Woods organizations (e.g. IMF and World Bank conditionality that mandates changes in the form of state and economic policy) and quasi-constitutional regional arrangements such as NAFTA or Maastricht, and the multilateral regulatory framework of the new World Trade Organization. It is reflected in the global trend towards independent central banks, with macroeconomic policy prioritizing the 'fight against inflation'.

New constitutionalism is a macro-political dimension of the process whereby the nature and purpose of the public sphere in the OECD has been redefined in a more privatized and commodified way, with its economic criteria defined in a more globalized and abstract frame of reference. The accountability of governments to 'markets' is mainly to material forces and sentiments of investment managers in the bond markets (i.e. of institutional investors such as pension funds, unit trusts, insurance companies) and to the conditionality of the Bretton Woods organizations. It has grown in a period of fiscal crisis and in accordance with the growing salience of 'new constitutionalist' discourses of global governance. The new constitutionalism can be defined as the political

---

since each one is defined by the place it occupies in a series and the gap that separates it from the others' (Foucault 1979: 145). An extreme form of discipline is the partitioning of space associated with the Panopticon, which, for Foucault, reveals the absolute power of total visibility, and the ability to render the human condition obedient and productive. The methods of separation, observation and experimentation provide a basis for both science and power, or power/knowledge (Blanchot and Foucault 1990: 85–6).

project of attempting to make transnational liberalism, and if possible liberal democratic capitalism, the sole model for future development.

New constitutionalist proposals are often implicit rather than explicit. Nevertheless, they emphasize market efficiency, discipline and confidence; economic policy credibility and consistency; and limitation on democratic decision-making processes. Proposals imply or mandate the insulation of key aspects of the economy from the influence of politicians or the mass of citizens by imposing, internally and externally, 'binding constraints' on the conduct of fiscal, monetary and trade and investment policies. Ideology and market power is not enough to ensure the adequacy of neo-liberal restructuring. It is worth noting the USA is the least likely of any country to submit to such constraints – although its leaders insist that they be applied systematically to other states. Nonetheless, even the autonomy of the USA, Japan and the European Union is constrained in matters of macroeconomic policy by the globalization of finance and production. Smaller and less self-sufficient states tend to be correspondingly more sensitive and vulnerable to global financial pressures.

In effect, new constitutionalism confers privileged rights of citizenship and representation to corporate capital, whilst constraining the democratization process that has involved struggles for representation for hundreds of years. Central, therefore, to new constitutionalism is the imposition of discipline on public institutions, partly to prevent national interference with the property rights and entry and exit options of holders of mobile capital with regard to particular political jurisdictions. These initiatives are also linked to efforts to define appropriate policy, partly by strengthening surveillance mechanisms of international organizations and private agencies such as the bond-raters. Governments in need of external financing are forced to provide data. One reason for this is to make domestic and economic and political agents and trends more transparent to global supervisors in the IMF or Bank for International Settlements (BIS) as well as to the increasingly influential private bond-rating agencies such as Moody's and Standard & Poor's. Indeed, initiatives based on new constitutionalist surveillance assumptions were launched at the G7 summit in Halifax, Nova Scotia, in June 1995. The G7 leaders opted to strengthen surveillance mechanisms under the *aegis* of the IMF, World Bank and BIS. This was after failure of existing methods of surveillance was revealed by the Mexican financial crisis of 1994–95.

By contrast, traditional notions of constitutionalism are associated with political rights, obligations, and freedoms, and procedures that give institutional form to the state. Constitutions define, describe and outline the rights and obligations of citizens; common policy-making institutions with authority over the entire polity; the limits to and the scope of action of these institutions; and of course, enforcement mechanisms and ratification and amendment procedures (Clarkson 1993).

Turning to recent examples of neo-liberal forms of regionalization, there is a difference in kind between North America and Western Europe. Here I represent both examples more as projects rather than as exemplars of the final crystallization of neo-liberal dominance. For example, questions of European unification have been made more complex by not only German unification, but also the accession of new Nordic members and the prospect of further enlargement to encompass former communist-ruled nations. NAFTA is also undergoing considerable turbulence and contestation, not only within each member nation, but also more broadly in Latin America.

The European Union has citizenship for individuals from member countries and has partly accountable mechanisms for negotiation, ratification, amendment and enforcement, and for incorporating and weighting the interests of the smaller European nations. However, although social and welfare policy and regulation has been institutionalized in the EEC since the Treaty of Rome, for example with respect to social security for migrant workers (Article 51); equal treatment of men and women (Article 119); protection of workers (Article 118); and health and safety of workers (Article 118 and 118a of the Single European Act), implementation has been patchy and uneven despite the influence of trades unions, some political parties and, in cases, the European Court for Human Rights, in large part because of employer opposition. A further reason is because of the development of unaccountable inter-governmental agencies, for example in the field of immigration, associated with the Schengen Convention (1985) and on freedom of movement between states and the Trevi Group (1976) on terrorism, radicalism, extremism and international violence. Nevertheless, the political centre of gravity of European political economy has tilted recently towards definitions that reflect a financial and free trade conception, that is a neo-liberal view of Europe – as opposed to the more social democratic idea of 'social Europe'. This is reflected in many of the Maastricht provisions especially the proposals for a largely unaccountable European central banking system, and fiscal/public debt provisions intended to be binding on all future governments in the Union.

North American arrangements are more hierarchical and asymmetrical, understood in both inter-state terms and in terms of the class structures of each nation. NAFTA is premised upon a low level of political institutionalization and a hub-and-spoke configuration of power, with the USA at the centre of a continentalized political economy. This is even more the case with the Caribbean Basin Initiative that can be terminated unilaterally by the USA. The USA has negotiated the implicit right to monitor and control large areas of Canadian political life in the USA–Canada Free Trade Agreement. It specifies that each side has to notify the other 'party' by advanced warning, of *intended* federal or provincial government policy that *might* affect the other side's interests as defined by the agreement. Because of its huge economic integration with the USA this is a situation that necessarily affects the vast majority of Canadian economic activity, but not *vice versa*. Thus Canadian governments can now no longer contemplate an independent or interventionist economic strategy. In NAFTA (and the USA–Canada Agreement), there are no transnational citizenship rights other than those accorded to capital, and these were defined to favour US-registered companies. Finally, NAFTA can only be amended by agreement of all signatories. Whilst these arrangements place binding constraints on the policies of Canada and Mexico, to a certain degree the USA retains constitutional autonomy and important prerogatives: its trade law is allowed to override treaty provisions, notwithstanding the rights of redress that are available to participants through the dispute settlement mechanisms.[13]

In other words, the US government is using access to its vast market as a lever of power, linked to a reshaping of the international business climate, by subjecting other nations to the disciplines of the new constitutionalism, whilst largely refusing to submit to them itself, partly for strategic reasons. Indeed, one of the arguments expressed by former European Union President Jacques Delors in favour of comprehensive west European economic and monetary union was strategic: to offset economic unilateralism from the United States, in matters of money and trade.

Thus an American-centred global neo-liberalism mandates a separation of politics and economics in ways that may narrow political representation and constrain democratic social choice in many parts of the world. New constitutionalism, that ratifies this separation, may have become the *de facto* discourse of governance for most of the global political economy. This discourse involves a hierarchy of pressures and constraints on government autonomy that vary according to the size, economic strength,

13. Clarkson notes that the USA 'maintained intact the sovereignty of Congress to pass new trade measures that could supersede the trade agreement. It avoided negotiating a definition of "subsidy" that might lessen the scope of its countervailing actions against Canadian producers or exempt Canadian exporters from the application of its other protectionist laws' (Clarkson 1993: 4).

form of state and civil society and prevailing national and regional institutional capabilities, and the degree of integration into global capital and money markets.

Panopticism and the coercive face of the neo-liberal state

Panopticon is a Greek word for 'sees all', coined by Jeremy Bentham, and popularized by Foucault.[14] We can define panopticism as 'a dystopia latent in modernity: the possibility of developing a system of control which reduces the individual to a manipulable and relatively inert commodity' (Gill 1995). Foucault's understanding of panopticism suggests that it is possible to render the human condition obedient and acquiescent to the various forms of observation, enquiry and experimentation that are demanded by scientific progress and social order in what he calls the disciplinary society – something which according to Maurice Blanchot, Foucault denounced and ultimately identified with Nazism (Blanchot and Foucault 1990: 86).

Use of panoptic practices antedates modern bureaucratic systems and technical innovations and goes back at least as far as the administrative, military, and labour control systems of ancient imperial China, or more recently the Ottoman Empire. Clearly there can be no all-seeing eye of power, merely mechanisms of surveillance that are intended to maximize discipline in the Weberian sense noted above. Indeed, these mechanisms of surveillance may be more intensive and important for the reproduction of the neo-liberal transnational historic bloc amongst its ruling classes and elites than among subordinate elements in society, who tend to resist them. As we shall see in Chapter 10 there is evidence of a recent tendency towards increasing use of technologically sophisticated surveillance capabilities by private firms and the state, whilst, of course, many new technologies are socially empowering, liberating and decentralizing in nature. However, it is crucial to stress that a technological 'revolution' does not necessarily entail or indeed imply a basic change in social relations, for example in the relations of exploitation and alienation in capitalism.

14. Published in 1791, the panopticon was a generic term for 'a new principle of construction applicable to any sort of establishment, in which persons of any description are to be kept under inspection; and in particular to penitentiary-houses, prisons, poor-houses, lazarettos, houses of industry, manufactories, hospitals, work-houses, mad-houses and schools' (Bentham 1843).

Contemporary surveillance practices by corporate and governmental bureaucracies are nevertheless important. Populations are constructed statistically as manipulable entities in databases, that is they are monitored and objectified for purposes of social control or profit, for example in the huge private data corporations that specialize in commercially useful information about individuals and households.[15] Some OECD social security ministries have shifted to more rigorous monitoring of clients, with some introducing 'workfare' programmes (analogous to Bentham's management schemes for paupers and prisoners) and ensuring the 'transparency' and 'inspectability' of claims and activities (Bentham 1843). More recently, because of restructuring of production and increased migration (and growth of transnational criminal networks), policing changes have involved reorganized surveillance capacities. In this process it is worth noting that the mobility of capital is not matched by a corresponding mobility or freedom of labour. Indeed, new OECD citizenship rights are increasingly regulated by a commodity logic and sold by governments to raise revenue and attract investment and, if possible, skills. Collection of information about populations may also be used to discipline individuals via sanctions or inducements, for example denial or provision of private credit (Gandy 1993), health and insurance, or genetic testing and biological monitoring of workers to identify and perhaps eliminate those who are unfit or potentially costly to corporate health plans.

One possible explanation for these surveillance tendencies is that pressures are placed on the state by the interaction between fiscal crises in local, regional and national governments (especially since the mid-1970s) and the globalization of financial markets and the mobility of transnational corporations. Driven to raise operating finance on the more globalized financial markets, governments are pressured into providing a business climate judged attractive by global standards in order to win and retain foreign direct investment.

Such developments have also accompanied major restructurings of tax systems in the OECD and elsewhere: these have reduced marginal tax rates on capital and high-income earners and have attempted to broaden the

15. Architectural counterparts are shopping malls that resemble fortresses or prisons, with internal galleries and central observation points. Some malls, like one in Edmonton, are also built like theme parks (as are new casinos in Las Vegas). In each case, interior space is illuminated and subject to video monitoring by guards. New shopping malls, unlike their Victorian antecedents (shopping arcades) are designed to prohibit 'inappropriate' consumers.

tax base, in order to create a more 'activist tax state' with increasingly regressive taxes. Traditional forms of state intervention in the economy to promote redistribution have declined, and socialization of risk for the majority of the population has been eroding. Indeed, on the basis of a comprehensive global survey, it has been suggested that the Swedish case is most striking since it signals a massive shift away from the redistributive welfare-nationalist form of state in a neo-liberal direction (Steinmo 1993). As noted, in the 1980s this has also gone with an emphasis on the restructuring of the state through the tactics of marketization and privatization. Governments have had to pay increased attention to collecting tax revenues and raising cash through privatization in an age where the ideology (but not the reality) of the balanced budget has come to prevail as a form of economic rhetoric. Such developments have allowed companies to allocate debt and investment strategies according to varying state policies.

In sum, governments in the OECD and elsewhere have invested heavily in new technologies to create and manipulate databases for tax collection, social security, immigration, social control and criminal enforcement.[16] Thus disciplinary neo-liberalism, under conditions of increasing fiscal crisis, may tend to make aspects of civil society, and the state form, more panoptic and indeed, coercive in nature.

Indeed, neo-liberal forms of discipline are hierarchical in both the sense of social classes and in terms of inter-state politics. At the heart of the global economy there is an internationalization of authority and governance that not only involves international organizations (such as the BIS, IMF and World Bank) and transnational firms but also private consultancies and private bond-rating agencies which act, as it were, as arbiters in the supply of capital for public finance and corporate investment, partly acting as private makers of global public policy. I call this politico-economic structure and the internationalization of authority that it entails, the G7 nexus. It tends to be represented in everyday political discourse and the mass media as an abstract, hyper-rational and largely uncontested set of social forces and processes. A technocratic representation of IMF surveillance and conditionality reinforces this, epistemologically and ideologically (see Chapter 9).

Discussing the bond-raters and allocation mechanisms in the capital markets, Timothy J. Sinclair notes that, 'more abstract investment standards will establish greater potential for ties between domestic and

---

16. On the privatization of crime control and incarceration, see Christie (1993).

foreign interests ... [perhaps] reinforcing the impression that investment is a neutral technical activity, rather than a struggle for resources between competing societal interests' (Sinclair 1994). Indeed in 1995, following the Mexican financial crisis, a draconian economic adjustment – indeed a 'shock therapy' programme – was undertaken, under US, IMF and World Bank supervision, provoking the worst Mexican recession since the 1930s and a massive rise in unemployment and social misery. The USA, the IMF and a less-than-unanimous G7 tended to represent the package as the only way in which Mexico could repair its tattered credit-rating and restore its credibility with foreign investors. This representation was also used later to justify the attempt by the G7 nations to increase the surveillance and economic veto power of the IMF with respect to its indebted Third World membership.

Neo-liberal contradictions and the movement of history

Neo-liberal forms of rationality are largely instrumental, concerned with finding the best means to achieve calculated ends. For neo-liberals, primary motivations are understood in a possessively individualistic framework. Motivation is provided by fear and greed, reflected in the drive to acquire more security and more goods. Yet any significant attempt to widen this pattern of motivation would entail intensification of existing accumulation and consumption patterns, tending to deplete or to destroy the eco-structures of the planet, making everyone less secure and perhaps more vulnerable to disease (even the powerful). Thus, if North American patterns of accumulation and consumption were to be significantly extended, for example to China, the despoliation of the global eco-structure would be virtually assured. Even so, the central ideological message and social myth of neo-liberalism is that such a possibility is both desirable and attainable for all: in so far as limitations are recognized this is at best through a redefinition of the concept of 'sustainable development' so as to make it consistent with the continuation of existing patterns of accumulation and consumption (Commission on Global Governance 1995).

Whilst existing patterns of consumption, have a more-or-less exclusive quality depending on the form and place of consumption, their very existence requires that public goods be provided locally and globally so as to underpin production, consumption and exchange processes. Governments throughout the world are required to regulate and to compensate for social, economic and ecological problems attendant upon existing patterns of consumption and production. This means the state must find ways to sustain the tax base and to police and regulate the market society. This may prove difficult when prevailing economic ideology and the organization of the world economy validate, on the one hand, cuts in public expenditure and reducing the scope of state action, and, on the other, a burgeoning black or informal economy and a tendency for organized criminal syndicates to grow in strength.[17] Nevertheless, as new constitutionalist arrangements suggest, capital depends on national and global public goods provision to extract surplus globally.

Therefore, the logic of neo-liberalism is contradictory: it promotes global economic integration (and hence the need for global public goods) but also generates depletion of resources and the environment as well as undermining the traditional tax base and the capacity to provide public goods. Indeed, neo-classical economic thinking that lies at the heart of neo-liberal discourse tends to ignore, with impunity, ecological constraints such as the laws of thermodynamics (Altvater 1993). Moreover, neo-liberal macroeconomic policies, aligned to the ideology of the competition state, may generate more conflict in inter-state dynamics in ways that may prolong economic stagnation for the vast majority of the world's population, through, for example, competitive austerity and beggar-thy-neighbour currency depreciation (Gill 1992).

According to Walter Benjamin, within myth the passage of time takes the form of predestination, such that human control is denied (Buck-Morss 1989). Thus the operation of the neo-liberal myth of progress in modernist capitalism is intended implicitly to engender a fatalism that denies the construction of alternatives to the prevailing order, and thus, negates the idea that history is made by collective human action. Whilst it might be argued that the generation of such a myth is central to the hegemony of capital, we might recast it in Polanyian terms: neo-liberalism holds out the reified prospect of a 'stark utopia'. As Adam Smith intimated in *The Theory of Moral Sentiments*, and as Polanyi pointed out in *The Great Transformation*, a pure market system is a utopian abstraction and any attempt to construct it fully would require an immensely authoritarian application of political power through the state. This would raise doubts about the viability of a minimal or 'night-watchman' state, as portrayed in liberal ideology. Indeed, it can be shown that many of the neo-liberal forms of state have been authoritarian. In some cases this has involved considerable coercive power to destroy opposition or eliminate the

17. The tax-evading 'informal sector' might be redefined to include all agents who evade taxes, e.g. transnational firms through transfer pricing and those that place funds in offshore tax havens.

possibility of a third way: such as in Chile in 1973 (see Chapter 4) or in post-communist Eastern Europe.

Restructuring along market-driven lines tends to generate a deepening of social inequality, a rise in rates and intensity of exploitation of labour, growth in social polarization, gender inequality, a widespread sense of social and economic insecurity, and, not least, pervasive disenchantment with conventional political practice. Such a situation may also open the door to the appeals of extremist political movements, whilst more broadly giving rise to resistance and counter-mobilization. Indeed, in the context of the growing salience of biological discourses concerning social life, one might suggest there may be a social Darwinist dimension to the neo-liberal world order. This proposition is supported by evidence of the renaissance of fascism and atavistic forms of nationalism.

Thus, whilst the restructuring of forms of state along neo-liberal lines has apparently accelerated in recent years there are indications that remaking state and society along these lines lacks moral credibility, authority and legitimacy. This is partly because the rule and the burdens of market forces are most frequently imposed hierarchically on the weaker states and social actors whilst the more powerful receive tax write-offs, state subsidies and other prerogatives. Indeed, one should be careful not to overstate the degree to which this represents the universalization of a new form of world order. Indeed, the very existence of neo-liberal structural adjustment programmes of the World Bank and IMF stabilization measures shows that economic liberalization has a very long way to go before it can be considered the new development paradigm for the majority of the world's population.

Indeed, such policies are contested within the ranks of the G7, and the conflicts between the different models of capitalist development this entails can be expected to continue. One reason for G7 conflicts is that the socio-economic systems of Germany and Japan are less attuned to pure market forces. For example, in Japan, important political forces seem to have the view that the very operation of capitalist market forces depends upon their restraint, and on the maintenance of traditional systems of obligations and institutions that cause people to behave *as if* they respect the law and accept not only the contractual but also the customary nature of market transactions (Hirsch 1976).

Thus, we should not conflate propaganda with history. History has not 'ended' and alternatives are created politically. Thus Polanyi argued that a 'double movement' of (free) economy and (self-protection of) social and political forces operated to configure global politics in the 1930s (Polanyi 1975). In various ways the New Deal, fascism and Nazism, and populist movements of left and right all reflected opposition to global *laissez faire* and the power of financial capital. For Gramsci, the 1930s involved the death throes of the old order, and the struggle of a new order to be born. By analogy, one can suggest that today we may be in, or entering into, a period of transformation that certainly manifests many morbid symptoms. The coming years will probably involve a substantial intensification of political conflict. It seems likely that this will incorporate the contradictory political tendencies associated with, on the one hand, democratic and progressive forces, and, on the other, the growing forces of reaction, such as the resurgence of fascism and certain forms of fundamentalist politics or criminal elements in world politics. Indeed, a new double movement would be different in character than that of the 1930s not least because its concerns would be more global and wide-ranging in nature, and might include nuclearism, the proliferation of conventional weapons, ecology, gender questions, the globalization of organized crime, re-regulation of new global information and financial grids.

Put differently, there is a growing contradiction between the tendency towards the universality of capital in the neo-liberal form and the particularity of the legitimation and enforcement of its key exploitative relations by the state. Whereas capital tends towards universality, it cannot operate outside or beyond the political context, and involves planning, legitimation and the use of coercive capacities of the state. This forms the key substantive problem for a theory of International Relations, at least as seen from a historical materialist perspective. In this context, one of the main tasks of Political Economy today is to understand and theorize the possibilities for the transformation of these dimensions of world order, in the context of consciousness, culture and material life.

This chapter has highlighted some of the terrain of struggle that will configure the politics of the emerging world order, which it has defined as a politics of *supremacy* rather than hegemony. It can also be read as part of a research agenda on the material and mental limits, contradictions and political opportunities for counter-supremacist forces that seek to redefine questions of International Relations by drawing on critical perspectives on epistemology, ontology, theory and practice, by highlighting the contestability of and contradictions in the practice of neo-liberal discourse. The chapter may contribute to a wider emancipatory project that seeks to use new forms and modes of knowledge to transcend the dominant economism and reductionism of our time and to contribute to the possibility for new intersubjectivities and intellectual and material networks. The motivation for this is that a critical and historicist reading of present trends suggests that, in the absence of major changes in lifestyle, consumption patterns and public goods provisions, the current configuration of world order and neo-liberal forms of global governance is unsustainable.

Finally, this chapter has posed the implicit question whether the phrase 'market civilization' is an oxymoron, in so far as the concept of civilization implies not only a pattern of society, but also an active historical process that fosters a more humanized, literate and civil way of life, involving social well-being on a broad and inclusive basis. Looking beyond the confines of this short chapter, that can only scratch at the surface of a huge and complex set of questions and problems, the key world order problem for the future might be said to involve the creation of a peaceful and tolerant co-existence between differentiated forms of civilization, in ways that provide material and political conditions of high quality. This requires effort to redress the vast inequalities of the present age and a double democratization of forms of state and civil society in both global and local dimensions of political life.

8
The Geopolitics of the Asian Crisis

This short chapter is a commentary on the world's worst economic crisis since the 1930s. Millions were impoverished, whilst much of the debt of private investors was socialized through government and IMF-led bailouts. However, largely overlooked at the time was how financial and economic crises have a strategic, geopolitical aspect. This aspect can be understood partly in terms of rival projects of capitalist development. Such projects involve the regional and global articulation of ideology, international organizations, state power, and capital.

At issue, as in earlier crises of restructuring in Latin America and in the former East Bloc in the 1980s and early 1990s were two strategic responses to the reshaping of conditions for accumulation, including ownership and control patterns. The first was a long-term Marshall Plan-like regional approach, linked to an Asian Monetary Fund proposal that allowed some national policy-making autonomy. This strategy was championed by Japan and supported by some of the other Asian governments. It concerned 'stakeholder' governance of companies and socially acceptable workouts in the management of bankruptcies. A second approach involved rapid macroeconomic stabilization with fiscal austerity ('shock therapy'), the usual formula associated with the so-called 'Washington consensus'. This formula also entailed market-based restructuring based on 'shareholder' corporate governance. In this approach, in a situation of bankruptcy, owners make all key decisions, if need be with little or no reference to the impact on workers and communities. The US Treasury and financial interests as well as elements of European capital opted for the latter approach, since it allowed opportunities for greater penetration of the region by foreign capital.

Crisis, danger and opportunity

The Chinese character for 'crisis' combines the ideas of danger and opportunity. In the span of about one year, a regional economic 'miracle', with its promise of continued high economic growth and opportunity for all, was transformed into a severe regional, and potentially global, economic collapse. It has seriously endangered the livelihood of millions of people, causing untold misery and suffering.

The Asian economic crisis has not been simply a matter of movements in the global markets. Geopolitical factors have also been at work. This chapter will consider the ways in which the crisis has been linked to the reassertion of US strategic power and supremacy in the region, through the increasing internationalization of capital. The East Asian crisis shows how, in the so-called new era of 'globalization', there is intense inter-state conflict over the form and direction of regional and global patterns of capitalist development. Central to US strategy is the imposition of a specific neo-liberal model of restructuring. In the context of recent crises, state-directed and controlled forms of political economy have been, and are being, pressured to liberalize. This general pattern can be identified not only in the recent developments in Asia, but also in the restructuring of Latin America following the debt crisis of the early 1980s, and in strategies to transform the communist-ruled states of Eastern Europe and the former Soviet Union in the early 1990s.

Thus, the East Asian crisis represents the third phase of a longer process involving the reassertion of US strategic dominance. So on one level, the crisis is that of an authoritarian state-directed capitalism that blocks a specific type of internationalization of capital. The US aim is a global free enterprise system, which allows large institutional investors and giant transnational corporations to gain greater control over future profit-flows in the region, insuring freer labour markets, so that capital can better exploit labour.

This scenario requires governments in the region to continue to act, and actually be able, to maintain political order, because the process of structural adjustment is, and will continue to be, a wrenching one. Whether these governments will succeed remains to be seen. It is in this context – despite the obvious dangers of repression in a region characterized by authoritarian and dictatorial governments – that the crisis is opening up opportunities for new political forces to organize further. It also allows for the possibility of alternative forms of development based, for example, on concepts of human advancement and democratization of the state and the economy.

The 'usual suspects' and the imposition of neo-liberalism

As in the Latin American and Eastern European cases, when crises emerged, there was a debate among the G7 nations (the advanced capitalist countries: Britain, Canada, France, Germany, Italy, Japan and the United States) about strategic responses. Ideology has played a major part in this debate, which has been dominated by strategists of the liberal approach. I call these strategists the 'usual suspects' – as in the phrase from the movie *Casablanca*, in which the French police inspector would routinely order his policemen to 'round up the usual suspects' when a crime had been committed, ostensibly so they would report to the occupying Nazi authorities.[1]

In the debate over East Asian restructuring, there is a line-up of experts who are regularly wheeled out whenever a crisis occurs. At least in the mass media and politics of the West, these usual suspects advocate a liberal framework for the internationalization of capital. They are invariably drawn from the IMF, the US Treasury and Federal Reserve, Wall Street, Ivy League universities, think tanks, mega-corporations, and the governments of North Atlantic nations.[2] All of the usual suspects advocate some form of structural adjustment, although there is some debate about the nature and scope of the role of the IMF in this process. What this effectively does – its negative ideological function – is to present the question as if there is no alternative to the orthodoxy of Wall Street and the so-called Washington consensus. The positive dimension of this ideology is that it gives identity and political direction to the processes of power, class formation, and restructuring.

Thus, the usual suspects have persistently criticized the East Asian model for giving unfair advantage to local (as opposed to foreign) firms, because East Asian firms obtain cheaper, state-subsidized supplies of capital while foreign firms are denied full market access. Some of the usual suspects have argued that the crisis is caused partly by too much overseas borrowing (especially of short-term funds) and bad investments linked not only to state-subsidized crony capitalism, but also to inadequately supervised and poorly regulated banking systems. Some of what they argue is true, of course, as the huge pyramids of bad debts in various countries indicate.[3]

1. At the end of the movie, the 'usual suspects' were rounded up by the Inspector to divert the attention of the Nazis away from leaders of the Resistance as they escaped from Casablanca.
2. Wider 'public' and 'private' efforts to construct a consensus commensurate with the geopolitical and economic interests of the world's largest corporations come together in forums like the Trilateral Commission and the World Economic Forum (see Chapter 9).
3. Debt defaults, like that of Russia in 1998, seem increasingly likely, despite the massive IMF-led bailouts. Total exposure of banks that reported to the Bank for International Settlements in 1998, for developing Asia, Latin America, and Eastern Europe, was approximately $800 billion; Russia owed about $140 billion in hard-currency debt; Brazil and China owed approximately $60–70 billion

For the usual suspects, however, the solution to the current crisis is self-evident: it involves a shift away from state capitalism toward a free market system based on investor interests and the maximization of shareholder value. They claim this system is more efficient. What they fail to emphasize is how deregulation, privatization and liberalization are a means of strengthening a particular set of class interests, principally the power of private investors. Structural adjustment allows for a redistribution of claims on future profit-flows that enable foreign capital to gain power and control over regional development patterns.

Thus, under conditions of crisis (when loans are required, to deal with balance of payments difficulties or a wider financial crisis), the usual suspects press the US government (and thus the IMF and World Bank), to deal with what are euphemistically called 'structural rigidities' on a 'case-by-case basis'; then they press for 'more fully developed securities markets' (so they are allowed to buy local assets and raise capital in those markets), arms-length bankruptcy laws (so that assets can be bought cheaply in distress and workers can be laid off), and the elimination of restrictions on insider influence and what they call 'crony capitalism' (so that foreign investors receive equal treatment).

Another issue the usual suspects rarely talk about – at least publicly – is the relationship between structural adjustment and fundamental questions of power and geopolitical strategy – that is, how the Asian crisis has been a means for the USA to strengthen its strategic interests worldwide.

Mystification and the East Asian model

There is much mystification about the nature of the regional political economy. In fact, despite what the usual suspects claim, there is no single East Asian model but a complex of national and regional development practices, developed in a particular geopolitical context. Between 1945 and the early 1990s, this context involved decolonization, the Cold War in Asia and, later, the growing influence of Japanese capital on export-led regional development. (By the 1990s, Asian exports accounted for roughly 30 per cent of GDP, making Asia the world's most export-dependent region.) Economic development generally took place under dictatorial or authoritarian governments. Nevertheless, not much

---

each; Korea nearly $100 billion in bank debt. European banks had much the largest exposure to emerging market debts. More generally, the 'identifiable debts at risk in the world [that is, risk of default] could easily total $1 trillion', including $500 billion in Japan and $250 billion in China (Group 1998: 16–17).

of the capital that flowed into the East Asian region from the West after World War II involved a large shift in the control over industrial structures, which allowed the state and local capitalists to forge a 'catch up' strategy of latecomer industrialization.

The post-1945 industrial and export-led expansions were associated with Cold War structures and were state-directed and -controlled. The Korean and Vietnam Wars each gave an economic boost to many of the nations in the region. Also, the anticommunist East Asian Newly Industrialized Countries (NICs) were supported by the USA, and dictatorships and authoritarian regimes, with strong militaries and secret police forces, were installed to sustain anticommunism. These regimes maintained local political conditions that allowed for the security of US military bases. Thailand also provided bases for 'rest and relaxation' for US troops – that is, the origins of today's regional sex trade.

In return, the USA and, more reluctantly, its Western European allies provided access to their markets, again partly for geopolitical reasons. Over time, this allowed for rapid industrialization in the region – or what some have called 'dependent capitalist development'. In this way, the political and class structures of each state interconnected around the central axes of primarily US, and secondarily Japanese power in this diverse region.

So what is changing in East Asia? As noted, what is at issue is not the presence or supply of foreign capital and power in the region as such, but a change in the form of that power, toward a more market-based system, or a shift from one pattern of capitalist development to another.

Leaving to one side the political differences between Anglo-American and state capitalist models (for example, the lack of democracy and individual freedoms in much of East Asia), both are 'capitalist' in the sense that each system is premised on the maximization of profit-flows over time. However, the differences between the two become apparent in conditions of crisis and restructuring, or what the IMF calls 'adjustment'. In situations of crisis, the Anglo-American financial markets tend to shape the economic response in the USA and the United Kingdom. They are characterized by what has been called a 'capital-market' system, sometimes known as a 'fluid' capital system (Zysman 1983). This means that the supply of capital for investment is provided mainly by stock and bond markets, and this in turn reflects the interests of shareholders or investors: the private property owners call the shots. In such a case, if a company fails, it is made bankrupt; workers are immediately unemployed, and the firm is liquidated.

By contrast, the Japanese and East Asian financial systems tend to be 'credit-based', or dedicated capital systems. Historically – in Japan and in the East Asian NICs – these have tended to be bank-centred, highly concentrated, and state-directed systems. In a crisis, the government generally has tended to negotiate adjustments amongst affected groups ('stakeholders') within society, including workers. This is also largely true in Germany. Here, the government, in conjunction with business networks and groups (e.g. Japanese *keiretsu*, South Korean *chaebol*), historically has organized a response to economic crises (like the oil crises of the 1970s) that is based on the general socialization of risk and informal workouts, with the help of business networks.

The restructuring of East Asia and the new geopolitics of capital

The Japanese and East Asian systems had been slowly moving in a liberal direction during the early 1990s, of course, but the key turning points (which accelerated liberalization) were probably 1994, when the Chinese renminbi was massively devalued to promote its intensive-intensive exports, and 1995, when the Japanese yen began to depreciate against the dollar.[4] This began to put pressure on exchange rates in the region. One reason for this was that when China devalued, it undercut rival Asian manufacturers in export markets like the USA, exposing the region's over-investment. (Investment levels were massively higher than anywhere else in the world.)[5] This immediately turned much of its production platform into surplus capacity – that is, it revealed chronic overproduction. At the same time, vast sums had been borrowed abroad, some of which were used to finance real estate and other high-risk forms of investment. That is, a business mentality more fully in tune with the gambling or casino aspect of capitalism had begun to take hold in the region. However, the economic dimension of the crisis was and is structural: it is fundamentally a problem of excess supply, or overproduction.[6]

4. The renminbi devalued by 50 per cent in 1994 and the yen depreciated by 50 per cent after mid-1995 (Group 1998: 4).
5. By the mid-1990s, investment spending accounted for an astonishing 40 per cent of GDP for the emerging Asian economies and, in 1996, reached 35 per cent for Asia as a whole. (The figure for the rest of the world was roughly consistent between 1980 and 1998 at around 24 per cent of GDP.) This led to excess capacity, increased competition, and a drop in rates of return, contributing to the build-up of problem loans for the banks in the region (Group 1998: 3–4; Chart 1).
6. For an account that links the problem of overcapacity in East Asia to overcapacity throughout the world, as well as to threats of global deflation and the potential for depression, see Tabb (1998).

When the crisis broke, under these conditions, the IMF moved in, not only to deal with questions of macroeconomic restructuring and exchange rates, but also to institute deeper structural reforms. As it had in Mexico in 1994 and 1995, the IMF assured foreign investors and banks that their debts would be repaid, and it moved to roll over short-term debt into long-term, compelling various governments in effect to socialize private debts. The fund also sought to break up the cartels, privatize or dismantle state-owned enterprises, create flexible labour markets (allowing workers to be fired more easily), and eliminate food subsidies in places like Indonesia, where per capita incomes have been halved to around $150, and where millions of farmers faced starvation because of drought.[7]

The socialization of private debts to foreign investors, accompanied by removal of food subsidies to the poorest, shows the limits of the commitment to pure free-market policies when the interests of Western capital are endangered. It also illustrates the class bias of the process as a whole.

So how does this process of 'economic' restructuring relate to the strategic issues facing the region? This question can be answered best by looking at the Japanese government's failure to create an Asian Monetary Fund (AMF) to deal with the economic crisis.

After the debt crisis in the early 1980s, the IMF subjected more than sixty countries to austerity measures under strict conditionality. In this way, liberal adjustment measures became relatively universal. In the 1990s, similar programmes were applied in Eastern Europe and the former Soviet Union. In the East Asian crisis, the IMF has applied harsh conditionality once again.

Of course, it is well known that it was the US Treasury that blocked Japanese proposals to create the AMF. The USA wanted to ensure that the international rescue operation was run on US lines. As the *Financial Times* put it on 15 January 1998, 'there was a dangerous moment before the Korean collapse, when the momentum was building in Asia behind a Japanese-led plan for a special regional bailout fund ... Mr. Summers [Deputy Secretary of the Treasury in the Clinton Administration] managed to kill off the proposal and leave the IMF at the forefront of the bailouts – the critical element of the US approach.'[8]

---

7. On some of these issues with special reference to Thailand, South Korea and Indonesia, as well as an insightful overview of the process as a whole, see Bernard (1999).
8. *Financial Times*, 15 December 1998.

What was significant about the Japanese plan was that it would have imposed a gentler form of adjustment in the region, while consolidating Japanese political influence. This was at a time when the relationship between Japan and the USA was under pressure. This was in part because of the chronically weak condition of the Japanese economy, as well as a result of the continued resistance of Japanese leaders to fully open up their society to deeper penetration by US capital.

The blocking of the AMF is analogous to the struggles over the future direction of Europe when communist rule collapsed in the late 1980s. For example, West Germany, because of its close economic links with and geopolitical proximity to Eastern Europe and the Soviet Union, proposed a gradual programme of reforms to make the former communist-ruled states into capitalist political economies. This proposal was a type of long-term Marshall Plan approach, which would have cemented the economic and political interests of Western Europe and Eastern Europe. The German plan contrasted with the strategy of rapid transformation or 'shock therapy' associated with Anglo-American proposals. In other words, there was a struggle over how these societies would be reintegrated into both regional and global capitalism. The process was eventually dominated by the Anglo-American approach, reflected in the policies of the IMF, the World Bank and the new European Bank for Reconstruction and Development.

What was at issue, in a geopolitical sense, was the prevention of a restructuring that would allow greater regional political cohesion (under a German leadership that promotes a form of 'stakeholder' as opposed to 'shareholder' capitalism), and thus would limit the prospect of European regionalisation developing beyond US control. These reform measures were therefore accompanied by NATO enlargement, so that the military and strategic context would continue to be under the control of an alliance structure dominated by the USA.

Another historical example is significant. In the Latin American debt crisis of the 1980s, a transnational political coalition which included the powerful G7 governments (led by the USA), international financial institutions, large banks and institutional investors in alliance with local political leaders, was able to force restructuring on these societies. This occurred in part so that these societies' debts would be repaid, and in part so that their markets and social structures would be open to exploitation by foreign capital. One universal result of these policies was a rapid widening of social and economic inequality in already extremely unequal societies. Greater external dominance was also a consequence.

Thus, in the context of the Asian regional crisis, the USA strengthened political and military links with China, partly as a means to influence

Chinese power, and partly to offset the potential for a Japan-centred regional bloc that might, like the European Union, create more autonomy in relation to the USA – a regional bloc that might, for example, eventually create its own currency as a rival to the dollar. However, particularly in the context of the humiliation Japan suffered in the Gulf War of 1991 (when it was forced, like Germany, to pay a huge financial tribute to support the US war effort), the defeat of the Asian Monetary Fund proposal showed once again the enormous subordination of Japan to US power. Thus the regional geopolitical situation now involves a strong element of realpolitik between the capitalist and communist superpowers: China increasingly needs US markets and supplies of high-technology equipment and weapons systems, the USA needs China to help to contain Japanese power and to prevent a form of regionalization that can threaten US globalism.

Conclusion

In the East Asian crisis, while many of the economic and social problems were clearly indigenous, an opportunity arose for the power of the USA and Western capital to be brutally exerted in the region. It is too early to know precisely how the political situation will develop. But at least now we know that the crisis is producing political contradictions because of, first, its impact on authoritarian governments (in so far as it undermines dictatorship) and second, its effects on the working classes and peasants of the region. While it creates demands for alternatives, it undermines the potential for real democracy as workers suffer.

The political situation is complex and the reactions to neo-liberal globalization come from both right and left. The political right in the region (Malaysia, for example) has used capital controls. The Japanese government has also actively considered controls. In mid-December 1998, the Japanese government revived the AMF proposal, but it remains to be seen whether the USA will once again block a regional effort.[9] Instead, intense Japanese and regional frustration with the USA was reflected on 22 January 1999, when the key official in the Japanese finance ministry, Eisuke Sakakibara (known in global financial circles as 'Mr. Yen'), delivered a speech entitled 'The End of Market Fundamentalism'.[10] Sakakibara cited Keynes and Polanyi in his indictment of the usual suspects and their

---

9. *Financial Times*, 16 December 1998. In fact, such regional proposals have not borne fruit.
10. Sakakibara's paper was presented at the Foreign Correspondents' Club, Tokyo, on 22 January 1999. I am grateful to John Mage for this reference.

Anglo-American, neo-classical approach to restructuring. So whether the USA will be able to sustain its regional dominance and block the Japanese challenge (or heresy) may turn out to be very much an open question. Others, on the left, have proposed taxes to regulate international capital mobility. In some contexts, remobilized labour movements and left-wing parties have started to co-operate with domestic capitalists to resist structural adjustment and austerity. In other words, they have opted implicitly for a return to a reformed state capitalism.

Thus the regional collapse is provoking some rethinking about alternative forms of development – considerations that were not seen as crucial in the hyper-materialist era of the 'miracle', when growth rates were rapid, incomes were increasing, and few leaders worried about democratization, the ecological and social costs of development, or the conditions of workers and peasants. Indeed, a fundamentally different alternative would have to involve democratization of the state and the economy. It would also presuppose some solution to the debt bondage that has gripped much of the world in the 1980s and 1990s (in Latin America, for example). This requires a challenge to the national and international structures of power. It also involves rounding up the usual suspects and informing them that they are no longer needed.[11]

11. For an account that stresses the emergence of 'An Asian Model of Resistance' linked to massive mobilization of workers, including increasing numbers of women workers, as well as social movements throughout the region, see McNally (1998). Bernard (1999) and McNally stress the importance of the massive ecological damage to the region and its role in forging resistance to neo-liberal globalization.

Part III

Global Transformation and Political Agency

Part II of this volume has shown how globalization involves a hierarchy of inter-state power with the USA at its apex, along with its G7 partners, and an increasingly global system of political economy that serves to redistribute social power and intensify inequality. The global political economy has both consensual and coercive mechanisms that serve to institutionalize the power of capital through extended property rights, legal and constitutional means – underwritten in part by the extended coercive capacity of the USA and its allies. Thus global restructuring has been accompanied by growing social polarization, human insecurity and widespread social dislocation.

Part III is therefore concerned with questions of political agency in the context of intensified globalization, and the limits to such agency that may be posed by the new relations of force in the early twenty-first century. The chapters in this part pay attention to how, on the one hand, there are new technologies of organized violence, extended surveillance and incarceration (disciplinary power) and, on the other hand, how new forms of global political innovation and collective action have nevertheless emerged to begin to pose alternatives to disciplinary neo-liberalism (often by using the very same technologies of global communication for organizational and persuasive purposes).

Marx once wrote that the new society is born, dialectically, within the womb of the old. For Marx a new form of society succeeding capitalism would involve collective forms of ownership and a high degree of participatory democracy. However, as Gramsci pointed out, in the struggle between the new and the old there may arise many 'morbid symptoms'. Indeed, there is nothing inherently inevitable about historical transformations, and Chapter 9 represents an attempt to theorize some of the movements and contradictions of political forces in the immediate aftermath of the collapse of communist rule in Eastern Europe and the former USSR. It argues that from the 1970s on there was a great transformation in not only the communist, but also the capitalist world, linked to the unravelling of post-World War II social hegemonies and political settlements. Changes were accelerated by the spatial expansion of market forces and an increase in the power of capital.

This contradictory but transformative process was partly associated with a directive element in globalizing capitalism: the 'globalizing elites'. This term refers to the political leaders and organic intellectuals associated with the internationally oriented fractions of capital (and some elements of privileged organized labour) and linked to the dominant public and private institutions of an embryonic global political and civil society. 'Globalizing elites' develop strategy and make policy recommendations to extend globalization as a political and historical project. Globalizing elites are formed politically at the intersection of national and transnational class and political formation drawn principally from the G7 and other OECD nations, although elements from much of the rest of the world are incorporated. Such transnational constellations are reflected in public-private forums such as that of Davos (World Economic Forum) and the wider 'G7 nexus', acting, as it were, as a type of loosely structured transnational political party or 'International' for capital.

However, the transnationalization of authority associated with the spread of capitalist social relations and accumulation strategies is only in an early form. This partly explains why global governance to sustain globalizing capitalism mainly requires powerful interventionist states, for example the US-led G7 (when Russia was added to this grouping in the mid-1990s it became the G8; however, Russian participation only relates to strictly selected military and political questions, not to fundamental questions of economic strategy). The G7 has been at the centre of the political project to constitutionalize disciplinary neo-liberalism. One reason for this use of state power concerns the effort to contain many of the contradictions involved in neo-liberal globalization, contradictions that may provide potentials and possibilities for counter-hegemonic projects. Indeed, as we have seen in Chapter 8, there is a great deal of rivalry and contestation within the ranks of the G7 states, as well as within the ranks of capital itself. There is no obvious class interest for capital-in-general. This is because in a capitalist world these forces must compete for state power, and to accumulate capital, which is their principal source of power and prestige.

At the same time, Chapter 9 offers a broader global conception of social stratification involving both a spatial as well as a structural exposition of global class formation, in ways that are similar to some of the radical geography literature. Radical geographers have increasingly discussed the ways in which space is socially constituted. In the new world order both the spatial and the structural are marked by both the contrast between centrality and marginality, as peripheries are formed in both the social and the spatial senses. Thus in global class formation beneath the capitalist class *per se* and the globalizing elites and cadres, there are also disparities between privileged, protected and unprotected workers. This is true both in the sense of their place within structures of production and accumulation, and in the literal sense of the places where they live. More generally, on a world scale there are small islands of privilege surrounded by vast human oceans of insecurity, marginalisation and poverty.

One of the most important, yet unexplored trends in the study of world order is the increasing institutionalization and exercise of surveillance. Drawing on Bentham's idea of the Panopticon, Chapter 10 seeks to highlight the dominant tendencies and contradictions in modern surveillance practices by introducing a series of hypotheses. The hypotheses are linked to capital's search for stable and predictable regimes of accumulation that minimize risk and uncertainty while facilitating present and future profit flows. This search to reduce uncertainty involves regimes of discipline and normalization of social and political subjects, so that they become more individualist, consumerist and politically passive.

Thus Chapter 10 looks at both social and geopolitical forms of power in the modern world, and how these are connected to the control of information flows and their links to extended surveillance power. Surveillance power is contrasted with some of the other key aspects of power in modernity, the power of collective action and the power of resistance. Thus chapter 10 helps us to sketch the real basis for the 'relations of force' at the start of the new millennium, and how these relations are reconfigured through the development of new apparatuses of organized violence and incarceration. New apparatuses are connected to a framework of ongoing social, economic and political surveillance that is built into the transactional and communication aspects of everyday life that leave traces (for example the use of credit cards, or surfing the Internet). However, although the state plays a central role in the process of information gathering, private firms are also intensifying efforts to collect and categorize information on consumers and their workers for the express purpose of generating profit and avoiding loss. In this context, panoptic practices are 'unequal in their effects' and never neutral in class-based societies. Thus modern panoptic practices have emerged in the context of 'crises of social reproduction' discussed by feminist political economy and the new apparatuses of surveillance are part of the intensified and more coercive forms of flexible accumulation that have created a 'double burden' for most women who work both in the home and as wage-labour in the formal and informal sectors of the global political economy.

Within this context there is geopolitical rivalry over the new technologies of surveillance and between states, with many governments seeking to resist American technological penetration. At the same time, Chapter 10 highlights the ongoing importance of political surveillance, not just of violent extremists, but also of peaceful groups seeking more democratic control. For example, prior to the suicide attacks on the USA of 11 September 2001, important aspects of the US security apparatus were in the process of being reconfigured to produce, in the Pentagon's inimitable jargon, 'full spectrum dominance': an extended, planetary form of extended surveillance designed to cope with new challenges to US security, including threats from new political forces.

Although new security structures seek to develop extended monitoring of the so-called anti-globalization movements, there is no such thing as an all-seeing Orwellian eye of power. Indeed, surveillance can be put to more democratic purposes. It can be used for planning, for monitoring changes in the ecosphere, and information structures could be used to produce a more equitable and sustainable social order. With this in mind Chapter 10 concludes by offering the reader some suggestions for future research on panopticism and the constitution of world order.

As becomes clear in Chapter 11, many progressive forces are often characterized, wrongly, as 'anti-globalization'. Indeed what most of these forces seem to want is a form of social justice and a more humane, better regulated and more democratically responsive form of globalization, not its elimination. By contrast the 1990s have seen the proliferation of reactionary, nationalist, fundamentalist and conservative forces that are opposed not only to both projects of globalization noted above but also to the frameworks of modernity/post-modernity. These anti-modernist forces often espouse pre-modern conceptions of social and political order and in particular, many of them reject and oppose what they perceive as an American-led globalization of culture and the political economy.

Chapter 11 mainly considers the social justice movements opposed to globalization-from-above. These forces are very broad-based throughout the world and are associated with a wide range of producers (workers and peasants), social movements (e.g. ecological, women's movements) and institutions (e.g. churches, grass-roots political organizations). Such forces are beginning to mobilize globally around shared concerns at the dislocations and contradictions associated with intensified globalisation, such as were experienced worldwide in 1997–98 during the Asian and global financial and economic crises when tens of millions were impoverished. This explains why such forces have led protests worldwide against the institutions associated with the administration of disciplinary neo-liberalism, in not only the OECD (e.g. Seattle in 1999 and Genoa in 2001) but much more frequently throughout the Third World (e.g. a series of anti-IMF riots). Indeed new forces are beginning to create forward-looking platforms and alternatives to globalization-from-above, such as at the World Social Forum that meets annually in Porto Alegre, Brazil.

The wider point therefore is that as capitalist social relations are being globalized, so too is resistance increasingly globalized. Indeed, whereas the neo-liberal globalization project is premised on a homogenization of social, cultural, political and economic forms, the collectivities challenging the new world order premise their struggles on diversity, democracy, and multiple forms and levels of participation. Indeed, this resistance is not simply negative but a positive, constitutive moment in global politics: indeed it entails transformative resistance. It should be understood as a set of social and political forces 'in movement'. Thus the neo-liberal project of the globalizing elites is opposed by rival projects we call 'globalization-from-below' (the latter involves dissenting forces from within the ranks of the elites and ruling classes).

Such forces in movement are called the Post-Modern Prince: an idea that seeks to represent the new forms of global political agency. This concept relates to Gramsci's *Modern Prince* that was modelled on the mass-based, democratic communist party. By contrast the Post-Modern Prince has, unlike the communist party, a diverse, multiple, non-hierarchical form. Although it converges around a shared sense of problems faced by peoples worldwide, it does not have a single ideology or doctrine, so it is not a conventional party as such. It is better understood in the plural, as a set of forces in movement, a kind of transnational political party of the future that combines the local and the global. In the new millennium, a key question for International Relations and global political economy will be how far and in what ways new forms of political agency are emerging to create real political alternatives and possibilities for progressive change.

9
Globalizing Elites in the Emerging World Order[1]

Global restructuring is generating increasing hierarchies of power and deepening social inequality in a process serving to both integrate and disintegrate key aspects of social life on the planet. Globalizing elites – intellectual and practical apparatuses within transnational capitalism – are at the apex of the social hierarchies that characterize the new, emerging world order.

Tendencies towards global integration and attempts to re-constitute power at the core of the world order are also bound up with tendencies towards social disintegration and chaos. Existing socio-economic structures and forms of state are mutating or are driven to collapse, in all three main categories of country. Both elites and social movements shape the historical dialectic. Thus consciousness and action, mobilization and strategy are involved. Thus an initial task is to identify 'the limits of the possible' for different groups, classes, coalitions, nations, within which, for example, forms of social reintegration can take place.

Global disintegration/integration and world order

One way to describe the present state of world order is as one of disintegration/integration. Old political, economic and social structures are under stress or breaking down and social chaos and disorder characterizes conditions in much of the world; new structures are only beginning to become perceptible. At the same time the ideas, institutions and material capabilities of the vanguard elements of the globalizing elites of contemporary capitalism are seeking to reconstruct new patterns of dominance and supremacy at the core of the system. A general

---

1. This chapter is based partly upon discussions held at Barboleusaz, Switzerland, 14–16 October 1991. Those present were Georges Abi-Saab, Robert Cox and Kees van der Pijl.

restructuring of power is occurring in a less consensual, more conflict-ridden and post-hegemonic world order.

Indeed, the collapse of the USSR has thrown into relief attempts by globalizing elites to re-constitute hegemony, under very different social conditions than those that prevailed following World War II. Here then, the collapse of the USSR is the most dramatic case of the 'descent from production into entropy'. What is meant by this phrase is a situation where a functioning economic system begins to self-destruct, partly because of its internal contradictions, and partly because of conscious choices which accelerate its road to collapse. Thus, although Soviet economic performance began to stagnate in the 1970s and 1980s, it was only in the latter part of the 1980s following Gorbachev's policies of *perestroika* (*glasnost*, or political openness, was quickly abandoned) that production began to decline and the physical capital and infrastructure of the USSR began to disintegrate, such that since 1989 the GNP of the former Soviet Union declined by over 50 per cent. Further decline and social atomization is to be predicted, particularly since existing political structures are inchoate and the pauperization of the population is accelerating. Indeed, the process in the former Soviet Union is an extreme example of key aspects of global structural change or 'global *perestroika*' (Cox 1992).

Thus, rather than being simply explicable in terms of conscious political decisions and the direct use of political power, global *perestroika* (that is the process beyond the former USSR) has produced a type of institutionalized chaos which is propelled by the restructuring of global capitalism. Of importance here are accelerating changes in production, finance and knowledge that have given rise to a relatively coherent, interrelated pattern. In this pattern there has been a cumulative if uneven rise in the structural power of internationally mobile capital, a rise that has brought with it certain limits and contradictions.

This emerging world order, then, can be contrasted with that which prevailed in the metropolitan nations in the 1950s and 1960s. From the vantage point of the early 1990s, it appears to be characterized by deepening social inequalities, economic depression for most parts of the world, and a reconfiguration of global security structures. These changes are strengthening the strong, often at the expense of the weak. The principle of distributive justice increasingly associated with this order is, to paraphrase *The Book of Matthew*: 'to him that hath shall be given, to him that hath not shall be taken away'.

In turn, certain aspects of contemporary development can be understood in terms of their deeper roots, as structures of material life. In the 1980s and 1990s, commodification and monetization of social life are extending and deepening. The current phase of transformation can be related to Braudel's concept of the *longue durée*, in so far as the structure and language of social relations is more systematically conditioned by the capitalist norms and practices that pervade the *gestes répétés* of everyday life (see Chapters 3 and 7). Tendencies towards the globalization of capitalism thus condition the limits of the possible for different agents and social movements in world order.

Historically, the form of state and the nature of economic and social regulation have varied according to the political relations and struggles between labour and capital, and the state's international position. In the post-1945 period, partly because of the development of socialism, trades unions, the gradual democratization of the liberal state, and because of the effects of World War II, the scope for capital mobility and unfettered, self-regulating markets was constrained substantially in a system premised upon state capitalist, welfare states. These forms of state, in North American and Western Europe, were products of the socio-political response to the austerity and economic depression of the 1930s. The contradictions of the inter-war period were associated with the application of 'pure liberal' orthodoxy of sound money and attempts to extend the logic of the self-regulating market at domestic and international levels.

By contrast, the post-1945 world order was politically reconstructed so as to give primacy to production over finance, and to consolidate the political centre against right- and especially left-wing forces, a struggle which intensified with the onset of the Cold War. Thus part of the social basis for the post-war hegemonic settlement (which many commentators argued existed in the 1945–70 period) was a rough balance between the demands and pressures of internationally mobile economic forces and those of domestic social welfare. Vulnerable, geographically immobile domestic groups and productive sectors were given protection that allowed time for social adjustment to demands of international competition. At the same time, the global security structure was configured primarily by two militarized alliance structures, led by the USA and USSR respectively, and a war of ideology was sustained between them.

Social structures of accumulation in the main capitalist countries rested upon Fordist production and consumption patterns, corporatism, Keynesian macroeconomic management, and a regime of very cheap energy (reflecting the subordination of the Third World) which assisted the vanguard industries (often associated with the military-industrial complex, such as arms production, oil, vehicle manufacture, aerospace, computing) in a period of unprecedented growth and prosperity in the West and Japan. Fordist production structures, albeit of a different type, also prevailed in the USSR, with heavy emphasis given in plans to military-industrial capacity and mass assembly-line production, in a Stalinist *Leviathan*.

Post-war economic liberalization in the West was partial and politically embedded in, and constrained by a consensus between labour, capital and the state. In Europe and to a lesser extent the USA this involved varied forms of state capitalism in the 'mixed' economy. Nevertheless, there were limits to state engagement in economic life in the 'Lockeian heartland' of transatlantic capitalism. The term 'Lockeian' is used here to reflect the fact that the system was premised on the existence of a vigourous and relatively self-regulating civil society (Pijl 1989). It reflected the formal separation of public and private, of state and civil society, in liberal democratic capitalist 'civil governance'. This contrasted with the mercantilist, interventionist 'Hobbesian' state form in the Soviet Union and China, and in a different way, in much of the Third World.

The international policy-making processes of the West and East differed in ways that partly reflected the two ideal-typical forms of state noted above. In the East, the USSR was dominant (and communism appeared to be unified, at least until the split with China in 1960), and the communist parties of the world tended to follow orders directly from the CPSU. In the Comecon countries, all economic and political roads led to Moscow. In the West, whilst the USA led, it did so through a less centralized process, involving a complex set of inter-state and ideological apparatuses, with ongoing bargaining over economic questions. Thus the USA and its allies built a political process to institutionalize international economic conflict in regimes and international organizations (such as the IMF, World Bank, Bank for International Settlements, OECD, UN) and in forums like the Group of 10. Crucial to this process were private, informal transnational apparatuses, such as the private international relations councils (e.g. Bilderberg) (Gill 1990: 122–42). Such 'private' councils reflected the post-1945 re-emergence of international civil society, after its relative decline in the inter-war years, partly modelled on the institutional pluralism of liberal democratic capitalism at the domestic level.

The development of international civil society had been curtailed in the 1930s with the rise of inter-capitalist and proto-Cold War rivalries, reflecting the near-collapse of international money and trade, and mass unemployment in much of the capitalist world. This was accompanied by the rise of new forms of state: for example on the right, authoritarian nationalism, fascism, Nazism, and on the left, Stalin's 'socialism-in-one-country'. Beggar-thy-neighbour economic policies of the 1930s in response to the global economic crisis were inimical to the development and extension of an international civil society of capitalist internationalism, although such an internationalism existed on a regional basis (e.g. the British-dominated sterling preference area, the empire and commonwealth; US dominance in the Americas; Japanese ascendancy in Asia), with Third World countries revolving politically and economically like satellites around their imperial planets (the republics revolved around Russia in the USSR).

In contrast to the quasi-autonomous financiers of the pre-Renaissance period, and *haute finance* in the nineteenth century, international civil society in the post-war era was less exclusive (and in some senses, less capitalist): organized labour, social democrats and members of what Kees van der Pijl calls the cadre class were included (Pijl 1989). This was because, from the 1930s onward, class interests associated with production (both labour and capital in manufacturing and extractive industries) asserted their political power so as to subordinate partly *rentier* or money capital in the making of economic and foreign policy. This process resulted in the emergence of the new forms of state noted above. The post-war settlements reflected how, with variations across countries, statist planners and productive forces pressed successfully for the creation of a national economic capacity (and policy autonomy), for the welfare state and for Keynesian macroeconomics. This included specific policies designed to inhibit the pure mobility of short-term speculative capital. The aim, in the words of the US Secretary of Treasury during the New Deal, was to make finance the 'servant' rather than the 'master' of production (Helleiner 1994). Thus, in the post-1945 period, following European and Japanese reconstruction, the public and private, national and international institutional apparatuses of capitalism sought to reconcile the economic and politico-strategic aspects of the post-war system of *pax americana*.

Liquidity for the international economy was provided by a seemingly endless supply of US dollars through its balance of payments deficits, themselves partly generated by US military expenditures overseas and by the foreign investments of US corporations. Nevertheless, the international mobility of money capital was more constrained in the Bretton Woods era than it had been in the inter-war years, at least until after 1931. The effects of the Great Depression and World War II were crucial in the (partially successful) attempts made at Bretton Woods to make international capital flows serve productive purposes and to finance directly trade and real investment in extractive industries and manufacturing.

Nevertheless, the appearance of stability in the transatlantic social structure of accumulation, and the relative coherence of the circuits of trade and investment was deceptive. Powerful forces linked to changes in the state and the internationalization of capital began to unravel the social hegemonies and politically centrist arrangements or compromises on economic and social policy.

The start of the 1970s saw the onset of a period of slower growth, higher inflation and unemployment, the recurrence and increasing severity of recessions and a growth in fiscal deficits at all levels of government (federal, regional, local). There were periodic crises for the dollar, resulting in President Nixon's decision in 1971 to decouple the dollar from gold and thus create a global dollar standard. This removed a key external constraint on US policy autonomy. However, Nixon's manoeuvre shocked the USA's key allies, who interpreted it as a shift towards economic nationalism and a return to 'beggar-thy-neighbour' economic policies. However, a key reason for the change in policy – apart from a perception of a decline in the competitiveness of US industries and the fact of rising unemployment – was that capital had found ways to evade the capital and exchange controls imposed during the Bretton Woods era. This was especially after convertibility of currencies was restored in Europe in 1958, when the EEC was created. Capital mobility and growing payments imbalances between the major economies undermined the sustainability of the system of fixed exchange rates.

Offshore financial markets began to grow rapidly during the 1960s. By the end of the 1970s these markets already constituted a vast pool of money capital, beyond the direct control of any one state. The Euromarkets were crucial in financing the spread of transnational companies during the 1960s, and in the 1970s, and they supplied funds to all categories of government for payments financing following the oil price 'shocks'.

Twin processes of globalization and economic liberalization quickened in the 1970s, with the shift in US monetary policy of 1979–80 a key catalyst for their acceleration. The US Federal Reserve raised real interest rates to unprecedented levels (breaking usury laws in some US states) to prevent a massive depreciation of the dollar. This precipitated the deepest global recession since the 1930s. Soon afterward, the US government combined very tight monetary policy with a Keynesian fiscal expansion, producing soaring budget deficits (partly caused by a military build-up aimed in large part at undermining the Soviet economy by intensifying the superpower arms race).

Reaganomics had the effect of sucking the bulk of the world's surplus savings into the US economy, forcing other countries to deflate: their interest rates rose to high levels to prevent even greater capital outflows to the USA. Part of the reason for this was structural: the integrated financial markets came to constitute a massive disciplinary force field, not only on firms but also on the policy autonomy of states. Thus international financial constraints forced the UK to go the IMF for a loan in 1976 (a move which split the ruling Labour Party and set the economic stage for Thatcherism), and anticipatory capital flight undermined Mitterrand's attempt at 'Keynesianism-in-one-country' economic expansion in France in the early 1980s.[2]

The monetarist deflations of the early 1980s meant globalization coincided with slower growth and recession, and for many governments growing indebtedness (much of which was caused by fiscal crisis at local, regional and federal levels of government and by higher interest rates on debt servicing). Driven by the imperatives of economic competition and inter-state rivalry this accelerated restructuring in a neo-liberal direction. The debt crisis of the 1980s was a part of a general fiscal crisis, as well as a crisis of development. The mechanisms through which the crisis was transmitted internationally were primarily financial. In the 1970s because of the glut of petrodollars recycled through the Euromarkets, Third World countries were able to borrow at very low real rates of interest (in some cases these were negative). In the early 1980s, their terms of trade deteriorated and recession lowered demand for their exports. Third World states were faced with much larger interest bills. Costs of repaying their debts went up at the very moment when their capacity to repay had declined. This set the stage for IMF and World Bank policies of 'structural adjustment'.[3]

2. The first experiment with market monetarism was in Chile, under the guidance of the so-called 'Chicago boys' following the military coup that installed Pinochet on 11 September 1973 (see Chapter 4).
3. Even the USA, as the world's biggest debtor (the Federal Government's cumulative debt at the start of 1992 was approximately $4 trillion) came to feel the constraints of the global financial system. For example, in the late 1980s, in the midst of recession, the USA was unable to finance its war effort in the Gulf by the means it had used in the 1960s. To finance the war in Vietnam, President Johnson decided to print more dollars, forcing others to hold IOUs in a depreciating currency, thus imposing an inflation tax on the rest of the world. In 1991 the USA was forced by its macroeconomic situation to press other countries for contributions to the so-called Defense Co-operation Account at the Treasury to pay its costs in the Gulf War. By raising interest rates to finance a war loan, it would have risked worsening a deep recession, and further weakening the fragile US financial system by tightening credit.

Since the late 1960s global restructuring has given added weight in the world economy to the OECD nations. The forces of transnational capital have been at the vanguard of this process. Restructuring has involved growing competitive and disciplinary pressures on states and economic agents (individuals, firms, unions, governments), speeding up the necessary response time for economic survival. The 1980s was associated with a 'Third Wave' of technological innovation, knowledge-intensification and organizational change. There was an accelerating shift away from Fordism to post-Fordism in the OECD region, and an associated secular decline in the power of traditional forms of organized labour. National systems of financial regulation and control were displaced by an integrated, 24-hour global financial system, which in some ways resembled a casino, beyond the control of any single government. By the late 1980s economic globalization approached levels that approximated those immediately prior to 1914, often considered to be the high-water mark of capitalist economic internationalism.

Nonetheless, trends in ownership, location and nature of economic activity suggests that the identity and allegiance of firms took on a less and less territorial aspect in the 1990s. This indicates potential contradictions between globalizing and more territorially bounded social forces and institutions, and between the economics and politics at the global level. The economic system is one of increasingly planetary reach, whereas political authority is still primarily constituted at the national level, although this situation is mutating since changes in economic conditions have served to reinforce political trends set in motion during the 1970s towards the restructuring of states into more neo-liberal forms. This process would appear now to be under way in the former communist states, where Poland was the initial laboratory for the social experiment supervised by the IMF. So far in the former East Bloc this experiment appears to have failed, abysmally, with the situation in the former East Germany appearing increasingly catastrophic. Unemployment in the former DDR may have reached 40 per cent in late 1992, and racist violence and Nazism are on the rise (see Chapter 8 on East Asian restructuring).

Such developments do not suggest a general weakening of state capacity. Rather it implies that some aspects of the state will expand in importance (for example to police markets, including labour markets; to sustain law and order) to sustain some of the social and economic conditions for accumulation, and to help legitimate a liberalizing capitalism. Nevertheless, especially in the Third World, the state's economic autonomy is being undermined once again *vis-à-vis* global economic forces, in so far as neo-liberal structural adjustment is forcing the abandonment of the statist mercantilism which developed, for example in Latin America, from the 1930s onward. Not only G7 governments, but also the IMF and World Bank, and the regional development banks, are demanding reductions in the size and scope of public sector intervention in the economy (which had been established to develop and sustain state capitalist strategic industries and to give protection to 'infant industries').

Despite the use of direct political power by G7 institutions, the key difference between this form of external domination and that which prevailed in colonial times is that it is ultimately structural and indirect, exercised primarily through creating new constitutional structures which serve to lock-in the power of market forces. At the same time, partly because of growing disparities of income and wealth, the sovereignty of the people is being reduced. Political pluralization and an incipient form of liberal democracy in the Third World, then, are not accompanied by an extension of capacities to participate. Social restructuring is accompanied by greater political and economic discipline, largely imposed from above and outside.

In sum, the international political economy of the immediate post-war period has evolved towards a global political economy. This change has transformed the former balance between finance and production, and the relations between capital, labour and the state. The current conjuncture, with neo-liberal forces in the ascendant, reflects a shift away from the integral hegemony in the transatlantic heartland. It reflects beginnings of erosion in the coherence of the 'organic' alliances organized under and directed by the USA. These alliances served to 'contain' communism within the major capitalist states, and restricted the geographical spread of the Soviet bloc during the Cold War era. Communist and Third World mercantilisms are giving way to neo-liberalism and the growing power of capital. ...

Perspectives, classes and elites

To give order to the remainder of my exposition two preliminary points are needed. My first point relates to the question of classes. I use the term in a Marxist sense but with a complex model of class stratification (see Figure 1 below). The concept of capital implies a social relation of inequality, involving a contrast between those who have a substantial and indeed privileged ownership or control of the means of production, that is physical or financial assets, and those who do not (most of society). In this sense, a class corresponds, at least methodologically, to a certain 'objective' reality, constituted primarily by a property relation (class-in-itself). In addition, we can distinguish subjectively and politically between classes, or fractions of classes: in terms of those which are, or are not, self-conscious of their common interests and attempt to unify their forces in a common struggle (class-for-itself).

In this chapter, then, the term 'globalizing elites' refers to a directive, strategic element within globalizing capitalism. It is not used in the reactionary and determinist sense of writers such as Gaetano Mosca and Wifredo Pareto, who stressed the inevitability of elite rule because of either their superior organization or innate ability, relative to the subordinated, inert, or inferior masses.

In what follows I distinguish between those far-sighted elements of internationally mobile capital that are self-conscious and seek long-term and politically stable conditions for global accumulation (generally associated with productive capital and what I call 'compensatory' liberals); and those which tend to take a more short-term view, with co-ordination and discipline indirectly achieved through the liberalization of market forces (often exemplified by financial interests and 'pure' liberals).

Each of these tendencies represents an alternative strategy towards the management of the emerging global political economy. In turn, the interests of transnational capital may be counterpoised to more nationally orientated forces, embodied by the US military-industrial complex, or the Japanese bureaucracy and *keiretsu*, which have been generally associated with a mercantilist or more state capitalist perspective, opposed to domestic liberalization, at least for 'strategic industries'. Thus, there is no concrete 'general' class interest of capital, and this implies the potential for significant intra-class struggles, particularly when conflict concerns the stability of the world economy and/or the question of national sovereignty and autonomy.

The second preliminary point to be made is that class perspectives are not merely ideologies, nor simply explanations, but *are a part of* the political economy. Perspectives guide conceptualization of problems and strategies, relative to other definitions and possibilities. Thus the term 'perspective' includes the theoretical and practical outlook, world-view and identity of a given set or constellation of social forces, movements and institutions. A perspective exists in political time and space and implies a particular standpoint, be it that of a group, nation or class. For a perspective to be both coherent and politically effective, it implies not only theoretical plausibility, but also an institutional and intellectual apparatus that can help to promote and reproduce certain interests.

A perspective becomes hegemonic when the theories and arguments it entails, and the social forces it embodies come to prevail in setting the agenda for debate and policy in a given historical situation. This does not imply a lack of contestation: merely that for practical purposes, alternatives are not fully considered because they lack weight, plausibility, credibility or practical effectiveness. Previously hegemonic perspectives may become partly or wholly discredited, such as mercantilism in the UK in the mid-nineteenth century and Stalinism in Eastern and Central Europe in the 1980s. ...

Globalizing elites and social stratification

Capitalist elites are representative of different interests within capitalism, a system that is of its nature, pluralistic (Pijl 1989). Indeed, the reproduction of capitalism on national and world scales requires an institutional pluralism that allows one disintegrating form to be challenged and replaced by another more securely based, newly leading form. This negates the thesis that a crisis of capitalism will necessarily lead to the replacement of capitalism by another socio-economic system.

At present, there is a struggle between at least two broadly defined, leading forms of capitalism, each of which has its own dynamics and contradictions. The first are the neo-liberal forms associated with the Anglo-Saxon countries. The second are the more varied state-capitalist, mercantilist forms that seek a more secure political basis in corporatist organization of production and welfare nets for the more disadvantaged. The neo-liberal form is most developed in the Anglo-Saxon countries, the state capitalist form in continental Europe and, in a modified variant, in Japan (see Chapter 8).

Globalizing elites can be defined as a grouping of organic intellectuals and political leaders within what can be called the transnational fraction of the capitalist classes of the world. As such they are located at the intersection of the two main forms of capitalism, and at the interface between territorial and globalizing aspects of world order. As organic intellectuals they seek to reconcile the contradictions of these aspects through a process of political synthesis. Such elites are in part constituted by their positions in key strategic locations in transnational companies, banks, universities, think tanks, media companies, governments and international organizations such as the IMF, World Bank and OECD, and by the discourse of neo-liberal globalization. Their activities seek to make transnational capital a class 'for itself' by theorizing the world order and by synthesizing strategy. Key members are located in organizations at the apex of global knowledge, production and financial structures, as well as in key political parties and government agencies in the major capitalist states, notably in the members of the G7. This grouping has a public and a private face. Its members drawn from the private realm of civil society are intimately related to and form part of 'political society' at both 'national' and 'international' levels.

The term elites is used in the plural so as to, on the one hand, avoid the implication of homogeneity, and on the other, to emphasize the vantage point and privileged perspective that the various members bring to bear. This reflects the plurality that inheres in the leading elements

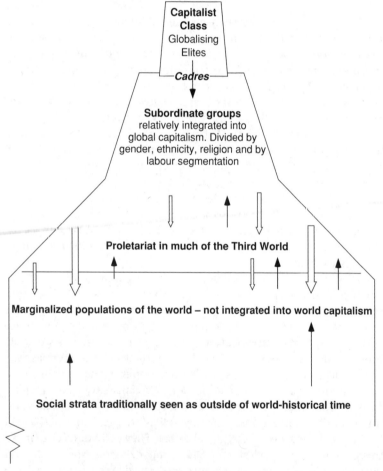

Figure 1   The structure of global social stratification

Note: arrows indicate the relations of force

of capitalism, even where globalization appears to take on the appearance of a totalizing set of social forces. The place of such elites in the social structure is sketched in Figure 1. This rough sketch represents the global structure of social stratification as a hierarchical series of layers in an ever-widening pyramid with a massive base (only the very top of the base is depicted in the diagram; it consists of perhaps two-thirds of the world's population – several billion people).

The upper, narrow cone, involving a privileged minority, again not to scale, would correspond to the globalizing elites and ruling classes and the cadre, directive element. The origins of this upper part of the social structure can be traced back to the early years of merchant capitalism, and to trade and financial links between 'world cities' such as Venice, Florence, Nuremburg, Lyons, Amsterdam, London, Delhi, Nanking and Osaka in the fifteenth to eighteenth centuries (Braudel 1982).

The second layer is normally subordinated within and from an urban centre. This corresponds to what Braudel calls 'market society' and it involves strata more or less integrated into world capitalism, usually both within, and surrounding the world cities.

Finally, there are the subordinated, marginalized zones of material existence. The latter are neither significantly articulated into the productive system and exchange circuits of global capitalism, nor into what I have called market civilization. Nevertheless, the marginal elements of society may disrupt the circuits of production and exchange, and change the configuration of power relations of both world capitalism and market society, partly since some of their members gradually become proletarianized. For example, worsening economic conditions in rich and poor countries, plus the prospect of wage-labour generates migratory movements to the urban centres of both 'North' and 'South'. At the same time, many Third World cities are overpopulated, with infrastructure collapsing and centres surrounded by shantytowns that threaten to paralyse economic activity. Indeed, within the most economically advanced world cities, such as New York and London today, there is a process of social marginalization reflected in the vast numbers of homeless people sleeping on the streets. In this sense, cities like Rio and Los Angeles serve as metaphors for the global social structure, with extremes of wealth and poverty, violence and instability, where the wealthy are protected by private security guards and live in walled enclave housing complexes (see Chapter 7).

In this model then, the capitalist class is viewed as not directly concerned with the question of different trajectories of capitalism. This task is performed by organic intellectuals drawn from the stratum broadly described as the cadres, as seen for example in the composition of the Trilateral Commission in which academics and senior civil servants and planners (cadres), mainly from the OECD countries, participate and prepare the analyses considered by the chieftains of transnational firms and government leaders.

The cadre stratum is divided between an upper layer, fully integrated with global capitalism and its ruling classes, and a broader lower layer less committed by interest and ideology to one or other form of capitalism. Within this lower layer, some stress the need for autonomous, technocratic management of production by cadres, some the potential for decentralization through the application of electronic technologies, some a concern for environmental degradation and the potential for new non-polluting and anti-pollution technologies, and so on. Social democratic cadres favouring not only socialized forms of ownership of the means of production, but also more systematic and accountable forms of public multilateralism to regulate important aspects of global activity (e.g. reflected in the debates over the New International Economic Order in the 1970s), including public control over international finance, have been marginalized from the upper echelons of the cadres.

Beneath the cadres, the labour force is increasingly segmented. Traditional organized labour is declining in strength, notably in the old Fordist mass-production industries with their industrial unions. The restructuring of production on a global scale is making 'flexible' use of a labour force located in many different places, separated not only geographically but also by nationality, ethnicity, religion and gender. To achieve a common consciousness, organization and strategy within this diversity has become very difficult, especially as unemployment has tended to rise in most OECD countries to very high levels during the last decade. In this sense, there has been 'peripheralization' within the OECD countries, as previously established and privileged workers lose their security of employment and suffer decline in their standard of living. The latter phenomenon has been very noticeable in the USA since the late 1960s, with real wages for the vast majority of US workers less now than they were then. This is the case not only for blacks and other ethnic minorities, but also the 'white' working class (see Chapter 10 on US social order/disorder).

There is still a proportion of the world's population only partially linked to global capitalism. Among these populations, traditionally conceived of as outside world-historical time and (and often written out of history), the indigenous populations are of particular interest:

They have in recent years achieved a new degree of self-consciousness and articulate political expression and organization on both national and global scales. Indigenous peoples have also perceived the opportunity of access to the United Nations system, e.g. on human rights issues, to press their claims, using transnational networks to press their claims in particular cases, e.g. against hydro-electric developments in northern Quebec and Japan. Indigenous peoples' organization may be a paradigm for marginalized people more generally.[4]

Globalism, territorialism and the USA

The reproduction of the neo-liberal order depends upon the most economically, politically and militarily powerful governments. Of these, the most important is the USA, followed by Japan and Germany. The G7, and other informal, private organizations such as the World Economic Forum and the process of international organization and law can be viewed as serving to constitute a partial internationalization of authority. This is not the same, however, as saying such authority is legitimate, or indeed unified. Part of the reason for this is the role of the USA in the world order: this increasingly takes on the character of a 'universal contradiction' (Nicolaus 1970).

In the USA, transnational liberalism vies for hegemony with territorially bounded sets of interests, identities and discourses (such as 'America first' nationalism). A key element of the contradictory role of the USA is that whilst its government is the key military enforcer of the functioning rules of the global economy of transnational liberalism, it is not prepared to play by the rules it seeks to set for others, partly because of the structure of the US political system, where key political forces prevent the government from deviating substantially from the logic of existing policy. The USA is a relatively inward-looking, ethno-centric and, in economic terms, undisciplined and consumerist nation (reflected in periodically high budget deficits and a low savings rate). Economic and political agents in the USA operate with very short time-horizons – in a country with a relatively short history. This inward-looking aspect contrasts with US global primacy, defined both in terms of its capacity for structural dominance that stems from US economic centrality, and its supremacy in global security. US economic policies can have disruptive consequences for the rest of the world, especially since the USA has become more integrated

4. Robert Cox, note on the Barboleusaz meeting, Switzerland, 14–16 October 1991.

into global circuits of production and finance in contrast to its previous situation of relative self-sufficiency.

Nevertheless, the US government is attempting to lead through reconstruction of an inter-state system and world economy that could become the political basis of the 'new world order'. Part of this strategy involves initiatives to restructure the relations between 'North' and 'South', 'West' and 'East', and between the USA and its major capitalist allies and rivals (the EEC and Japan). In this regard, central to elite debates in the 1980s and 1990s is the question of to what degree the world order is perceived as evolving towards 'three blocism' or, conversely, towards a more interdependent 'trilateralism', between the three dynamic poles of contemporary capitalism.

In these debates there is a cleavage between transnational liberals and the increasingly influential geoeconomic strategists. Edward Luttwak summarizes the perspective of the latter grouping as an 'admixture of the logic of conflict with the methods of commerce' (Toal 1992). The strategists tend to interpret history in terms of cycles of rise and decline of great powers and stress inter-state rivalry and the need for state control over economic policy, for example using ideas drawn from the new literature on strategic trade theory. In sum, in what is perceived as a 'declining' US, much of the focus of attention has been on the 'rising' power of Japan and the 'problem' this poses for US policy.[5] Other elements in the USA are attempting to replace the 'lost enemy' (the USSR) with new 'demons' or new forms of 'otherness' so as to galvanize US foreign policy. Examples here are the (leaders of) 'rogue regimes' (e.g. Saddam Hussein, Moamur Gadaffi). (See Chapter 5 for earlier discussion of the strategy problématique.) ...

The salience of American mercantilist perspectives was reflected in the 1988 Omnibus Trade Act, in the US positions in the Strategic Impediments Talks and in the Yen-Dollar Committee during the 1980s, and most recently in President Bush's decision to take a large group of US corporate chief executives to Japan. This group was intended to influence the Japanese government to show favour towards 'American' producers like GM and Chrysler (both of whom have joint ventures and co-production agreements with their erstwhile Japanese competitors, reflecting a more general transnationalization of the US economy). A more centrist variant of the geo-economic, mercantilist argument is that of Michael Porter. This

---

5. In the late 1980s and early 1990s obsessive concern with Japan's threat to US pre-eminence was a feature of American political discourse. This concern subsided later in the 1990s because of the continued economic slump in Japan.

influential work – since revised – applies business strategy concepts to economic and foreign policy, and advocates more comprehensive state engagement to ensure the competitive success of enterprises operating within and from a given territory (Porter 1998). Here it is worth noting that mercantilist thought has a long lineage in the USA, going back to Alexander Hamilton's *Report on Manufactures*. Indeed the great theoretician of German mercantilism, Friedrich List, was an advisor to the US government during the nineteenth century.

Linked to this debate is one concerning the likelihood of a resurgence of quasi-Leninist forms of inter-imperialist rivalry, after the 'glue' of the Cold War had been dissolved, especially between the USA and Japan. In this regard transnational liberals have sought to dampen potential frictions between the USA, the EEC and Japan. For example, the New York Council on Foreign Relations, Trilateral Commission, Brookings Institution and many of the Ivy League universities have sought to preserve the integrity of the USA–Japan relationship and protect Japan from the criticism associated with the geostrategic thinkers. They have sought to demonstrate the importance of foreign investment in the USA, whilst minimizing the strategic threats this might pose.

A parallel current is the concerted critique of the thesis of US relative decline associated, for example, with Paul Kennedy (Kennedy 1988). In particular, Joseph Nye argues that the USA has maintained its economic position since the early 1970s noting the tremendous internationalization of the US economy in that period, and how the USA consolidated its strategic primacy considerably as the USSR weakened. Nye maintains that US power and capabilities are more comprehensive than that of any previous hegemonic power. Thus, the USA is bound (destined) to lead the major capitalist states (Nye 1991).

Nye was the key author of a recent Trilateral Commission report that argued that the 1990s would not see the emergence of three rival politico-economic blocs, despite the possibility of a growth in centrifugal forces among the trilateral (North America–EU–Japan/East Asia) countries. Thus whilst the USA is viewed as being too profligate by trilateralists, Japan is seen as being too large to be a 'free rider', or simply a banker. 'Japan, with due sensitivity to historical and legal constraints, should be more involved in international financial institutions, decision making in the United Nations and in other informal mechanisms of world order.' If Europe's trilateral partners treat Europe as an entity they can encourage the integration process (and retard this process if they seek to play off European states against each other). European integration should be linked to NATO and the USA in light of the November 1990 Transatlantic

Declaration. With regard to European security 'Navigation and a sense of direction will be more important than the details of architecture. We should head in the direction of a greater European capacity to contribute to its own defence without removing the residual insurance policy provided by the American security guarantee' (Nye et al. 1991: 45).

On the other hand, trends in technology and economics, and in security (with Europe and East Asia still needing US support), as well as the nationalism of many 'smaller, non-trilateral nations, fearing dominance from a large trilateral neighbour', would serve to sustain many forces in favour of trilateral and global co-operation. For this possibility to be enhanced it would require political action on a transnational basis, requiring the making of *'transnational coalitions* that advance the common good ... the wealthy countries ... as the largest players in the world economy, should see themselves as *trustees of the public good* of sustainable economic growth. As trustees, they need to *resist domestic veto groups*, keep their markets open, and promote sustainable growth in the poorer parts of the world' (Nye et al. 1991: xiii; 41).[6]

The latter is a quintessential – although somewhat patronizing and paternalistic – statement of the perspective of the transnational liberal, globalizing elites, and the prerogatives which its members feel they ought to possess. On the other hand, many leading organic intellectuals, in the USA, and even larger numbers of their counterparts within the ranks of globalizing elites in Europe and Japan, would like to see a USA not just 'bound to lead', but also, like Ulysses forgoing the temptations of the Sirens, 'bound to the mast'. In other words, they see it as being in their collective interest, as well as in the particular interest of the USA, that it 'puts its own house in order', for example with respect to its economic and social policy.

From other elements in the globalizing elites comes the argument that 'trusteeship' of international public goods is not enough. They argue that what is needed is a set of mechanisms which will tie the hands of future politicians in the OECD countries (and elsewhere), lock in neo-liberal constitutional and economic reforms, and thus lengthen the 'shadow of the future' for economic agents, and provide a predictable politico-economic environment for internationally mobile capital.

These arguments relate to what I call the 'new constitutionalism', in so far as many of the debates over neo-liberal restructuring have been framed around the reformulation of concepts of sovereignty and discipline, in

6. Emphasis added.

matters of political economy. Associated political initiatives – like the EEC's 1992 programme and the North American Free Trade Agreement (NAFTA) – are intended to promote the reconfiguration of global political and civil society – and global governance – along Lockeian lines (see Chapter 7).

The key concepts of neo-liberal constitutionalism are market efficiency, discipline and confidence, policy credibility and consistency viewed from the standpoint of new theories in neo-classical economics in a world of international capital mobility. One aspect concerns the institutional arrangements designed to insulate key aspects of economic life from the interference of (elected) politicians: to impose binding constraints on democratic authority over the economy in the future. Thus new constitutionalist arguments usually stress the need to strengthen surveillance mechanisms and institutional capabilities to reinforce, respectively, microeconomic and macroeconomic market discipline at the multilateral level, and to help to sustain the legal and political conditions for transnational capital (Gill 1992). For example, such new constitutionalist thinking lies at the heart of the Maastricht Agreements for European unification and a single currency. If ratified they would tie the hands of future governments with regard to their control over much of their economic policy.

A second set of elite debates relates to tactics and strategy with regard to the incorporation and subordination of the Third World, and more recently towards the restructuring of former communist states. Here, matters of strategy, economics and politics are intimately connected.

For example, under US influence, debates concerning World Bank and the IMF structural adjustment policies in the Third World have changed to place more emphasis on state-building so as to be better able to restructure states along the lines noted earlier. New forms of conditionality involve political and constitutional demands, including control of arms proliferation in the Third World. These developments, then, reflect reconsideration of how the dominant institutions of the 'North' can better incorporate the 'South' in the attempt to re-constitute hegemony, that is, how to extend neo-liberal hegemony beyond the core. Thus it is noteworthy that many of the 'best and brightest' of the Third World have been trained by the UN economic institutions and form part of transnational elite cadres that seek to implement and sustain the policies of liberalization and structural adjustment which have characterized the last decade.

As we have noted, the wider aspect of new constitutionalism is strategic: attempting to make (where possible or necessary, liberal-democratic) capitalism the sole model for future development. Involved here are attempts to redefine 'public' and 'private' spheres in the economy, for example in ways which guarantee both investment and the entry and exit options for international capital in different nations. The military forces of the major G7 countries are being reconfigured in ways that, in conjunction with the deepening of market forces and commodification of social life, add a further disciplinary aspect. The economic initiatives concerning the Third World are related to new forms of military mobilization by the USA and its NATO allies, in the form of European as well as US Rapid Deployment forces for swift intervention, especially in the Gulf to control the strategic resource of oil. Western strategy towards the former Soviet republics involves attempts to weaken or incorporate them militarily.

On the 'economic' front, perspectives can be analysed in terms of 'compensatory' and 'pure' liberal models of transition. Compensatory liberals range from those who called for substantial aid transfers to the former USSR in the form of a 'second Marshall Plan' to more modest proposals such as those who argued for debt write-offs plus limited levels of transitional and humanitarian aid. Pure liberals are more likely to be 'shock therapists', who blooded their Eastern strategy in Poland in 1989–90, following previous experiments in Latin America earlier in the decade. So far the aid actually offered to Poland and Russia has been meagre, mainly in the form of 'advice'. This suggests either that the pure liberals have the upper hand, or that the key strategic objective is to further weaken the former USSR and its former allies, perhaps for decades to come, or a combination of the two. Since 1988, all the former Comecon states have been in a spiralling economic depression, involving the physical liquidation of capital and massive falls in output.

The medicine which has been applied in practice by the IMF in Poland (and mooted in Russia) has stressed the need for independent central banks, swift convertibility of currencies in the former USSR (post-war convertibility was only restored in the most powerful West European states in 1958), the creation of markets for labour and capital, with rapid development of a system of private property rights and privatization programmes and the promotion of an 'enterprise culture' which goes beyond gangsterism and the former black economy.

Finally, it perhaps needs to be emphasized that the politics of the transition from communism to capitalism involves much more than the G7, IMF, OECD and other public institutions. A wider 'transnational historic bloc' of public and private neo-liberal forces is leading the restructuring process, in concert with its counterparts within the former Soviet bloc. The key individuals in this process are bound together by a shared framework of thought (economic liberalism) and economic necessity (he who pays the piper calls the tune). In the transition, the 'West' has refused to countenance any alternatives to Anglo-Saxon-style liberal capitalist institutions (for example the 'third way'). This is despite the fact that a growing number of commentators, including myself, economists warned that the structural adjustment/shock therapy was likely to prove more lethal than the original disease.[7]

Concluding reflections

Class interests are contestable and are linked to the perspectives of different fractions of capital. Intra-class as well as inter-class struggles take place at both domestic and international levels, and any set of ideas, institutional proposals and policy arrangements will favour some interests rather than others. At the present point in time, the prevailing perspectives appear to be those associated with large internationally mobile elements of capital in the metropolitan countries.

These perspectives stress economic efficiency, competition and global factor mobility, and the need to constrain some of the intervention capacity of the state that might impede globalization. Nevertheless, in both political and economic terms these policies may prove to be profoundly contradictory. By this I mean that the deflationary thrust of policy and the impoverishment of masses of people in many countries, and the marginalization of labour and the cadres from policy-making circles in the OECD substantially narrows the social basis for hegemony. In this sense, the legitimacy and political durability of neo-liberal dominance can be seen as sowing the seeds of its own contradictions.

Economic depression and spiralling decline has become a fact of life in much of Latin America and Africa for at least ten years, and the situation in Eastern Europe and the former USSR is grim. Economic and political deterioration in many parts of the world is becoming chronic. Moreover, in the context of the restructuring of global production, massive migratory movements are occurring, mainly from South to North. With the collapse of the USSR, there are likely to be more migrants and refugees from East to West, and more political conflict as the privileged countries seek to impose limitations on the movement of these peoples into their economies. All of these developments, along

---

7. This literally proved to be the case as death rates soared and life expectancy shrank to pre-industrial levels in the former Soviet Union during the 1990s.

with environmental, security and other problems suggest a turbulent decade to come.

Nevertheless, the political agenda of globalizing elites – despite political conflicts within the ranks of G7 leaders – is to consolidate the political and geographical core of the system whilst extending the power and penetration of capital into previously closed territories, such as China, India and the former USSR. This extension of capital into new territories reflects the fact that an aspect of its structural power is the division of the globe into rival sovereign states. It also explains why the globalizing elites in general do not favour a world state or even a more minimal global institution such as a world central bank: this might prove to be an object of global class struggle, and institutional pluralism and innovation provides greater political flexibility to the powerful.

All in all, this is a world that can be described as post-hegemonic in Gramscian terms. Its political appeal, and capacity to include and incorporate subordinate elements is being replaced by a politics of dominance and supremacy. In response counter-hegemonic movements and political organizations must mobilize capabilities and democratize power and production. There is, of course, no guarantee that this will materialize, given the power and reach of transnational capital. Nevertheless we might witness remobilized social movements forming not only to protect society from the unfettered logic of disciplinary neo-liberalism and its associated globalizing forces but also, perhaps to imagine new social projects. As in the 1930s, we can anticipate that not all of these new forces will be progressive: there are already signs of reaction and authoritarianism in many former communist states, in the context of a resurgence of inter-communal violence and political chaos, fuelled by the descent into economic entropy. The role of the IMF and the G7 is becoming bitterly controversial in Russia and the consequences of a deepening of resentment at the 'shock therapy' need careful reflection. In this sense, the G7 initiatives in Russia may come to be seen, in retrospect, as the low point of capitalist internationalism in the twentieth century.

10
Surveillance Power in Global Capitalism

This chapter is a hypothetical exploration of one of the most fundamental forms of modern social power: that of extended surveillance and its exercise. In particular, this chapter asks questions about how panopticism – involving, as was noted in Chapter 7, both the self-discipline of elites and state cadres and their extended surveillance of populations – is related to the constitution and contradictions of global capitalism, and how this may set limits to emancipatory forms of collective action.

In a world where the perception and reality of uncertainty and insecurity seem to have increased since the breakdown of the post-war social settlements, intensified efforts are being made by both state and capital to institutionalize panoptic practices. Such practices are intended, along with hedging and other means of risk management, to minimize uncertainty, and maximize profit opportunities for business, on the one hand, and to maintain order and 'discipline' under rapidly changing social conditions, on the other. However, although new network technologies facilitate new forms of military-political surveillance and military tactics, they also allow for new forms of political agency, and the relative empowerment of 'non-state actors' who would otherwise be relatively weak in traditional economic and military terms (this is elaborated in Chapter 11). This is because network technologies have a dual quality: they may therefore constitute a relatively universal power resource for communication on a global basis by individuals and groups who would otherwise have little capability to impart their message or argument. Of course, in a global political economy characterized by growing inequality, they may generally serve to widen, rather than narrow the gap between the information-rich and the information-poor.

In what follows then, are a series of hypotheses, rather than a fully worked out set of arguments. They are intended to identify tendencies, not laws, that is the tendencies in question can be shaped and redefined through democratic collective action to produce, among other things, a more democratic and accountable form of surveillance in our societies and in world order. My hypotheses mainly concern the frameworks of discipline and punishment associated with the coercive reproduction of globalization. In particular, they concern how panopticism in global capitalism can be understood as part of an effort to re-constitute the social and political subject by means of neo-liberal disciplinary discourse. Prioritized in this discourse is not an active, democratic political subject or citizen, but rather an individual as worker and consumer, rendered transparent in the political and economic marketplace.[1]

Our first hypothesis is that recent extension of US power in the new world order is linked to its leading edge in panoptic, networking technologies and this is used to monitor governments, populations and economic activity. A second hypothesis is that extension of panoptic power to maximize predictability and minimize uncertainty is related to an acceleration of the intensive and extensive expansion of capital. The third hypothesis is that these new, intensified patterns of accumulation create contradictions for processes of social reproduction in our societies. As a result, this may cause governments to engage increasingly in coercive processes of intensified surveillance – as well as discipline, punishment and incarceration – to sustain order in society. Our fourth hypothesis is that the world order counterpart to these carceral and disciplinary strategies are new systems of military-political surveillance associated with the US-led alliance systems.

We begin our discussion with earlier conceptualizations of panoptic power – those of Jeremy Bentham and those of the French revolution-aries who sought to create 'a new constitution for nature' organized along hyper-rationalist principles. Time, space and nature generally would be subjected to forms of uniform categorization and control, such as metrication. I then argue that ancient and modern forms of surveillance are both concerned with the production of identities and the maintenance of order. In the modern moment (and also in the context of the post-modern condition) American power harnesses these twin objectives (identity and order production) to the pursuit of capital accumulation, partly through surveillance technologies and other mechanisms that increasingly privatize risk.

Panoptic power

Let us initially outline the conceptual framework that guides our hypotheses. As I noted in Chapter 7, Panopticon is the Greek term for

---

1. As recent scandals such as the bankruptcy of Enron reveal, what is generally rendered transparent is not capital. In much political discourse capital is assumed to be akin to a life-giving force, central to the meaning and successful reproduction of accumulation patterns.

'sees all'. The Panopticon idea allows us to understand one of the fundamental forms of 'disciplinary' power in modern societies and indeed how it may be used to counteract another of the fundamental forms of modern power: the power of collective action. (Gill 1995; Gill 1997).

Bentham's Panopticon and the Industry-Houses

Although never built, the Panopticon that was invented by the British utilitarian philosopher Sir Jeremy Bentham was intended to be a new economy of power achieved through the disciplining and normalization of subjects (Bentham 1995). The primary purpose of the Panopticon blueprint was to create a secure establishment that would be productive, in effect a type of manufacturing unit with cheap labour. Its effectiveness was to be premised upon surveillance of two types. First, it would operate through the eyes of the warders in a central watchtower who would always be able to observe inmates in cells that were constantly illuminated. Second and more subtly, because their cells were always transparent to the warders, and because prisoners would never know whether or not they were under observation (inmates could not see into the watchtower), inmates would tend to exercise self-discipline, to act, as it were, as surrogate warders. Power was therefore both visible (prisoners were aware that warders were present in the watchtower) as well as unverifiable (they would not know if they were being watched from the watchtower). The Panopticon was a model not only for a prison, but also for institutions of education, medicine, mental health, and so on. Bentham sought a way to make institutions function productively in a way that was efficient, automatic and profitable, and of course in the case of the Panopticon prison, 'secure'.

As I have noted earlier the origin of disciplinary projects and practices of this type was, according to Foucault, early modern systems to control the plague and spread of epidemics. Elaborate classification systems and other devices (e.g. use of quarantine; systems of permanent registration) were used to control threatened populations and contain the spread of disease. As such disciplinary practices were associated with the protection of a particular social order from the threat of internally and externally generated chaos. Moreover as Fernand Braudel showed in his study of European development between the fifteenth and the eighteenth centuries, the poor were the principal victims of the plague (Braudel 1982). Albert Camus also demonstrated this in respect to twentieth century conditions, in the existentialist novel based in Algiers, *La Peste* (*The Plague*). The effects of the plague – and indeed the epidemics that are once again now part of the conditions of globalization – are not neutral.

Under conditions of social inequality, a hierarchy of power and of social order, partly a racialized one, determines the systems of quarantine and treatment – and thus who is most likely to survive. As such, such systems become objects of intense resistance.

Bentham proposed the Panopticon as an alternative to the transportation of British prisoners to New South Wales. Bentham considered transportation to be inhumane, ineffective and expensive. The Panopticon was thus, on one level, a social innovation that could be linked to a more rational and secure system of British imperialism. As I have noted, however, it is important to emphasize how Bentham's approach to incarceration and penal reform was meant to be not only productive of integrated and normalized members of the population, but also profitable (the original idea for the Panopticon, devised in 1792, was based on a factory in Russia that was run by his capitalist brother, Sir Samuel Bentham). Thus the issue with respect to panoptic power was not only how to 'secure public order' and avoid chaos through the construction of rationalized systems of medical practice, pedagogy, treatment of the mentally ill, and so on, but also how to make the response profitable, perhaps in ways that would serve to constitute more 'productive' members of society.

Indeed, by 1794 Bentham intended to use the prisoners and paupers (poor and unemployed people) on a large scale to run machinery, since it had occurred to the Bentham brothers that it would be cheaper to employ convicts and paupers than using steam to drive the machinery. Bentham then envisaged a joint stock company to make profits from the poor. Thus, the Panopticon Plan for Industry-Houses was modelled on the Bank of England, with its voting powers allocated according to ownership of shares. Overseen by one board of directors, it was intended to comprise 250 Houses with approximately 500,000 inmates. It was to be called the National Charity Company. Inmates/paupers would be controlled and organized according to elaborate classification systems. For example the unemployed would be categorized according to the type and nature of their unemployment. 'Out of place hands' (those recently dismissed from jobs) were differentiated from 'periodical stagnation' (seasonal workers) and from 'superseded hands' (the technologically unemployed) and 'disbanded hands' (unemployed as a result of bankruptcy). The key category was, however, 'casual stagnation' (unemployment because of general stagnation of demand). In this way, 'Bentham's plan amounted to no less than the levelling out of the business cycle through the commercialization of unemployment on a gigantic scale' (Polanyi 1975: 107).

If we reflect upon these innovations from the vantage point of the early twenty-first century, we can see how Bentham anticipated many of the aspects of modern penal systems, such as those associated with the American prison industrial complex discussed below. He also anticipated modern systems for managing unemployment and finding ways to make it productive and profitable, for example recent trends associated with the shift from welfare to 'workfare' states that we noted in Chapter 7.[2]

Of course, for such schemes to be imaginable, as opposed to being actually possible (Bentham's joint stock company was never floated), it presupposed a powerful and strong state apparatus that could not only effectively incarcerate prisoners, but also manage the indigent and the unemployed on a large scale. This required detailed surveillance of populations. Thus, in the context of nineteenth century British liberalism and utilitarianism, Bentham understood that in order to sustain a society with economic freedom it required sophisticated forms of state surveillance ('inspectability') of the population on an ongoing basis. Thus he advocated a range of techniques and innovations, including the census, as a means to maximize inspectability. In sum Bentham's imagination suggested the need for transparency to be built into the architecture of power to make surveillance both economical and effective over a large subject population.

In this way the concept of the Panopticon also allows us to understand some of the meaning of the concept of 'transparency' central to recent discourses on governance of the global political economy, for example as reflected in a series of initiatives by the international financial institutions to ensure Third World governments provide effective accounting techniques and data about fiscal and other economic policies, partly as a means of ensuring that they finance their debts and obligations to foreign investors. This is part of the so-called 'new international financial architecture' developed after the Asian crisis of the late 1990s.

2. Moreover, we might also draw a further analogy between Bentham's view of a global solution to the problem of poverty, as something that could be tackled in ways that generated profits, and the perspective of the international financial institutions and their strategies of Third World debt management. Over the past two decades there have been net transfers of resources, via these institutions, from the Third World into first world countries. This modern type of debt bondage has extracted resources, often from the very poorest members of Third World societies, in order to pay interest on loans to the IMF and World Bank, in many cases whilst their rulers have looted billions and placed their money in offshore bank accounts.

Surveillance power: ancient and modern

As I have mentioned, transparency relates to one of the most fundamental forms of power in modern society: that of extended surveillance based upon particular knowledge forms that allow for the rational classification and ordering of populations. Today's transparency and surveillance practices differ from pre-modern forms of surveillance associated with ancient China where it was supervised by the imperial bureaucracy with its capillary forms of surveillance down to the smallest village. This imperial surveillance system was effective for centuries across large territories and populations, not just in maintaining order, but also producing different forms of identification with the imperial centre. In this sense, ancient and modern forms of surveillance are both connected to the production of identities as well as maintaining order.[3]

Indeed many of the roots of modern panoptic practices (particularly associated with computerization and mechanized control systems) can be traced back to what might be called the 'First Information Revolution' in early modern Europe. After movable type was invented during the Renaissance, it allowed for printed books and the diffusion of literacy across the population in ways that began to give rise to a shift in the nature of European consciousness. One aspect of the shift was an erosion of the relative monopoly on knowledge of the Roman Church and of local feudal authorities. This undermined aspects of the medieval political consciousness associated with a fixed, hierarchical chain of being. As I noted earlier in Chapter 3, from the late fifteenth century onwards an epistemological and ontological transformation began to embrace new concepts of the political. This was reflected in the gradual emergence of what today we would call early nation-states, with new concepts of sovereignty and property associated with 'national territories' and the gradual emancipation of the bourgeoisie. It began to encompass new notions of progress and science: a new epistemological perspective linked to the emergence of new forms of politics. By 1700 empiricism and atomism, and a new social perspective of possessive individualism based on the emancipation of those who held private property, allied to a Newtonian view of the universe, began to hold increasing sway across Europe.

---

3. Imperial classification systems, and censuses are productive of identities in complex ways. For example, immigrants from different South and Central American countries become 'Hispanics' according to the census classification schemes of the USA, and indeed in broader political discourse. However when such immigrants move to Canada, they become Canadian-Colombians, Canadian-Venezuelans or Canadian-Hondurans etc.

However it was the French Revolution that took this process of rationalization a step further, under the banner of liberty, equality and fraternity for the citizens of 'the nation'. The Revolution introduced the decimal system that was, as Eugen Rosenstock has noted, part of a wider attempt to create a 'new constitution for nature' in the tradition of Voltaire's rationalism. In 1821 John Quincy Adams (later US President) noted its revolutionary scope and how metrication was in conflict with varieties of the forms of nature and human practice (Rosenstock-Huessy 1969). Decimalization involved all of life's necessities, every individual, each family, each industry, and so on. It required vast legislative and administrative effort across all social institutions to implement, so that:

> The whole system should be equally suitable to the use of all mankind ... [With] every weight and every measure ... designated by an appropriate, significant, characteristic name, applied exclusively to itself ... so as to form an era in human science in order to approach the ideal perfection of uniformity. (John Quincy Adams cited by Rosenstock-Huessy 1969: 203)

Of course, it is important to stress that many of the innovations mentioned above had progressive and not simply repressive elements since they were part of a relatively universal social and epistemological transformation that went with new concepts of the political, including the ideas of freedom, equality and emancipation, as well as the ways that the French Revolution also stressed the sanctity of private property rights. These rights were enshrined in the Declaration of the Rights of Man and the Citizen, where the basic principle was that 'all men are born free and equal in rights' (e.g. in Article 1), which were specified as the rights of liberty, private property, the inviolability of the person, and resistance to oppression (e.g. Article 2). The Declaration was adopted between 20–26 August 1789, by France's National Assembly, and it duly served as the preamble to the Constitution of 1791.

American informational capitalism and world power

In this section I move our historical focus from the nineteenth century to the early twenty-first century and discuss new panoptic technologies and their links to American power in the new world order.

Our first hypothesis relates to the shifting forms of power in the world order of the early twenty-first century. In this context, American power in an increasingly network-based world order is linked to its leading edge in panoptic technologies. One of the key aspects of resurgent American power is the so-called new economy that integrates networking and other knowledge-enhancing capabilities in ways that permit expanded capital accumulation.

Contradicting the expectations of many theorists of International Relations and International Political Economy who predicted that the USA would continue its relative decline, the USA experienced a long boom during the 1990s that only really came to an end – or indeed a pause – in 2001. This resurgence was not simply economic: following the collapse of the Soviet Union it also entailed remobilization of American military power. One characteristic of this resurgence was connected to how the liberalized world financial system served to recycle trade surpluses of other nations (especially Japan and South Korea and capital exports from the European Union) to help fund American expansion. The external funding combined with higher public investment from the mid-1980s focusing on the academic-military complex and high-technology innovation (e.g. the Internet; military projects such as DARPA[4]). Thus foreign capital supplemented shortfalls in domestic private savings needed to fund the increases in American investment in the 1990s – and much of this investment took place in the emerging core technologies of the information age. In industrial terms, much innovation was *within* computing, communications and control systems. In the past few years, however, although at uneven speeds of change, it has spread to virtually all industries in the USA. Of course, many other factors and forces were at work in this transformation, but nevertheless it is widely acknowledged that the USA has established a massive lead in core technologies associated with the information, communications and other industries of the so-called 'new economy'. At the same time, it is worth remembering that the shift to the so-called new economy, has also been linked to changing patterns of liberalization and deregulation in the global political economy, whilst at the same time American corporations and the American government have sought to gain control over the new international standards that determine many of the infrastructures of the so-called network and communications industries.

One of the reasons for this is that network industries today facilitate enhanced capacities for the surveillance, categorization, incorporation and normalization of (affluent) consumers, so as to create and reproduce markets for goods and services. This normally takes place within the

---

4. DARPA is the central research and development organization for the US Department of Defense. See <http://www.darpa.mil/>.

context of constitutional protections and specific laws on data protection. On the other hand, what is often overlooked is how these new technologies are associated with efforts at greater social control, via the introduction of systems of surveillance of government systems and populations as well as economic activity and transactions more generally. Indeed, since the early 1980s the US government has aggressively sought to promote a shift from state capitalism towards a more liberalized order in both telecommunications and broadcasting, as well as in software, with intellectual property rights now treated increasingly as commodities (Correa 1999; Sell 1997). With respect to the world's communications industries, for much of the post-war period, models of state capitalism tended to prevail. As part of the post-World War II reconstruction and nation-building process, information and cultural industries were highly regulated and state-directed. Large national public broadcasting services and telecommunications grids (often with monopoly powers) were typical. From the late 1980s this pattern began to change rapidly and this meant new opportunities for American capital under conditions of intensified globalization (Lash 1994).

Thus communications systems are evolving towards more flexible, market-driven structures, particularly as new media of communication become more widely available (e.g. via the Internet) and national telecoms are privatized. This situation is being ratified in the negotiations to institutionalize the General Agreement on Trade in Services (GATS) in the World Trade Organization (WTO) – negotiations that have been spearheaded by American interests. GATS is intended to advance the liberalization process across not only communications services, but also in education, broadcasting and other social and cultural realms, and correspondingly to potentially constrain certain types of public health and social welfare policies (Sinclair 2000).

Network capitalism of the 'new economy' focuses on the control of abstract objects, partly through intellectual property rights.[5] Under massive pressure from American government and corporate lobbying, these rights have been made subject to the jurisdiction of not only national government, but also the WTO, the latter an organization ostensibly dedicated to the liberalization of trade. The period of globalization of intellectual property rights began when the USA succeeded

5. Intellectual property rights are generally divided into (i) industrial property rights (patents, designs, trademarks) and (ii) rights in artistic and literary works (copyright).

in linking trade to intellectual property rights in the Uruguay Round trade negotiations in 1994. American software, entertainment and pharmaceutical companies successfully lobbied for an agreement with global coverage and enforcement mechanisms. Strikingly this has involved, with little discussion, 'increasing use of criminal law in an area that has traditionally been a civil matter' (Braithwaite and Drahos 2000: 85). Ironically TRIPS has little to do with free trade since it involves locking in the rights of private monopolies over innovations, and so on, for example through patents. This is why even some neo-classical economists have argued that TRIPS undermines global welfare by preventing competition, an argument used frequently by Third World governments. Many developing countries and NGOs have strongly denounced particular aspects of TRIPS and have called for its removal, for example because of ethical objections to specific provisions such as Article 27.3(b), which deals with the patenting of life forms.

In addition, new standards are also being set with respect to economic policies and accounting, for example Fiscal Codes of Conduct and binding regulations to promote 'transparency' of government policies to investors and market agents – and thus to create the regulatory conditions for extending and consolidating the world market. Of course, the Enron scandal of 2002, involving the world's largest ever bankruptcy, showed the dubious practices of large international accounting firms, and illustrated that we are a long way from universal accounting standards and regulatory frameworks that make capital fully accountable.

Expanded reproduction of capital and social order

This section relates to our second hypothesis: modernist surveillance of systems and populations in order to maximize predictability and minimize uncertainty is connected to the intensive and extensive expansion of capital. By 'intensive', I mean the way that capital penetrates into, and makes its profits from not only work but also leisure and indeed, ever-more aspects of social life (thus corresponding to what Marx called a shift from the formal to the real subordination of labour to capital). We have seen recently how parts of the human body can become commodities. We have also witnessed how fundamental social institutions such as the family, education and churches operate increasingly under market-based principles associated with the making of profit. In other words capital has the tendency to alienate and to subsume the social in its patterns of accumulation, provided that profit opportunities are available. By 'extensive' I have in mind the spread of the commodification process into new territories, such as the former Soviet Union and China: as Marx and Engels put it in the *Communist Manifesto*, capital engages in a universal revolution, 'battering down all Chinese walls', unsettling and transforming social relations (see Chapter 7).

Indeed, partly because of contradictions engendered by these processes we might add that this expansion of capital is accompanied by a growing tendency towards the increasing use of surveillance capabilities by modern states, such as by the liberal democratic state to regulate the new market society and exercise social control in a period of rapid social change. Of course it is very important to note that certain types of surveillance are both necessary and beneficial for social reproduction and for world order. For example with respect to global issues, such technology is crucial in the verification of arms control agreements, in monitoring ecology: such as depletion of rain forests, climate patterns, and so on. On the other hand, the post-Cold War era involves acceleration in military/political surveillance, policing a world where social inequality, social dislocations, political polarization and commercial rivalry are intensifying, and where proliferation of weaponry continues. The key point is that technology is implemented in a given social and political context, where it becomes not a neutral technical apparatus but part of an architecture of power.

In this context, much of the scope and nature of panopticism today is driven by the dialectic between state and capital. Indeed much of today's innovation in surveillance practice and technology is driven by state apparatuses – like that of the USA – gathering information about populations and firms, and collecting data on legal and illegal activities for reasons of planning, taxation and control – a process that has intensified in very significant ways since the attacks on the World Trade Center and Pentagon on 11 September 2001. On the other hand, capitalist enterprises have long deployed panoptic techniques as a means of profit maximization and/or to try to eliminate or to hedge risk. The improved capacity of telecommunications and software systems to gather, centralize and analyse data – much of which was difficult to process or that was previously stored separately, either geographically or functionally – clearly lies at the heart of these developments.

With this wider framework in mind in this section we focus mainly on the private or commercial aspects of surveillance associated with informational or network capitalism. The driving force of the new capitalism is consumption and consumer confidence, which in turn rests upon the use of credit as a means of decreasing the turnover time of capital. In an extended economic structure, the successful accumulation of capital depends partly upon a complex system that monitors transactions and calibrates risk and credit in real time. This is why much of the method of modern business panopticism is premised on actuarial techniques associated with insurance: that is, the management and if possible the avoidance of risk.

It is also worth noting that within a given population set, modern techniques serve to eliminate 'unproductive', 'unprofitable' or high-risk individuals, and to identify those who can be 'constructed', normalized or profitably captured as workers and consumers. Genetic screening techniques plus lie detector and other tests are also often coupled to credit ratings and criminal checks as part of the hiring process in big US corporations, as well as (not just sensitive) areas of the state bureaucracy.[6] US corporations seek to sort out potentially 'risky' workers who may become 'sickly' and thus a financial burden on corporate healthcare plans (and who therefore may be a negative influence on a company's stock price because of potential financial liabilities). Some theorists have argued that there now seems to be a trend towards a surveillance process that focuses on the worker viewed as a risk, and not simply as a tool of production. According to the American Management Association 75 per cent of the American private sector monitors its employees electronically; 33 per cent of workers who use the Internet at work have their online browsing monitored.[7]

As has been widely reported, consumer profiling is widely practised on an ongoing basis and it is linked to credit rating applied with respect to each transaction (e.g. when we wait for a computerized credit approval for our transaction to be made at a cash register). Expensive purchases (for example autos, PCs) are often financed through larger loans that require detailed credit checks. Data for such evaluations is collected through forms of transactional activity that leaves electronic traces, including not only use of charge or credit cards but also use of the Internet. Database technologies manage files on the credit histories and financial status of consumers (and in some cases criminal records as well as insurance and health histories) (Gandy 1993). In turn, manufacturers use these integrated databases to help design new models with consumer profiles in mind, as well as using them to target potential customers who are deemed credit-worthy. Thus these technologies facilitate networking

---

6. In many respects – as recent discussions on human cloning and other linked technologies has illustrated – this is linked to a broader tendency of our times, the rising use of genetic explanations for social phenomena.
7. Based on a report by the Privacy Foundation. See also 'Judges Ease Surveillance of Web Use', *New York Times*, 20 September 2001.

across industrial sectors and a deeper and more flexible integration of finance, production and consumption – that is to say that they are central to the political economy of flexible accumulation. These techniques also create what has come to be regarded as valuable commodities: information sets about (consumer) populations. In turn such information can be bought and sold in the extended reproduction of the circuits of capital. These are some of the reasons why, in production and commerce, common information standards have emerged. Production-in-general has come to rely increasingly on the same information architectures and infrastructures, and in a very broad sense, the cognitive frameworks within which a whole series of transactions and symbolic representations take place. Thus, as an information technology specialist has put it: 'Neural networks and data mining software can now mimic human thought when processing vast amounts of sales data, thus enabling companies to save millions of dollars, enter new markets, retain customers, track fraud and generally become more competitive.'[8] This process thus relates to the way that new technologies enable enhanced capacities for the surveillance and the normalization of affluent consumers, so as to create and reproduce markets for goods and services. By the same token, the processes that capture and include the normalized segments of the population can serve to exclude or marginalize others.

The Internet in some significant ways facilitates this sorting, categorization and evaluation process, as well as acting as a kind of offshore cyberspace beyond the reach of many national regulation and taxation structures. For example, surfing the Web involves, simultaneously, the creation and storage of records of activity. It thus helps indirectly in the construction of consumer/user profiles. This is why a recent investigation by the *New York Times* illustrated how 1994–95 was a turning point in the accelerated gathering of such data through the Internet. In 1994 'cookies' were invented: Web-memories/programs placed on individual computers. In 1995 cookies were placed in the Netscape browser, a move emulated by other major online companies, including American Online and Microsoft (done initially without alerting users). Cookies enable the automatic recording of the online activity of shoppers and browsers, such that Websites have become spaces 'capable of extraordinary monitoring'.[9]

8. Paul Taylor, 'Breakthroughs in business intelligence', *Financial Times*, Special Report: Information Technology. 7 May 1997.
9. John Schwartz, 'Giving Web a Memory Cost its Users Privacy', *New York Times*, 4 September 2001.

Of course, use of the Internet by business has been accelerating exponentially, as has the practice of using cookies for data collection on customers, allowing for product advertising to be customized to individual computers when they visit the Web. And because the Web is a borderless cyberspace, this process is transnational and transcends particular regulatory jurisdictions. This aspect of the Internet is important in the context of the liberalization measures associated with GATS and TRIPS.

What happens in the USA of course is crucial to future developments with respect to the use and potential abuse of such data flows. In this context is important to note that the USA – where the biggest and most aggressive data-corporations are located – has no protections in the Federal Constitution for individual rights to privacy. In the USA, private corporations have created massive databases on citizens and indeed, much of this is sold to them in the first place by governments (usually at bargain prices). Regulation of these practices lies with the individual States, allowing for significant variations or, as one journalist put it, a system that resembles a 'quilt with many holes'.[10] Much of it involves self-regulation by business through voluntary codes of conduct. Indeed much of the focus of privacy bills before Congress in 2001 was on privacy invasions by government rather than business, although of course this pattern changed following September 11th.[11] As such, an important facet of human security is jeopardized, namely the right to freedom from the invasive behaviour of corporations or federal government agencies.

> Although only a few US States such as Maryland 'actively hawk' their public records to private firms 'every state ... has opened its filing cabinets to information brokers who have copied and computerized millions of records'. For example Maryland has sold its driving records, car registrations, property deeds, and records of 'court cases linked to the individual'. Private firms' databases often include not only credit and sometimes health records but also 'unlisted phone numbers, Social Security numbers, physical details such as height and weight, as well as the description and value of the person's house'.[12]

This type of development has given rise to enormous numbers of complaints in the USA not least because American (as well as other)

10. Robert O'Harrow Jr., 'Laws on Use of Personal Data Form a Quilt With Many Holes?' *Washington Post*, 9 March 1998.
11. Ibid.
12. Ibid.

data-corporations can now expand more aggressively (and offshore) partly because of the new phase of trade and investment liberalization associated with GATS and TRIPS:

> In Texas a company called Public-Data.com last year paid $1600 to buy a database with the records of about 14 million drivers and 3 million others with state-issued identification cards, which the company posted on the Web. But when the state legislature passed a law ... requiring anyone purchasing motor vehicle information to pledge not to post the data without approval from individuals, Public-Data simply moved abroad – to the British West Indies – and kept the information on the Web.[13]

In sum, many private agencies in the USA now have massive centralized databases, or data warehouses containing public and private information accessed by powerful, increasingly high-speed computers. In the past decade, the number of these data warehouses in the USA has risen from 100 to over 1,000, also reflecting the tenfold increase in the number of private firms engaged in what the *Washington Post* calls the 'surge in aggressive data gathering' in the period 1993–98.[14] This type of business has become a hot commodity in the USA. One of the biggest firms is Experian, formerly TRW, a US-based credit-rating and marketing organization which by 1994 boasted detailed economic and social data on 170 million American citizens (the US population was then about 254 million). By March 1998 Experian executives claimed that a database enquiry that took 6 minutes on a giant mainframe in 1994 now only took 19 seconds. Experian sold for $1 billion in late 1996 and seven weeks later it was resold for $1.7 billion. About $10 billion a year was spent in the USA in the 1990s on building or maintaining private data warehouses.[15]

In conclusion, the Internet and new forms of communication offer not only increases in efficiency and lower costs for business but also more opportunities for scrutinizing information flows. Some government agencies (particularly intelligence agencies) are pleased at the growth of the Internet since the ordered convergence of the net, electronic messages and other data flows allow for the transmission, collection and analysis

13. Robert O'Harrow Jr., 'Laws on Use of Personal Data Form a Quilt With Many Holes?' *Washington Post*, 9 March 1998.
14. Robert O'Harrow Jr., 'Data Firms Getting Too Personal?' *Washington Post*, 8 March 1998.
15. Ibid.

of potentially vast amounts of (sensitive) information.[16] In similar ways, the public sector seeks to monitor the financial system and to pursue tax claims and in some cases track down fraud and money laundering as well as 'enemies of the state' (see below).

Production and social reproduction

Our next hypothesis concerns the way that new patterns of accumulation may be in contradiction to the processes of social reproduction in our societies, such that one response is more coercive processes of intensified surveillance. This hypothesis is explored in the next two sections of this chapter.

With respect to the accumulation of capital, 'discipline' is associated with a certain type of normalization, that is into certain forms of possessively individualistic, consumerist behaviour that support the extension of the world market under the rule of capital. Thus systems of surveillance as well as legal mechanisms associated with the regulation of trade and investment, money and finance, are premised, as the World Bank put it in its *World Development Report* of 1997, on 'locking in' the rights of capital and thereby 'locking out' democratic control over key aspects of the political economy. As I have indicated elsewhere, in the 'new constitutional' frameworks of 'disciplinary neo-liberalism' public policy is increasingly premised on the goal of increasing the security of property (owners) and minimizing the uncertainty of investors partly through placing populations and governments under constant surveillance. Indeed, where individuals are not integrated and normalized into the circuits of global capitalism, strategies of incarceration, military surveillance, organized violence and intervention may be used as ultimate forms of power.[17]

With this in mind, our hypothesis is more specifically that panopticism is a means to coercively contain the contradictions between capital accumulation and social reproduction, and where this fails, strategies of

16. The USA even monitors online activity and e-mail of its own judges. Indeed the Judicial Conference of the US Courts (chaired by Chief Justice William Rehnquist of the Supreme Court) ruled that the Federal Government must relax surveillance of approximately 30,000 judges and related employees. See 'Judges Ease Surveillance of Web Use', *New York Times*, 20 September 2001.
17. Following the terrorist attacks on the US on 11 September 2001, there was a shift in public opinion in most nations in support of greater state surveillance of the population, particularly of certain types of immigrants.

incarceration and punishment are increasingly used (see the following section for elaboration). As feminist theorists have pointed out, social reproduction involves not only the reproduction of the commodity labour power but also the structures of socialization in the family, the community and the state that create the social foundations upon which all production must necessarily rest (Picchio 1992). However, in the era of neo-liberal globalization, for most of the Third World over the past 20 years – with the crucial exception of China and East Asia – living standards have stagnated for the majority as capital and resources have been drained from the very poorest nations to the wealthiest, and from the many to the few. The period of the reassertion of American global power and liberalization has coincided with a steep increase in global inequality, social dislocation and political polarization. Not only has global inequality grown, so has inequality within the USA itself, in ways that have tended to re-privatize the mechanisms of social reproduction and the so-called care economy, as public provisions have been reduced because of austerity programmes and greater fiscal restraints on governments (Bakker 1999). These points also help explain why the American-led strategy of neo-liberalism necessarily involves the use of coercive power, allied to practices of intensified surveillance ('transparency') of populations. This also explains why the often repressive use of surveillance structures and technologies is important in these struggles, and why the control over their development – in the communications, software and other information industries – is so crucial for the inter-state politics of the post-Cold War era.

In this context, such processes of panopticism (surveillance and normalization) are not neutral or generic. Rather they are unequal in their effects. Moreover in a world of intensifying economic crises, burdens of restructuring are felt most strongly by vulnerable members of society. These people are generally marginalized from privileged circuits of production and consumption in a socially and politically polarizing world order. That is to say that globalization is stratified along lines of class, race and gender, with poor women particularly hard-hit because of their dual role as commodified labour and providers of care within families. This is made more acute since we have experienced a period when many of the social provisions of welfare states (social security and pensions; socialization of risk more generally) have been downsized and privatized. As such the general conditions for social reproduction have been undergoing fundamental change.

This is also true with respect to other aspects of socialization of risk and the structures of social reproduction. For example, US executives not only have huge salaries, bonus and stock options, they also receive generous pensions devoid of the risk inherent in typical retirement plans. Whilst executive pensions have escalated, other American employees have seen their pensions shrink in size in recent years. The common pattern between 1983 and 1998 was that the amount of money held in retirement accounts by the typical household with people aged between 47 and 64 fell by 11 per cent after being adjusted for inflation (this includes both private pensions and the value of anticipated government Social Security benefits). The decline seems to have been caused by a shift from guaranteed traditional pensions (both public and private) with predetermined annual benefits to voluntary savings/investment programmes such as the 401(k) that are entirely subject to privatized market risk.[18]

US social order/disorder: enclavisation and incarceration

As I have noted, panoptic practices of American society, in the sense of normalizing populations, apply mainly to people who are exemplars of the commodified and normalized society *par excellence*. They are largely the beneficiaries of the increasingly privatized structures of the market and personal security. They hold gold and platinum credit cards and as market-place, transactional beings, their personal and pecuniary information is assessed and manipulated in the 'panoptic' databases. At the same time, whilst normalized and incorporated in the Foucauldian sense, they are nevertheless protected from the marginalized members of society by means of legal and coercive systems as well as spatial segregation. In many respects, they are the beneficiaries of a new world social order in which there is increasingly both social and spatial concentration of affluence (for example gated communities) and poverty (growing ghettoization). According to recent demographic research there is a new global politics of inequality where class lines are growing more socially and spatially rigid. This process in the USA was, in the past, attributed mainly to race, obscuring its class dimensions (Massey 1996: 403–4).

In most American cities, as in many Third World cities, gated communities and armed guards provided by private security services protect the affluent. I call this the process of *social enclavization*. One of the effects of enclavization is to undermine the capacities for the social reproduction of less affluent communities. The reason for this is that as

18. See D. Leonhardt, 'For Executives, Nest Egg is Wrapped in a Security Blanket', *New York Times*, 6 March 2002.

the affluent flee the big cities to the suburbs and to their gated communities, the urban tax base is eroded. Poorer communities are caught in a vicious cycle: the poor get worse and worse services, whilst the rich pay a smaller proportion of taxes but get much better services on a *per capita* basis than was the case when they lived in communities where rich and poor both lived. Increasingly, the rich never see or indeed ever meet or confront the poor. These developments in the USA have been connected to a new form of increasingly nihilistic, violent 'social ecology' in many cities (Massey 1996).

In order to contain the repercussions of this new social ecology, in the USA there has being a massive growth in the so-called prison industrial complex. In the last two decades the number one growth industry in the USA has been crime control and American incarceration rates have risen almost exponentially. The most vibrant sector of this industry has been private prisons, especially in rural locations where economic conditions are depressed. Such prisons provide jobs and enhance the local tax base as well as providing new settings for the expansion of capital and the hyper-exploitation of labour, since many prisoners are employed as very cheap labour under repressive conditions. And as is well known, the USA now has the world's highest rates of incarceration of any large country at 702 per 100,000 people (based on US Census Bureau estimate of national population of 275.1 million at mid-2000). At the end of 2000, American prisons and jails held 1,933,503 inmates, up from 330,000 inmates in 1972. The USA's rate of incarceration is five to eight times higher than that of Canada and the European Union and slightly higher than Russia's.[19] Moreover, the American prison population is disproportionately black and male. The incarceration rate for young black males aged 25–29 years was 13,118 per 100,000 in 2000, an astonishing 13 per cent of young men in that age group.[20] Similar racial- and gender-specific patterns are also manifest in the use of the death penalty in the USA.[21]

19. The 2000 incarceration rate for Japan was 40 per 100,000, Sweden 60, Switzerland 85; Netherlands, France and Italy 90, Germany 95, Canada, Australia and Spain 110, the UK 125, South Africa 400 and Russia 699. See <http://www.sentencingproject.org/news/usno1.pdf>.
20. The recent US prison population trend (year, prison population total, prison population rate) is 1992 1,295,150 (505) 1995 1,585,586 (600) 1998 1,816,931 (669). http://www.prisonstudies.org/.
21. The largest contrast is of course with white collar crime, i.e. the crimes of the powerful, usually involving huge sums of money accruing to people who are already very rich; such people often manage to avoid conviction or imprisonment and in some cases as fugitives from US justice even receive Presidential pardons, e.g. Marc Rich in 2001.

Homeland security

Following the destruction of the World Trade Center and attack on the Pentagon, the Federal Government moved quickly to expand its authority to monitor the population, including much greater video, telephone and Internet surveillance, and with the support of the majority of the public. Indeed, not only fingerprint but also retina, voice and facial scanning technologies are in development by biometrics firms, for example to confirm the identities of airline passengers. The stock of such firms rose rapidly in the aftermath of the attacks on the USA, and this despite a plunge of 10–15 per cent in the stock markets, as over a trillion dollars of investors' assets were wiped out.[22] Some of these surveillance techniques are now being incorporated into US federal laws governing immigration and monitoring of aliens.

On 6 June 2002, President George W. Bush proposed the creation of a Department of Homeland Security. This was partly to offset an increasingly aggressive inquiry from two key Congressional committees (Senate Judiciary and a Joint Intelligence Committee). The Congress was acting following the mounting public concern that the Administration had failed to heed warnings of direct threats to the USA prior to the attacks on the Pentagon and World Trade Center on 11 September 2001. As was noted by many sources outside of the USA at the time:

> Evidence from countless sources [suggests] that the 'colossal failure of intelligence' described by several senior politicians was not entirely the result of ignorance. In the three weeks before the attack, the FBI was actually looking for two suspected associates of Osama bin Laden who turned out to be among the 19 suicide hijackers. That search was part of a pattern of alarm signals sounding in intelligence circles from late August onwards ...[23]

Indeed, much earlier in the year, in January 2001 a bipartisan Congressional Commission had warned:

> 'The relative invulnerability of the US homeland to catastrophic attack' was coming to an end. The report said: 'A direct attack against American

---

22. Barnaby J. Feder, 'Exploring Technology to Protect Passengers With Fingerprint or Retina Scans', *New York Times*, 19 September 2001.
23. Andrew Gumbel, 'Bush Did Not Heed Several Warnings of Attacks', *Independent Digital* (UK), 17 September 2001.

citizens on American soil is likely over the next quarter century.' A series of 50 recommendations was made, including a greater reliance on human intelligence rather than espionage equipment and the creation of a new domestic security agency marshalling the forces of the CIA, immigration, the border patrol, the Coast Guard and the FBI. Rather than accept the report, which was unanimously approved by all seven Republicans and seven Democrats involved in its drafting and which led to the introduction of congressional legislation advocating the creation of a National Homeland Security Agency, the Bush administration chose to put it to one side and work out its own strategy from scratch.[24]

So it is clear that irrespective of the outcome of the new Congressional inquiries, the Department of Homeland Security has already received wide bipartisan support. If implemented it will represent the most extensive reorganization of the American security apparatus since World War II. It will go well beyond the present *ad hoc* system that combines over 20 separate executive agencies concerned with border and transportation security; emergency preparedness; countermeasures for weapons of mass destruction; infrastructure protection; and information analysis normally associated with the policing and intelligence agencies. The latter include a counter-terrorism centre established in 1986 with staff from both the CIA and the FBI, supposedly to achieve 'fusion' of intelligence sources and methods concerning threats to US interests. Congressional leaders seem to be convinced that this fusion never took place. Indeed the new Department of Homeland Security seems likely to be very strongly influenced by the results of extensive investigation of intelligence failures over the last ten years that has just been launched by the Congress. The hearings and inquiry will go well beyond the CIA and FBI to involve scrutiny of the highly secret National Security Agency (NSA), for example including the degree to which its interpretations of the huge amounts of electronic data and communications traffic it collects and intercepts is adequate to American security needs.[25] Some of the implications of this extended apparatus of electronic surveillance and military-political monitoring are discussed in the following section.

24. Andrew Gumbel, 'Bush Did Not Heed Several Warnings of Attacks', *Independent Digital* (UK), 17 September 2001.
25. Patrick L. Tyler, 'Reaction, then Action. With Intelligence Lapses Under Scrutiny, White House Acts to regain the initiative', *New York Times*, 7 June 2002; David Johnston and Neil A. Lewis, Bush, 'As Terror Inquiry Swirls, Seeks Cabinet Post on Security', *New York Times*, 7 June 2002.

'Future Image Architecture': monitoring enemies and friends

In this section I hypothesize that the international counterpart to the coercive strategies mentioned in the two previous sections are the new systems of surveillance associated with the US-led alliance systems. Indeed, it appears that the goal of the US apparatuses relates to the modernist dystopia noted earlier – to place both friends and enemies alike under total surveillance. The attacks of 11 September 2001, whilst showing how far this goal remains elusive, will likely mean an intensification of US surveillance efforts and more effective co-ordination of the different agencies involved.

An ironic example of the type of thinking that underlines the ideology of total surveillance was given following the capture of the EP-3E spy plane by China in April 2001, when a veteran of US Navy surveillance remarked to journalists that an officer in his squadron had business cards inscribed with the motto: 'In God we trust. All others we monitor.'[26]

This type of thinking, of course has a much longer lineage. Geopolitical theorist George Kennan anticipated some of it immediately after World War II. He argued that an American strategy of containment should be launched to sustain the world economy as it was, with its very unequal distribution of wealth and power skewed heavily in favour of the USA. In 1997, US Space Command released a strategy document premised on the concept of 'full spectrum dominance', maintained well into the future through 'full force integration'. The goal was military superiority over land, sea, air and space. Indeed, the rapid militarization of space was heralded as the most important single strategic initiative for the USA in the twenty-first century. The strategy is designed to protect 'US national interests and investments' across the globe in the new millennium, not from traditional rivals, but also from new challenges:

> Although unlikely to be challenged by a global peer competitor, the United States will continue to be challenged regionally. The globalization of the world economy will also continue, with a widening between 'haves' and 'have-nots.' Accelerating rates of technological development will be increasingly driven by the commercial sector – not the military. Increased weapons lethality and precision will lead

---

26. Christopher Drew, 'Listening, Looking: Old Methods Still Work', *New York Times*, 14 April 2001.

to new operational doctrine. Information-intensive military force structures will lead to a highly dynamic operations tempo.[27]

In other words, following the demise and the final collapse of the Soviet Union, the conventional strategic wisdom that arose in Washington was that challenges to US primacy were likely to be more diffuse, which means that even US 'friends' are a potential target of surveillance. Needless to say this has created concerns in the European Union and elsewhere, given the extensiveness of American intelligence networks.[28] Here it is worth recalling that under the influence of the US government and coalitions of transnational corporations, international organizations have embarked on a huge effort to create uniform databases and universal standards for data protocols and for other forms of information provision. Of course standards do not determine the content of what is transmitted through the new information structures, although control over the basic infrastructure of networks can be considered to be an important power resource. Thus network development has a strategic aspect, and indeed several American military theorists have sought to emphasize the need for US economic and military control over strategic nodes within the global systems of interlocking networks, thus controlling the rules of access to and participation in these networks. Thus some of the changing context for strategy – in the so-called information age – is viewed by one US military theorist as follows:

> Another way of assessing the changes in the ways of strategy is to compare World War I and II warfare to information age warfare. Whereas the world wars used attrition (WWI) and maneuver (WWII), information age war emphasizes control. Whereas the world wars attempted to exhaust (WWI) and annihilate (WWII), cyberwar seeks to paralyze. And whereas the tools of the world wars were firepower weapons (WWI) and mechanization (WWII) produced in mass, the tools of information war are limited numbers of inexpensive computers linked via global communication systems. (Fast 2001)

27. US Space Command, *Vision for 2020*. Washington DC: US Department of Defense, 1997. <http://www.gsinstitute.org/resources/extras/vision_2020.pdf>. I am grateful to Tim DiMuzio for this example.
28. E.g. Steve Wright, *An Appraisal of the Technologies of Political Control*. Omega Foundation Report to European Parliament Scientific and Technological Options Assessment (STOA) updated September 1998. <http://www.iptvreports.mcmail.com/ic2kreport.htm>.

Indeed, notwithstanding its now central commitment to the 'war on terrorism' the George W. Bush Administration has made it consistently clear that its military priorities lie not only in developing its new version of Star Wars (missile defence) but also in increasing its space-based satellite and terrestrial surveillance structures. It has also stressed the need to build up American capacities to engage in cyber-war and information warfare more generally, including plans to create a new secret agency located in the White House and in the Pentagon, called the Office of Strategic Influence (OSI). This Orwellian initiative was strongly criticized by many Americans, after members of the Bush Administration made it clear that OSI would use black propaganda and disinformation campaigns in order to combat the influence of anti-American forces throughout the world. However at the time of writing OSI seems set to continue, with an undisclosed budget. With respect to issues of surveillance, the leadership at the Pentagon reflects the new emphasis on high-technology strategy. For example President Bush's Chairman of Joint Chiefs of Staff is General Richard B. Myers. Myers was commander in chief of the USA's space forces during the late 1990s and oversaw the development of the military's computer network, becoming a champion of cyber-war tactics.[29] Indeed, it was reported in 2001 that the US government propaganda agencies were seeking to accelerate the use of computer technologies to carry their information war to the Internet in an effort to evade Chinese (efforts at Web) censorship. Some of this is being carried out under a programme funded by the venture capital arm of the CIA, In-Q-Tel.[30]

By contrast, President Clinton extended US intelligence support to commercial organizations by creating the National Economic Council, paralleling the National Security Council. In many respects, however, the Bush and Clinton Administrations are two sides of the same coin, since there is considerable continuity in American military and surveillance practices. Put differently, whilst the USA has used its capacities for aerial bombardment and intervention, the actual use of organized violence is only part of its new architectures of military power. The other side is relentless and ongoing surveillance of 'enemies and friends' by important agencies such as the NSA with a budget several times larger than that of the CIA (its overall direction is under the authority of the Director of the CIA). NSA gathers information of all types.

29. James Dao, 'Low-key Space Buff: Richard Bowman Myers', *New York Times*, 25 August 2001.
30. Jennifer Lee, 'US May Help Chinese Evade Net Censorship', *New York Times*, 30 August 2001.

So for example, in April 2001 it was announced that the secret National Reconnaissance Office of the USA was authorized by the Clinton Administration and the Congress to undertake a massive expansion of its spy satellite systems, partly because other nations such as Russia, France, India and closer American allies such as Israel and Canada have satellite surveillance systems.

The US initiative entails the most expensive venture ever undertaken by American intelligence agencies, called 'Future Image Architecture' (FIA). FIA will cost $25 billion over 20 years – by contrast the Manhattan Project to build the atomic bomb during World War II cost $20 billion in inflation-adjusted dollars. The new systems are intended to supplement other surveillance systems to give the USA a unilateral capacity for certain types of military action. This new system also fits well with the Bush Administration's priority of developing the military uses of space and the use of cyber warfare. The new system will orbit 2,000 miles (3,200 km) high, will collect between 8 and 20 times more imagery and detail than present systems, and it will be more difficult to evade. It will be able to keep any target within camera range for about 30 minutes (as opposed to the present limit of about 10 minutes) and be more precise and 'able to track objects as small as a baseball anywhere, any time on the planet'.[31] The *International Herald Tribune* noted:

> The truly revolutionary feature, however, is not in the sky but in the ground station computers that will capture the downloads of electronic imagery, process the data into useable intelligence and then distribute pictures to a growing throng of US government agencies – the official consumers of the material ... [including] detailed battlefield pictures ... Until now these high-resolution images, which can be taken at night or through clouds, have taken days to reach down to the officers ...[32]

Here it is worth noting that the USA benefits from intelligence inputs from its major allies. Many of the electronic surveillance facilities of the English-speaking countries are combined in the so-called ECHELON system, created in the 1970s and enlarged between 1975 and 1995. Tens of billions of messages are analysed every day, for example through data-

31. Joseph Fitchett, 'Spying from Space: US to Sharpen the Focus', *International Herald Tribune*, 10 April 2001.
32. Ibid. 4. In the global surveillance system co-ordinated by NSA, the US is allowed all the 'raw' intelligence data of its main partners in the UKUSA alliance intelligence system that was created in 1947 (UK; Canada; New Zealand; Australia). In exchange the US returns 'processed data'.

mining software operating through Internet servers. ECHELON feeds the data into huge computers known as Dictionaries that automatically select written communications using lists of target numbers, subjects and keywords.[33] Virtually all the messages that are selected by Dictionary computers are automatically forwarded to NSA or other users without being read locally. ECHELON is designed primarily for non-military targets: governments, businesses, organizations and individuals.

Since most nations make it illegal to spy on their own citizens, UKUSA arrangements may allow this to be circumvented.[34] In addition, many intelligence practices are undergoing changes following the 2001 attack on America by terrorists. Many of these changes have crucial implications for civil rights and human security, for example the right to asylum and non-coercive migration – and not just in the USA. For example, in the aftermath of the attacks, the USA pressed Canada to agree to a unified and truly continental security system (i.e. accept the US framework as its own) in immigration, anti-terrorism and policing of borders, despite the fact that Canada has different policies on asylum, refugees and immigrants. This is, in other words an area where the Bush Administration's penchant for unilateralism will necessarily be curbed since for anti-terrorist measures to succeed they require global co-operation of police and intelligence services, and forms of policing that operate effectively at the capillary level of particular districts.

This co-operation may be made easier by recent events but it is by no means automatic in the future – particularly when there are ongoing concerns about the use of surveillance systems for the benefit of American capital. For example, continental Europeans do not believe American claims that ECHELON has not been used for commercial espionage and for spying on their citizens more generally. Led by France in collaboration with Germany, they have begun to set up rival systems, partly for commercial and mercantilist reasons, and partly for reasons of privacy. Public opinion in the European Union seems to be increasingly concerned at how American surveillance routinely intercepts its phone calls, faxes

33. Proof was found in 1998–99 by US intelligence specialist Jeffrey Richelson, via the Freedom of Information Act. He obtained documents that confirmed the existence, scale and expansion of the ECHELON system. See <http://www.zdnet.co.uk/news/2000/25/ns-16204.html>.

34. Law enforcement agencies normally intercept a specific line/lines, and must justify this by requests to a judicial or administrative authority and gain a specific warrant for action before proceeding. Communications intelligence (Comint) agencies conduct 'trawling' activities, under general warrants that do not require that intercepted parties be criminals.

and e-mail. However, UKUSA arrangements give the USA a massive bridgehead into Europe, and ability to place much of European telecommunications and data flows under constant surveillance.

Conclusion

What this chapter attempts to do is to point towards the need for an exploration of how surveillance processes ('panopticism') are connected to broad developments in political and civil society, both from the vantage point of its historical roots and the deepening of the mechanisms associated with the present world order. What is at issue here is the reconfiguration of civil society, and the re-privatization of aspects of risk (both market risk and credit risk) that were largely socialized in the OECD countries between c.1950 and c.1980.

Whilst this chapter has focused mainly on the USA and other OECD nations, it has implications for much of the rest of the world, since developments in the USA have global repercussions and these need to be placed in the context of worldwide trends towards the increased privatization of not only state-owned industries, but also of social reproduction and the provision of public goods, as recent World Bank and UNDP annual reports have amply documented (UNDP 2000; World Bank 2002). On the one hand risk is shifted increasingly down to the personal level, and the hedging of risks takes a market form, for example the provision of private healthcare arrangements, private security guards, and so on. On the other hand risk is increasingly generalized (e.g. environmental or market risks, such as a fall in the stock market undermining life-savings of workers, or the collapse of a massive corporation, such as Enron, or a wider financial collapse impoverishing millions, as in the global economic meltdown of 1997–98. Here the class-based nature of systems of justice is exposed as the chief criminals often escape going to trial, or even avoid prosecution altogether.[35]

35. In 1989 the US Sentencing Commission recommended much harsher penalties – up to one-third of a billion dollars – for crimes committed by multi-billion dollar corporations, including that of the individuals who run them. However, it was halted by fierce corporate lobbying, resulting in maximum penalties being scaled back by 97 per cent in 1990, and it was made easier for corporations to reduce their fines even more based on a set of mitigating factors. In an article of the same title, social theorist Amitai Etzioni, a former member of the Commission, noted that 'Enron-type scandals will end when penalties fit crimes', *USA Today*, 26 March 2002. Etzioni doubted whether any of the key Enron executives would be charged, let alone go to trial, given their 'high powered lawyers and invocation of the Fifth Amendment'.

Of course there is nothing new about the surveillance of populations by the imperial powers and their state apparatuses – the ancient Chinese Empire combined surveillance by its bureaucratic apparatus and local, capillary forms of normalization and observation of populations at the village level with systems of policing of its borders to prevent the encroachment of enemies. In other words such pre-modern forms of surveillance were extensive and they constituted an efficient economy of power across social and political space and time, although they could not overcome all forms of local resistance. In the Chinese case, its system lasted for well over 1,000 years. However, what may be distinctive about modern and indeed post-modern forms of panopticism is the way in which they are linked to the ongoing surveillance of domestic and foreign populations, as well as political leaders, in the context of 'real time'.

One conclusion is that the logic of panopticism in the post-modern condition has roots in a process to overcome and incorporate, on the one hand disorder and chaos, and on the other hand, resistance of various kinds to its discipline, for example based in the particularities of culture/local systems of social reproduction. In the same way that the French revolutionaries sought to supplant localized orders with a more 'rational' form of production, capital takes on a panoptic form. Capital does not simply depend upon states and international organizations to create the epistemological and ontological categories that define its fields of relevancy. Indeed, it does not depend upon the state to collect all of the data on populations, activities and transactions that it needs. Thus capital as well as the state and international organizations, defines what is formal, or legal, or indeed informal and illegal, what is included and what is excluded within the field of normalized practices.

What seems to be missing, and sorely needed is the democratic and accountable use of surveillance capabilities and transparency practices in order to better regulate the global political economy, and to increase the capability of countries to sustain their tax base and thus capacities for social reproduction. What is needed is surveillance of the commanding heights of political and economic power.

So in conclusion, how might a research agenda further explore and interpret some of these questions?

First, as we have argued, if we were to look at this issue from the perspective of recent developments in Feminist Political Economy, the issue would be whether there is a process whereby fundamental processes of social reproduction are being subjected to and subordinated by extended commodification and intensified surveillance. Put differently, the question that would be posed is whether there is a contradiction between the expanded and global reproduction of capital, and the continued social reproduction of labour, which by definition occurs within particular communities. Second, if we add to the issue of social reproduction a transnational class perspective, we would need to know more about the link between transformations in patterns of power and social reproduction associated with changing ownership structures of capital. For this to happen we need both a better research apparatus and more democratic forms of surveillance based on, for example, greater transparency of capital. Indeed, one of the salient features of the emerging patterns of intensified globalization is the emergence of complex transnational ownership structures, associated with integrated capital and other asset markets offering more global opportunities for investment. Thus institutional investors such as pension funds routinely invest in a range of jurisdictions using a variety of assets to both minimize risk and to maximize profits, and as has been increasingly noted, increasing numbers of American firms are incorporating in offshore jurisdictions such as Bermuda in order to avoid taxes. Whilst this may increase profits flows over time, it may reduce the incentive, and indeed the need, for business to show any *loyalty* to any particular country, and indirectly, any incentive to contribute to its system of social reproduction (e.g. through the payment of taxes or by training workers). In other words, whilst by definition in a capitalist system, capital as a class force has a very powerful *voice* in the policy-making process, capital, particularly financial forms of capital, also has the capacity to exercise *exit* from particular jurisdictions if it perceives that the business or investment climate has deteriorated. On the other hand, immobile producers and workers more generally, are tied to particular locations, and lack this exit option, which is an aspect of the structural power of capital. Thus democracy, and the continued ability for societies to sustain their structures of social reproduction requires both more extensive and democratic surveillance as well as greater capability to enforce taxation on capital.

Finally, in a world where there seems to be ever-greater perception of insecurity, even for the very powerful, we need to know much more about the relationship between social dislocation, economic crisis and the propensity to new forms of violence. This is unlikely to be delivered by the existing forms of surveillance since they are constructed on the basis of crude, dichotomous methods of categorization and classification. This issue is as much epistemological as it is social. The emergence of transparency capitalism has coincided with a world of cascading economic and financial crises, as well as growing economic inequality. One of the manifestations of this globalizing contradiction may well be irrational and violent dissent – including terrorism of the weak. One explanation for this may well be that as states have tended to retreat from engagement in the provisions associated with social reproduction (welfare, education and health) and have focused upon creating an enabling environment for market forces, deeply conservative political forces have stepped into a vacuum created by the state's retreat from human development and human security. Some of these new forces, albeit in a reactionary way, attempt to provide frameworks of meaning and order at the fringes of survival, whereas others indoctrinate their followers into cults of martyrdom propelled against the West in general and the USA and Israel in particular. In sum, whilst the attacks on America on 11 September 2001 seemed to be the work of middle-class fundamentalist radicals, acting as martyrs to their cause, it is important not to lose sight of this more structural context that seems to be linked to the intense popular resentment against American power and imperialism in many parts of the world. To contain this type of resentment will require much more than military-surveillance capabilities, even if they are allied to a more extensive American propaganda machine in the Islamic world. What is needed is a set of policies that can address the pressing issues of human insecurity, economic dislocation and the privatization of risk.

11
The Post-modern Prince[1]

> The modern prince, the myth-prince, cannot be a real person, a concrete individual. It can only be an organism, a complex element of society in which a collective will, which has already been recognized and has to some extent asserted itself in action, begins to take concrete form. (Gramsci 1971: 129)

This chapter analyses recent protests against aspects of neo-liberal globalization, as for example at the World Trade Organization (WTO) Ministerial Meeting in Seattle in late 1999 and in Washington, DC in spring 2000 to coincide with the IMF and World Bank Annual Meetings. I first examine the reasons for the failure of the Seattle talks, and second, evaluate the protests and their political significance. Finally, I analyze some emerging forms of political agency associated with struggles over the nature and direction of globalization that I call the 'the Post-modern Prince'. This concept is elaborated in the final section. It is important to stress at the outset, however, that in this chapter the term 'post-modern' does not refer, as it often does, to a discursive or aesthetic moment. In my usage, 'post-modern' refers to a set of conditions, particularly political, material and ecological that is giving rise to new forms of political agency whose defining myths are associated with the quest to ensure human and inter-generational security on and for the planet, as well as democratic human development and human rights. As such, the multiple and diverse political forces that form the Post-modern Prince combine both defensive and forward-looking strategies. Rather than engaging in deconstruction, they seek to develop a global and universal politics of radical (re)construction.

The battle in Seattle took place both inside and outside the conference centre in which the meetings took place; the collapse of the discussions was partly caused by the greater visibility of trade issues in the everyday lives of citizens and the increasing concern over how international trade

1. © *Millennium: Journal of International Studies.* This article first appeared in *Millennium*, 29 (1) 2000: 131–41. Excerpts reproduced with the permission of the publisher.

and investment agreements are undermining important aspects of national sovereignty and policy autonomy, especially in ways that strengthen corporate power. These concerns – expressed through various forms of political mobilization – have put pressure upon political leaders throughout the world to re-examine some of the premises and contradictions of neo-liberal globalization.

Why the WTO talks failed

Why specifically did the Seattle talks fail? The first and most obvious reason was US intransigence, principally in defence of the *status quo* against demands for reform by other nations concerned at the repercussions of the liberalization framework (the built-in agenda) put in place by the GATT Uruguay Round.[2] The GATT Uruguay Round was a 'Single Undertaking', a generic all-or-nothing type of agreement that meant signatories had to agree to all its commitments and disciplines, as well as to the institutionalization of the WTO. The wider juridical-political framework for locking in such commitments can be called the new constitutionalism of disciplinary neo-liberalism (Gill 1998). This encompasses not only trade and investment, but also private property rights more generally (and not just intellectual property rights). It also involves macroeconomic policies and institutions (for example independent central banks and balanced budget amendments) in ways that minimize, or even 'lock out' democratic controls over key economic institutions and policy frameworks in the long term.

In this context, the USA mainly wanted to sustain commitments to existing protections for intellectual property rights and investment and stop any attempts to weaken the capacity of existing agreements to open new markets for American corporations. The US position was based on intelligence work by government agencies, academics, and corporate strategists co-ordinated by the CIA.[3]

So it would be easy to say that protests outside the Seattle Convention Centre and confronted by the Seattle riot police, the FBI and the CIA had little or no effect on the failure of the talks, other than the fact that many delegates could not get into the building because of the disruptions outside. However, this would be to misunderstand the link between

2. Scott Sinclair, 'The WTO: What Happened In Seattle? What's Next In Geneva?' Briefing Paper Series: Trade And Investment No. 2. Ottawa: Canadian Centre For Policy Alternatives, 2000: 6.
3. See 'CIA Spies Swap Cold War for Trade Wars', *Financial Times*, 14 August 1999.

public concern and the negotiating positions of states in the WTO. Indeed, it is becoming clear that the central reasons for the failure of the Seattle Ministerial were linked to the fact that the establishment of the WTO has gone well beyond the traditional role of the GATT in ways that have begun not only increasingly to encroach on crucial domestic policy areas and national sovereignty, but which also have repercussions for international law. In addition, key areas of concern to the public such as food safety, biotechnology, the environment, labour standards, and broader questions of economic development add to the popular disquiet and mobilization over cultural, social and ethical questions linked to the globalization project.

In this regard – and this is very relevant to the concerns of the protesters as well as many governments – the new services negotiations that will occur in Geneva as a result of the 'Single Undertaking' have a wide mandate and the new trade disciplines will have potentially vast impact across major social institutions and programmes, such as health, education, social services, and cultural issues. This will allow for wider privatization and commercialization of the public sector and indirectly, of the public sphere itself, for example in social programmes and education.[4] The logic of the negotiations will likely inhibit many government programmes that could be justified as being in the public interest, unless governments are able to convince WTO panels that these programmes are not substantially in restraint of trade and investment on the part of private enterprise. Indeed, because the built-in agenda will proceed in Geneva, many divisions among governments, especially between North and South, are emerging. The North–South divisions also revolve around dissatisfaction on the South's part at concessions made in the earlier GATT Uruguay Round, coupled with their frustration in failing to open Northern markets for their manufactured and agricultural exports.

With this agenda in mind, the protesters – although drawn from a very diverse range of organizations and political tendencies – believe there is a centralization and concentration of power under corporate control in neo-liberal globalization, with much of the policy agenda for this project orchestrated by international organizations such as the WTO, the IMF and the World Bank. Thus, it was not surprising that the battle in Seattle

---

4. 'New Trade Rules Target Education'. Editorial. *Canadian Association of University Teachers Bulletin*, 7 September 1999. The Bulletin added that Education International, representing 294 educational unions and associations worldwide, expressed great concern about how WTO initiatives would undermine public education.

moved to Washington DC in mid-April where the same set of progressive and environmental activists and organizations, including trade unions, protested the role of the IMF, World Bank and the G7.

What is significant here is that the new counter-movements seek to preserve ecological and cultural diversity against what they see as the encroachment of political, social and ecological monocultures associated with the supremacy of corporate rule. At the time of writing, the protests were set to move on to lay siege to the headquarters of Citicorp, the world's biggest financial conglomerate.

The contradictions of neo-liberal globalization and the Seattle protests

Implicitly or explicitly, the failure of the talks and indeed much of the backlash against neo-liberal globalization is linked to the way that people in diverse contexts are experiencing the problems and contradictions linked to the power of capital and more specifically the projects of disciplinary neo-liberalism and new constitutionalism. So what are these contradictions and how do they relate to the Seattle protests?

The first is the contradiction between big capital and democracy. Central here is the extension of binding legal mechanisms of trade and investment agreements, such as the GATT Uruguay Round and regional agreements, such as NAFTA. A counter-example, which pointed the way towards Seattle in terms of much of its counter-hegemonic political form, was the failed OECD effort to create a Multilateral Agreement on Investment (MAI). The MAI was also partly undermined by grass-root mobilization against corporate globalization, as well as by more conventional political concerns about sovereignty. The protesters viewed agreements such as NAFTA and organizations such as the WTO as seeking to institutionalize ever-more extensive charters of rights and freedoms for corporations, allowing for greater freedom of enterprise and worldwide protection for private property rights. The protesters perceived that deregulation, privatization and liberalization are a means to strengthen a particular set of class interests, principally the power of private investors and large shareholders. They are opposed to greater legal and market constraints on democracy.

Put differently, the issue was therefore how far and in what ways trade and investment agreements 'lock in' commitments to liberalization, whilst 'locking out' popular-democratic and parliamentary forces from control over crucial economic, social and ecological policies.

The second set of contradictions is both economic and social. ②
Disciplinary neo-liberalism proceeds with an intensification of discipline
on labour and a rising rate of exploitation, partly reflected in booming
stock markets during the past decade, whilst at the same time persistent
economic and financial crises have impoverished many millions of
people and caused significant economic dislocations. This explains the
growing role of organized labour – for example American-based trade
unions such as the Teamsters – in the protests, as well as organizations
representing feminists, other workers, peasants, and smaller producers
worldwide. In this regard, the numbers do not lie: despite what has been
the longest boom in the history of Western capitalism, the real incomes
of average people have been falling. So if this happens in a boom, what
happens in a bust? This question has been answered already in the East
Asia crisis when millions were impoverished.

Third, for a number of years now, the discipline of capital has become ③
linked to the intensification of a crisis of social reproduction. Feminist
political economy has shown how a disproportionate burden of (structural)
adjustment to the harsher more competitive circumstances over the past
20 years has fallen on the shoulders of the less well-paid, on women and
children, and the weaker members of society, the old and the disabled.
In an era of fiscal stringency, in many states social welfare, health and
educational provisions have been reduced and the socialization of risk
has been reduced for a growing proportion of the world's population. This
has generated a crisis of social reproduction as burdens of adjustment are
displaced into families and communities that are already under pressure
to simply survive in economic terms and as risk becomes privatized,
redistributed and generalized in new forms (Bakker 1999).

The final set of contradictions are linked to how socio-cultural and ④
biological diversity are being replaced by a social and biological
monoculture under corporate domination, and how this is linked to a
loss of food security and new forms of generalized health risks. Thus, the
protesters argued that if parts of the Seattle draft agenda were ratified, it
would allow for a liberalization of trade in genetically modified crops,
provisions to allow world water supplies to be privatized, and the
patenting of virtually all forms of life including genetic material that had
been widely used across cultures for thousands of years. The protesters
also felt particularly strongly about the patenting of seeds and
bioengineering by companies like Novartis and Enron, and other firms
seen to be trying to monopolize control over food and undermine local
livelihood and food security.

Hence protesters opposed the control of the global food order by corporate interests linked to new constitutionalism. These interests have begun to institutionalize their right 'to source food and food inputs, to prospect for genetic patents, and to gain access to local and national food markets' established through the GATT Uruguay Round and World Trade Organization (McMichael 1999: 3). Transnational corporations have managed to redefine food security in terms of the reduction of national barriers to agricultural trade, ensuring market rule in the global food order. The effect is the intensification of the centralization of control by 'agri-food capital *via* global sourcing and global trading', in ways that intensify world food production and consumption relations through 'unsustainable monocultures, terminator genes, and class-based diets premised on the elimination of the diversity of natural resources, farm cultures and food cultures, and the decline of local food self-sufficiency and food security mechanisms' (McMichael 1999: 2).

Together, these contradictions contribute to what might be called a global or 'organic crisis' that links diverse forces across and within nations, specifically to oppose the ideas, institutions and material power of disciplinary neo-liberalism. Much of the opposition to corporate globalization was summed up by AFL-CIO President John Sweeney, who alongside President Clinton was addressing the heads of the 1,000 biggest transnational corporations at the annual meeting of the self-appointed and unelected World Economic Forum in Davos in February 2000. Sweeney stated that the protests from North and South represented 'a call for new global rules, democratically developed' to constrain 'growing inequality, environmental destruction, and a race to the bottom for working people', warning that if such rules were not forthcoming 'it will generate an increasingly volatile reaction that will make Seattle look tame'.[5] Indeed Clinton's remarks made at Davos 'seemed designed as a reminder that these fears – even expressed in unwelcome and sometimes violent ways, as they were in Seattle – have a legitimacy that deserves attention in the world's executive suites and government ministries'.[6]

We know by now, of course, that the violence in Seattle was almost completely carried out by the heavily armed police militias who took the battle to the protesters. In Washington in April 2000, police pre-emptively arrested hundreds of demonstrators, in actions justified by the local

5. John Sweeney, 'Remember Seattle', *Washington Post*, 30 January 2000.
6. Ann Swardson, 'Clinton Appeals for Compassion in Global Trade; World Economic Forum Told Don't Leave "Little Guys" Out', *Washington Post*, 30 January 2000.

police chief as a matter of prudence. Another example of this was the repression of peaceful protests at the Asia-Pacific Economic Co-operation meeting in Vancouver in 1998. The protests focused on the contradiction of separating free trade from political democracy, dramatized by the presence of the Indonesian dictator, President Suharto. In sum, state authorities will quickly act to restrict basic political rights and freedoms of opposition by alternative members of civil society – rights supposedly underpinned by the rule of law in a liberal constitutional framework – when business interests are threatened. At Seattle, the anonymous, unaccountable and intimidating police actions seemed almost absurd in light of the fact that the protests involved children dressed as turtles, peaceful activists for social justice, union members, faith groups, accompanied by teachers, scientists and assorted 'tree huggers' all of whom were non-violent. Indeed, with the possible exception of a small number of anarchists, virtually none of the protesters was in any way violent. In Washington, the police protected the meetings wearing heavy armour from behind metal barricades, in face of protesters carrying puppets and signs that read 'spank the Bank'. Moments such as these, however, illustrate not only a comedy of the absurd but also the broader dialectic between a supremacist set of forces and an ethico-political alternative involved in a new inclusive politics of diversity.

Indeed, since the Seattle debacle the protesters have been able to extend their critique of what they see as the political monoculture by showing how one of its key components, the 'quality press' and TV media, reported what occurred. In the US, for example, the mainstream media found it impossible to represent the violence as being caused by the authorities in order to provoke and discredit the opposition as being Luddite, anti-science and unlawful. Seen from the vantage point of the protesters, 'the *Washington Post* and the *New York Times* are the keepers of "official reality", and in official reality it is always the protesters who are violent'.[7]

Toward a Post-modern Prince?

In conclusion, I advance the following hypothesis: the protests form part of a worldwide movement that can perhaps be understood in terms of

7. Posted on <http://www.peoples@post4.tele.dk> 26 April 2000 on behalf of the NGO network that organized the Washington protests: Mobilization for Global Justice, 1247 E Street SE, Washington DC 20003, <www.a16.org>. At the time of the protests this Website passed 250,000 visitors. It was the subject of a *Washington Post* article on 1 April 2000, 'Rally Web Site also Interests the Uninvited: This revolution will not be televised: It will be downloaded.'

new potentials and forms of global political agency. And following Machiavelli and Gramsci, I call this set of potentials 'the Post-modern Prince' which I understand as something plural and differentiated, although linked to universalism and the construction of a new form of globalism, and of course, something that needs to be understood as a set of social and political forces in movement.

Let us place this hypothesis in some theoretical context. Machiavelli's *The Prince* addressed the problem of the ethics of rule from the viewpoint of both the prince (the *palazzo*, the palace) and the people (the *piazza*, the town square). Machiavelli sought to theorize how to construct a form of rule that combined both *virtù* (ethics, responsibility and consent) and fear (coercion) under conditions of *fortuna* (circumstances). *The Prince* was written in Florence, in the context of the political upheavals of Renaissance Italy. Both Machiavelli and later Gramsci linked their analyses and propositions to the reality of concrete historical circumstances as well as to potential for transformation. These included pressing contemporary issues associated with the problems of Italian unification, and the subordinate place of Italy in the structures of international relations. And it was in a similar national and international context that Gramsci's *The Modern Prince* was written in a fascist prison, a text that dealt with a central problem of politics: the constitution of power, authority, rule, rights and responsibilities in the creation of an ethical political community. Nevertheless, what Gramsci saw in *The Prince* was that it was 'not a systematic treatment, but a "live" work, in which political ideology and political science are fused in the dramatic form of a "myth"' (Gramsci 1971: 125). The myth for Machiavelli was that of the *condottiere*, who represents the collective will. By contrast, for Gramsci *The Modern Prince* proposed the myth of the democratic modern mass political party – the communist party – charged with the construction of a new form of state and society, and a new world order.

In the new strategic context (*fortuna*) of disciplinary neo-liberalism and globalization, then, a central problem of political theory is how to imagine and to theorize the new forms of collective political identity and agency that might lead to the creation of new, ethical, and democratic political institutions and forms of practice (*virtù*). So in this context, let me again be clear that by 'Post-modern Prince' I do *not* mean a form of political agency that is based on post-modern philosophy and the radical relativism it often entails. What I am intending to communicate is a shift in the forms of political agency that are going beyond earlier modernist political projects. So 'the Post-modern Prince' involves tendencies that have begun to challenge some of the myths and the disciplines of modernist practices, and specifically resisting those that seek to consolidate the project of globalization under the rule of capital.

Thus, the battles in Seattle may link to new patterns of political agency and a movement that goes well beyond the politics of identity and difference: it has gender, race and class aspects. It is connected to issues of ecological and social reproduction, and of course, to the question of democracy. This is why more than 700 organizations and between 40,000 and 60,000 people – principally human rights activists, labour activists, indigenous people, representatives of churches, industrial workers, small farmers, forest activists, environmentalists, social justice workers, students and teachers – all took part collectively in the protests against the WTO's Third Ministerial on 30 November 1999. The protesters seem aware of the nature and dynamics of their movement and have theorized a series of political links between different events so that they will become more than what James Rosenau called 'distant proximities' or simply isolated moments of resistance against globalization (Rosenau 1997).

In sum, these movements are beginning to form what Gramsci called 'an organism, a complex element of society' that is beginning to point towards the realization of a 'collective will'. This will is coming to be 'recognized and has to some extent asserted itself in action'. It is beginning to 'take concrete form' (Gramsci 1971: 129). Indeed the diverse organizations that are connected to the protests seek to go further to organize something akin to a post-modern transnational political party that is one with no clear leadership structure as such. It is a party of movement that cannot be easily decapitated. This element puzzled mainstream press reporters at Seattle since they were unable to find, and thus to photograph or interview the 'leaders' of the protests. However, this emerging political form is not a signal of an end to universalism in politics as such, since many of the forces it entails are linked to democratization and a search for collective solutions to common problems. It seeks to combine diversity with new forms of collective identity and solidarity in and across civil societies. Thus the organizers of the April 2000 Washington demonstrations stated that 'Sweeney's prediction' made at Davos was in fact a description of events that were going on right now, but that are largely ignored by the media:

> The Zapatista uprising in Mexico, the recent coup in Ecuador, the civil war in the Congo, the turmoil in Indonesia, and the threat of the U'Wa people to commit mass suicide, are all expressions of the social explosion that has arisen from the desperation caused by the policies of the World Bank, IMF, and their corporate directors ... Fundamental change does not mean renaming their programs or other public

relations scams. Fundamental reform means rules that empower the people of the world to make the decisions about how they live their lives – not the transnational CEO's or their purchased political leaders.[8]

In this regard, the effectiveness of the protest movements may well lie in a new confidence gained as particular struggles come to be understood in terms of a more general set of interconnections between problems and movements worldwide. For instance, the Cartagena Protocol on Biosafety on genetically modified life forms was signed in late January 2000 in Montreal by representatives from 133 governments pursuant to the 1992 UN Convention on Biological Diversity for the trade and regulation of living modified organisms (LMOs). The draft Protocol ensures that sovereign governments have rights to decide on imports of LMOs provided this is based on environmental and health risk assessment data. The Protocol is founded on the 'precautionary principle', in effect meaning that where scientific uncertainty exists, governments can refuse or delay authorization of trade in LMOs. Apart from pressure from NGOs, the negotiations were strongly influenced by scientists concerned at genetic and biological risks posed by the path of innovation. The process finally produced a protocol with significant controls over the freedoms of biotechnology and life sciences companies. Indeed, linkages and contradictions between environmental and trade and investment regulations and laws are becoming better understood by activists worldwide, for instance how the Biosafety Protocol and the rules and procedures of the WTO may be in conflict.

Nevertheless, it must be emphasized that, although they may represent a large proportion of the population of the world in terms of their concerns, in organized political terms the protest groups are only a relatively small part of an emerging global civil society that includes not only NGOs but also the activities of political parties, churches, media communications corporations, scientific and political associations, some progressive, others reactionary. Transnational civil society also involves activities of both transnational corporations, and also governments that

8. Posted on <http://www.peoples@post4.tele.dk> 26 April 2000. In May 2002 it was announced that the U'wa people had forced the giant energy corporation, Occidental Oil, off their lands. This was despite huge reported reserves of oil valued at over $50 billion and after over $100 million had been spent on seismic and other feasibility studies. The U'wa reflected their epistemological and political alternative when, following their successful act of resistance, they commented: 'the money king is only an illusion. Capitalism is blind and barbaric.' John Vidal, 'Colombia's U'Wa Have Their Prayers Answered', *Guardian Weekly*, 23–29 May 2002.

are active in shaping a political terrain that is directly and indirectly outside the formal juridical purview of states. Indeed, as the UN Rio conference on the environment and its aftermath illustrated, corporate environmentalism is a crucial aspect of the emerging global civil society and it is linked to what Gramsci called *trasformismo* or co-optation of opposition. For example, 'sustainable development' is primarily defined in public policy as compatible with market forces and freedom of enterprise. When the global environmental movement was perceived as a real threat to corporate interests, companies changed tack from suggesting the environmentalists were either crackpots or misguided to accepting a real problem existed and a compromise was necessary. Of course a compromise acceptable to capital was not one that would fundamentally challenge the dominant patterns of accumulation partly through strategies of transformative resistance.

I have not used the term post-modern in its usual sense. Rather, I apply it to indicate a set of conditions and contradictions that give rise to novel forms of political agency that go beyond and are more complex than those imagined by Machiavelli's *The Prince* or Gramsci's *The Modern Prince*. Global democratic collective action today cannot, in my view, be understood as a singular form of collective agency, for example a single party with a single form of identity. It is more plural and differentiated, as well as being democratic and inclusive. The new forms of collective action contain innovative conceptions of social justice and solidarity, of social possibility, of knowledge, emancipation and freedom. The content of their mobilizing myths includes diversity, oneness of the planet and nature, democracy and equity. What we are discussing is, therefore, a political party as well as an educational form and a cultural movement. However, it does not act in the old sense of an institutionalized and centralized structure of representation. Indeed this 'party' is not institutionalized as such, since it has a multiple and capillary form. Moreover, whilst many of the moments and movements of resistance noted above are at first glance 'local' in nature, there is broad recognition that local problems may require global solutions. Global networks and other mobilizing capabilities are facilitated with new technologies of communication.

A new 'Post-modern Prince' may prove to be the most effective political form for giving coherence to an open-ended, plural, inclusive and flexible form of politics and thus create alternatives to neo-liberal globalization. So, whilst one can be pessimistic about globalization in its current form, this is perhaps where some of the optimism for the future may lie: a new set of democratic identities that are global, but based on diversity and rooted in local conditions, problems and opportunities.

Bibliography

Altvater, Elmar. 1993. *The Future of the Market: An Essay on the Regulation of Money and Nature after the Collapse of 'Actually Existing Socialism'*. London: Verso.

Arrighi, Giovanni. 1993. The Three Hegemonies of Historical Capitalism. In *Gramsci, Historical Materialism and International Relations*. Edited by S. Gill. Cambridge: Cambridge University Press.

Ashley, Richard K. 1988. Untying the Sovereign State: A Double Reading of the Anarchy Problématique. *Millennium: Journal of International Studies* 17 (2): 227–62.

Augelli, Enrico, and Craig Murphy. 1988. *America's Quest for Supremacy and the Third World: An Essay in Gramscian Analysis*. London: Pinter.

Axelrod, Robert M., and Richard Dawkins. 1990. *The Evolution of Co-operation*. Harmondsworth: Penguin.

Bakker, Isabella. 1999. Neoliberal Governance and the New Gender Order. *Working Papers* 1 (1): 49–59.

Bell, Daniel. 1975. The End of American Exceptionalism. *The Public Interest* 41 (3): 193–224.

Bentham, Jeremy. 1843. *The Works of Jeremy Bentham: Published under the Superintendence of His Executor, John Bowring*. Edinburgh: William Tait.

Bentham, Jeremy. 1995. *The Panopticon Writings*. London; New York: Verso.

Bernard, Mitchell. 1999. East Asia's Tumbling Dominoes: Financial Crisis and the Truth about the Regional Miracle. In *Socialist Register, 1999: Globalisation and Democracy*. Edited by L. Panitch and C. Lees. London: Merlin Press.

Blair, John Malcolm. 1976. *The Control of Oil*. New York: Pantheon Books.

Blanchot, Maurice, and Michel Foucault. 1990. *Foucault/Blanchot*. Translated by J. Mehlman and B. Massumi. New York: Zone Books.

Braithwaite, John, and Peter Drahos. 2000. *Global Business Regulation*. Cambridge: Cambridge University Press.

Braudel, Fernand. 1980. *On History*. Chicago: University of Chicago Press.

Braudel, Fernand. 1981. *The Structures of Everyday Life*. Translated by S. Reynolds. London: William Collins and Sons.

Braudel, Fernand. 1982. *Civilization and Capitalism, 15th–18th century*. III vols. New York: Harper and Row.

Buck-Morss, Susan. 1989. *The Dialectics of Seeing – Walter Benjamin and the Arcades Project*. Cambridge, MA: The MIT Press.

Calleo, David. 1982. *The Imperious Economy*. Cambridge MA: Harvard University Press.

Chase-Dunn, Christopher. 1982. International Economic Policy in a Declining Core State. In *America in a Changing World Political Economy*. Edited by W. Avery and D. Rapkin. New York: Longman.

Christie, Nils. 1993. *Crime Control as Industry: Towards Gulag Western Style?* London: Routledge.

Clarkson, Stephen. 1993. Constitutionalizing the Canadian-American Relationship. In *Canada Under Free Trade*. Edited by D. Cameron and M. Watkins. Toronto: Lorimer.

Correa, Carlos María. 1999. *Intellectual Property Rights, the WTO, and Developing Countries: The TRIPS Agreement and Policy Options*. New York: Zed Books.

Cox, Robert. 1983. Gramsci, Hegemony and International Relations: An Essay in Method. *Millennium: Journal of International Studies* 12 (2): 162–75.

Cox, Robert W. 1987. *Production, Power, and World Order: Social Forces in the Making of History*. New York: Columbia University Press.

Cox, Robert W. 1992. Global Perestroika. In *Socialist Register 1992: New World Order*. Edited by R. Miliband and L. Panitch. London: Merlin.

Davies, Matt. 1999. *International Political Economy and Mass Communications in Chile: Transnational Hegemony and National Intellectuals*. Basingstoke: Macmillan.

Davis, Mike. 1984. The Political Economy of Late Imperial America. *New Left Review* (143): 6–38.

Davis, Mike. 1985. 'Reaganomics' Magical Mystery Tour. *New Left Review* (149): 45–65.

De Vroey, M. 1984. A Regulation Approach to the Interpretation of Contemporary Crisis. *Capital and Class* 23 (1): 45–66.

Fast, William R. 2001. Knowledge Strategies: Balancing Ends, Ways, and Means in the Information Age. Washington DC: Institute for National Strategic Studies.

Foucault, Michel. 1972. *The Archaeology of Knowledge, World of Man*. New York: Pantheon Books.

Foucault, Michel. 1979. *Discipline and Punish: The Birth of the Prison*. Translated by A. Sheridan. New York: Vintage Books.

Foucault, Michel, and Colin Gordon. 1980. *Power/Knowledge: Selected Interviews and Other Writings, 1972–1977*. New York: Pantheon Books.

Frieden, Jeffry A. 1987. *Banking on the World: The Politics of American International Finance*. New York: Harper and Row.

Fukuyama, Francis. 1992. *The End Of History and the Last Man*. New York: Avon Books.

Galbraith, John Kenneth. 1992. *The Culture of Contentment*. Boston: Houghton Mifflin.

Gandy, Oskar Jr. 1993. *The Panoptic Sort: A Political Economy of Personal Information*. Boulder: Westview Press.

Gill, Stephen. 1990. *American Hegemony and the Trilateral Commission*. Cambridge: Cambridge University Press.

Gill, Stephen. 1992. The Emerging World Order and European Change: the Political Economy of European Union. In *Socialist Register 1992: New World Order?* Edited by R. Miliband and L. Panitch. London: Merlin.

Gill, Stephen. 1995. The Global Panopticon? The Neo-liberal State, Economic Life and Democratic Surveillance. *Alternatives* 20 (1): 1–49.

Gill, Stephen. 1997. Finance, Production and Panopticism: Inequality, Risk and Resistance in an Era of Disciplinary Neo-liberalism. In *Globalization, Democratization and Multilateralism*. Edited by S. Gill. New York: Macmillan, United Nations University Press.

Gill, Stephen. 1998. European Governance and New Constitutionalism: EMU and Alternatives to Disciplinary Neo-liberalism in Europe. *New Political Economy* 3 (1): 5–26.

Gill, Stephen. 2002. Constitutionalizing Inequality and the Clash of Globalizations. *International Studies Review* 4 (3): 47–65.

Gill, Stephen, and David Law. 1988. *The Global Political Economy: Perspectives, Problems, and Policies*. Baltimore: Johns Hopkins University Press.

Gilpin, Robert. 1981. *War and Change in World Politics*. Cambridge: Cambridge University Press.

Governance, Commission on Global. 1995. *Our Global Neighbourhood*. Oxford: Oxford University Press.

Gramsci, Antonio. 1971. *Selections from the Prison Notebooks of Antonio Gramsci*. Translated by Q. Hoare and G. Nowell-Smith. New York: International Publishers.

Group, Bank Credit Analyst Research. 1998. The Asian Crisis After One Year. Montréal: Bank Credit Analyst.

Gunnell, J.G. 1968. Social Science and Political Reality: The Problem of Explanation. *Social Research* 31 (1): 159–201.

Habermas, Jürgen. 1976. *Legitimation Crisis*. London: Heinemann.

Halliday, Fred. 1984. *The Making of the Second Cold War*. London: New Left Books.

Harvey, David. 1989. *The Condition of Postmodernity*. Oxford: Blackwell.

Helleiner, Eric. 1994. *States and the Reemergence of Global Finance – From Bretton Woods to the 1990s*. Ithaca, NY: Cornell University Press.

Hill, Christopher. 1980. *The Century of Revolution – 1603–1714*. 2nd edn. London: WW Norton and Co.

Hirsch, Fred. 1976. *The Social Limits to Growth*. Cambridge, MA: Harvard University Press.

Hobsbawm, Eric. 1994. *Age of Extremes – The Short Twentieth Century – 1914–1991*. London: Michael Joseph.

Jones, I. Deane. 1931. *The English Revolution*. London: William Heinemann.

Kennedy, Paul M. 1988. *The Rise and Fall of the Great Powers: Economic Change and Military Conflict from 1500 to 2000*. London: Unwin Hyman.

Keohane, Robert O. 1984. *After Hegemony: Cooperation and Discord in the World Political Economy*. Princeton, NJ: Princeton University Press.

Keohane, Robert O., and Joseph S. Nye. 1977. *Power and Interdependence: World Politics in Transition*. Boston: Little Brown.

Keohane, Robert, and Joseph Nye. 1985. Two Cheers for Multilateralism. *Foreign Policy* 60 (2): 391–412.

Kindleberger, Charles. 1973. *The World in Depression, 1929–1939*. London: Allen Lane.

Kornai, Janos. 1980. *Economics of Shortage, Contributions to Economic Analysis*. Amsterdam; Oxford: North Holland.

Kornai, Janos. 1990. *The Road to a Free Economy: Shifting from a Socialist System, the Example of Hungary*. New York; London: Norton.

Krasner, Stephen D. 1983. *International Regimes*. Ithaca, NY: Cornell University Press.

Lash, Scott, and John Urry. 1994. *Economies of Signs and Space*. London: Sage Publications.

Lindblom, Charles Edward. 1977. *Politics and Markets: The World's Political Economic Systems*. New York: Basic Books.

Maier, Charles. 1987. *In Search of Stability: Explorations in Historical Political Economy*. Cambridge: Cambridge University Press.

Marx, Karl. 1973. *Grundrisse: Foundations of a Critique of Political Economy*. Edited by D. McLellan. New York: Paladin.

Massey, Douglas S. 1996. The Age of Extremes: Concentrated Affluence and Poverty in the Twenty-First Century. *Demography* 33 (4): 395–412.

McCormack, Gavan. 1991. The Price of Affluence: The Political Economy of Japanese Leisure. *New Left Review* (188): 121–34.

McMichael, Phillip. 1999. The Crisis of Market Rule in the Global Food Order. Paper read at British International Studies Association, 20–22 December 1999, at Manchester.

McNally, David. 1998. Globalization on Trial: Crisis and Class Struggle in Asia. *Monthly Review* 50 (4): 1–14.

Mills, C. Wright. 1961. *Images of Man: The Classic Tradition in Sociological Thinking*. New York: G. Braziller.

Morera, Esteve. 1990. *Gramsci's Historicism: A Realist Interpretation*. London: Routledge.

Murphy, Craig. 1994. *International Organization and Industrial Change: Global Governance Since 1850*. Cambridge: Polity Press.

Nicolaus, Martin. 1970. The USA: The Universal Contradiction. *New Left Review* (59): 3–18.

Nye, Joseph S. 1982. US Power and Reagan Policy. *Orbis* 26 (2): 391–412.

Nye, Joseph S. 1991. *Bound to Lead: The Changing Nature of American Power*. New York: Basic Books.

Nye, Joseph S., Kurt Biedenkopf, Bernard Wood, and Motoo Shiina. 1991. *Global Co-operation after the Cold War*. New York: Trilateral Commission.

Pearce, Frank. 1989. *The Radical Durkheim*. London, Boston: Unwin Hyman.

Picchio, Antonella. 1992. *Social Reproduction, the Political Economy of the Labour Market*. Cambridge: Cambridge University Press.

Pijl, Kees van der. 1984. *The Making of an Atlantic Ruling Class*. London: Verso.

Pijl, Kees van der. 1989. Ruling Classes, Hegemony and the State System. *International Journal of Political Economy* 19 (1): 7–35.

Pijl, Kees van der. 1993. Soviet Socialism and Passive Revolution. In *Gramsci, Historical Materialism and International Relations*. Edited by S. Gill. Cambridge: Cambridge University Press.

Polanyi, Karl. 1975. *The Great Transformation: Political and Economic Origins of our Times*. New York: Octagon Books.

Popper, Karl R. 1976. *Conjectures and Refutations: The Growth of Scientific Knowledge*. London: Routledge and Kegan Paul.

Porter, Michael E. 1998. *The Competitive Advantage of Nations*. Basingstoke: Macmillan.

Resnick, Stephen A., and D. Wolff Richard. 1987. *Knowledge and Class: A Marxian Critique of Political Economy*. Chicago; London: University of Chicago Press.

Rosenau, James N. 1997. Imposing Global Order: A Synthesized Ontology for a Turbulent Era. In *Innovation and Transformation in International Studies*. Edited by S. Gill and J.H. Mittelman. Cambridge: Cambridge University Press.

Rosenstock-Huessy, Eugen. 1969. *Out of Revolution: Autobiography of Western Man*. Norwich, VT.: Argo Books.

Ruggie, John Gerard. 1982. International Regimes, Transactions and Change – Embedded Liberalism in the Post-War Order. *International Organization* 36 (3): 379–415.

Russett, Bruce. 1985. The Mysterious Case of Vanishing Hegemony. Or, is Mark Twain Really Dead? *International Organization* 39 (2): 219–33.

Sell, Susan K. 1997. The Agent-Structure Debate: Corporate Actors, Intellectual Property and the World Trade Organization. Paper read at Non-State Actors and Authority in the Global System, 31 October–1 November 1997, at Warwick University.

Sinclair, Scott. 2000. *GATS: How the WTO's New 'Services' Negotiations Threaten Democracy.* Ottawa: Canadian Centre for Policy Alternatives.

Sinclair, Timothy. 1994. Passing Judgement: Credit Rating Processes as Regulatory Mechanisms of Governance in the Emerging World Order. *Review of International Political Economy* 1 (1): 133–59.

Steinmo, Sven. 1993. *Taxation and Democracy: Swedish, British, and American Approaches to Financing the Modern State.* New Haven; London: Yale University Press.

Strange, Susan. 1985. Protectionism and World Politics. *International Organization* 39 (2): 233–59.

Strange, Susan. 1986. *Casino Capitalism.* Oxford; New York: Blackwell.

Tabb, William K. 1998. The East Asia Financial Crisis. *Monthly Review* 50 (2): 24–38.

Thompson, E.P. 1980. *The Making of the English Working Class.* Harmondsworth: Penguin.

Toal, Gerard. 1992. Japan as Threat: Geo-Economic Discourses on the US–Japan Relationship in US Civil Society 1987–91. Paper read at Institute of British Geographers, 7–10 January, at Swansea.

UNDP. 1994. *Human Development Report.* New York: Oxford University Press.

UNDP. 2000. *Human Development Report.* New York: Oxford University Press.

UNRISD. 1995. *States of Disarray. The Social Effects of Globalization.* Geneva: United Nations.

Wallerstein, Immanuel M. 1974. *The Modern World-System: Capitalist Agriculture and the Origins of the European World-Economy in the Sixteenth Century.* New York: Academic Press.

Weber, Max. 1963. *From Max Weber: Essays in Sociology.* Edited by H. Gerth and C. Wright Mills. New York: Oxford University Press.

World Bank. 2002. *Building Institutions for Markets.* Washington, DC: Oxford University Press.

Wriston, Walter. 1992. *The Twilight of Sovereignty: How the Information Revolution is Transforming Our World.* New York: Scribner's.

Zysman, John. 1983. *Governments, Markets and Growth: Financial Systems and the Politics of Industrial Change.* Ithaca, NY: Cornell University Press.

Index